This book addresses the problem of the precariousness of justice in relations between non-equals (men, and men and women), via an analysis of Rousseau which uses techniques of reading associated with literary theory, and draws particularly on the work of Derrida, de Man and Starobinski. The best possible relationship between un-equals, according to Rousseau, is one of *bienfaisance*, giving, receiving and repaying benefits. To function successfully the practice of beneficence should be inspired by a passionate impulse and governed by a rational code. It should be distinct from aristocratic magnanimity and from a market economy, starting from an assumption of hierarchical difference but working to mitigate that inequality. The book includes study of classical sources for eighteenth-century thinking on beneficence; including Seneca, Cicero, Aristotle and Plato.

Rousseau also notoriously claims that to preserve social existence women must adhere to the code of *pudeur*. Dr Still argues that ultimately it is sexual difference, constructed defensively as a fixed opposition, which disturbs bene-ficence. This emerges through analysis of the conceptual underpinnings of Rousseau's ethics and of the gaps and contradictions in some of his 'minor' texts which present more excessive scenes of transgression than his lengthier, more harmonious and more influential works. Rousseau's reworking of the classical inheritance on ethical and political issues in a revolutionary historical moment, his peculiar combination of Enlightenment rationality and near-pathological sensibility, his oscillating self-identi-fication with virility and femininity, make his work a particular pressure point for the question whether it is possible to have just and generous relations where there is difference.

Cambridge Studies in French 39

JUSTICE AND DIFFERENCE IN THE
WORKS OF ROUSSEAU

Cambridge Studies in French

Recent titles in this series include

A complete list of books in the series is given at the end of the volume

JUSTICE AND DIFFERENCE IN THE WORKS OF ROUSSEAU

Bienfaisance and *Pudeur*

JUDITH STILL

Lecturer in Critical Theory, Department of French, University of Nottingham

CAMBRIDGE
UNIVERSITY PRESS

Published by the Press Syndicate of the University of Cambridge
The Pitt Building, Trumpington Street, Cambridge CB2 1RP
40 West 20th Street, New York, NY 10011–4211, USA
10 Stamford Road, Oakleigh, Victoria 3166, Australia

First published 1993

Printed in Great Britain at the University Press, Cambridge

A catalogue record for this book is available from the British Library

Library of Congress cataloguing in publication data
Still, Judith, 1958–
Justice and difference in the works of Rousseau: *bienfaisance* and *pudeur* /
Judith Still.
p.   cm. – (Cambridge studies in French; 39)
Includes bibliographical references and index.
ISBN 0-521-41585-3
1. Social justice. 2. Equality. 3. Sex role. 4. Rousseau, Jean-Jacques,
1712–1778 – Political and social views. I. Title. II. Series.
HM216.S764   1993
305.3 – dc20   92-3203 CIP

ISBN 0521 415853 hardback

To my mother

Contents

ix

Acknowledgements

I should like to thank all those who have read the manuscript of this book at various stages and made helpful comments; all those with whom I have discussed ideas; and all those who have given love, comfort and support.

Earlier or expanded versions of sections of chapters have already appeared as follows: from Chapter 2, 'Elements of the Classical Code of Beneficence Presupposed in Rousseau's Writing' in *Studies on Voltaire and the Eighteenth Century*; from Chapter 5, 'From Eliot's "Raw Bone" to Gyges' Ring: Two Studies in Intertextuality' in *Paragraph*; from Chapter 6, 'Lucretia's Silent Rhetoric' in *The Oxford Literary Review* and 'Rousseau's *Lévite d'Ephraïm*: The Imposition of Meaning (on Women)' in *French Studies*. I am grateful to the editors of these journals for permission to reprint.

A preliminary note on vocabulary and conventions

I have generally chosen to translate Rousseau's term *pudeur* by
the rare English term 'pudicity' (from the Latin *pudicitia* or
'shamefacedness') when *pudeur* is used to refer to a code
structuring the possibilities of virtuous feminine identity or
women's adherence to a strict moral reserve in order to protect
men from the consequences of unbridled amorous passion. The
usual modern translation of *pudeur* is 'modesty' (from the Latin
modestia or 'moderation'), but the primary and secondary
meanings of modesty are 'moderation; freedom from excess; self
control; clemency; the quality of being modest' (defined as
'well-conducted, orderly; not domineering; having a humble
estimate of one's own merits'). Only the third meaning listed by
the *Shorter Oxford English Dictionary* suggests 'womanly propriety
of behaviour; scrupulous chastity of thought, speech and
conduct'. By employing 'pudicity' as well as Rousseau's *pudeur*
I want to reverse the order of connotation for the English
reader, tie *pudeur* closer to the feminine, and, by the strangeness
of 'pudicity' to the modern ear, reinforce a point which can
easily be elided, namely that here *pudeur* is understood as a social
construct and not simply as a natural emotion. Feminine *pudeur*
or 'pudicity' is unusual amongst the virtues which Rousseau
prizes, as there can be no split between inner assent and outer
appearance: the veil of pudicity is a social display (or rather
non-display) with crucial apotropaic and economic functions,
saving men from excessive expenditure and thus enabling
reproduction. By employing a somewhat alienating archaism I
am emphasising the seemingly archaic quality of Rousseau's
analysis of (his fears and fantasies around) femininity; but I

hope that it is obvious to readers that the fears and fantasies survive in various forms, reworked in modern vocabularies of provocation, negligence or emasculation, for example. To trace the genealogy of the policing of specifically feminine thought, reading, speech, conduct, dress and so on to control and to excite desire is unfortunately beyond the scope of the present work.

Wherever possible citations from Rousseau will be from the *Œuvres complètes de Jean-Jacques Rousseau*, edited by Bernard Gagnebin and Marcel Raymond, 4 vols. (Paris, 1959–69). Citations from the *Lettre à d'Alembert* will be from the edition by M. Fuchs (Geneva, 1948). Citations from the *Essai sur l'origine des langues* will be from the edition by Charles Porset (Paris, 1970). Citations from Rousseau's correspondence will be from the *Correspondance complète*, edited by Ralph A. Leigh, 40 vols. (Oxford, 1965–82).

All page references will be given in the text. All spelling in quotations from seventeenth- and eighteenth-century authors has been modernised. Publication details of all works cited are in the bibliography.

Introduction

Rousseau is one of the most important moral and political philosophers of the modern era. He is, at the same time, a leading figure in the canons of literature. A great deal of secondary material has been produced on both sides of the divide, some of which helps us to have a finely nuanced and sophisticated approach to Rousseau's work. This book is located in the tradition which attempts to work in both of those fields simultaneously in the belief that disciplinary segregation can lead to political readings which seem naively inattentive to the rhetorical structures of the text or to literary readings which seem to ignore the very questions which the text prioritises, those issues of justice, freedom and virtue which Rousseau considered to be of primary importance. I wish to analyse certain moral (and hence political) questions in Rousseau by using the techniques of reading which are currently associated with literary criticism or theory. The specific questions which will be addressed are those of the functioning of *bienfaisance* (beneficence) and of *pudeur* (pudicity), also of the relationship between the social codes which govern each of these practices, and of the extent to which that relationship casts light on each of the codes individually.

The code of beneficence, which regulates the giving, receiving and repaying of benefits, used to be a central topic of moral philosophy and of applied ethics, but has been afforded little close critical scrutiny in recent times. This is partly due to the fragmentation of disciplines; topics which impinge on a number of distinct fields – anthropology, sociology, political science, economics, moral philosophy, literature – often seem to be

treated in a partial and limited manner and may even fall in
between stools. It is also partly due to a confident assumption
(unfounded in my view) that the question of beneficence is now
largely a historical one, thanks to a more egalitarian society, to
the advent of the Welfare State, and to a breaking down of
certain traditional, stable relations between individuals, as
capitalism has become ever more advanced. And yet, the
present fragility of Welfare States apart, beneficence is still an
issue in many people's lives, and a feature of many interpersonal
relationships: parent–child, child–aged parent, teacher–pupil,
spouses, neighbours, to name but a few.[1]

One way of questioning the continuing relevance of the study
of beneficence has been via the argument that all human
relations are economic – and have always been economic – in
the sense that they are all governed by the same criterion as
market transactions, that is to say, rational profit maximisation
on the part of the individuals concerned.[2] Some traditions have
sought to counter that argument by identifying a sphere of
activity which is governed by a different kind of economy,
locating this sphere in societies which are distant from us in time
or space, often 'primitive' societies – the very name suggesting
some of the dangers associated with that kind of thinking.[3] In
Economie libidinale, Jean-François Lyotard suggests that any such
opposition between capitalism and some other primitive lib-
idinal economy should be deconstructed.[4] However, the attempt to identify a kind of relationship which is not governed by
rational profit maximisation and located not in some other time
or place, but accessible alongside the market seems to me to be
particularly valuable. In the final analysis any such attempt
may be shown to be doomed to failure or irremediably
metaphysical if not both. However, the path to that final point
may be a very useful one, and holding the possibility of a non-
market relationship in suspense is at the least a device which
works against a cynical acceptance of the inevitability of profit
maximisation in all relationships.

I would argue that this question cannot progress beyond a
certain level without paying attention to sexual difference, and
that the Rousseau texts bring that point home. The relation of

women to exchange has historically been quite different to that
of men, and that difference is an important one in the context of
a discussion about (disinterested) gift exchange as defined
against market exchange. Furthermore, in any purportedly
egalitarian moral or political theory, the issue of women raises
in an acute form the question of equality's relationship to
difference.

The question of codes, such as pudicity, which are intended to
structure feminine identity, is incontrovertibly alive and a
burning topic of debate thanks to the efforts of those feminists
not yet ready to agree that postfeminism is the order of the day.
However, where Rousseau's pronouncements on the subject of
women seem particularly offensive today, analysis can give way
to ritual condemnation of a kind prone to charges of ana-
chronism. Indignation had its historical place as a strategy, and
many denunciations were also enlightening about the assumptions and effects of certain normative texts. However, this
reading response should not be reiterated *ad infinitum* lest it blind
us to useful lessons which can be drawn from the case.
Consequently this book will be less concerned to dwell dis-
approvingly on Rousseau's inegalitarian assertions regarding
the best conduct for women as opposed to that for men, than to
analyse the gaps and contradictions produced where sexual
difference is at stake. These gaps and contradictions sometimes
arise from a 'femininity' which cannot be contained in the way
that Rousseau prescribes, and which persists in my reading of
seemingly universal ('man') questions.

This book in no sense attempts to be exhaustive nor even to
summarise a history of ideas or practices of gift exchange or of
pudicity. Instead I wish to focus my analysis on a certain
pressure point, located in the works of Rousseau: the in-
tersection of beneficence with sexual politics. In Chapter 1 I
introduce the problematic relationship between beneficence
and pudicity which is the subject of the book. In Chapter 2 I
elaborate the intricacies of the code of beneficence at greater
length and set it in the context of the classical tradition of
writing about beneficence, which had an enormous influence on
eighteenth-century thinking. The very use of the term 'code',

with its legislative implications, becomes more self-evident through study of a text such as Seneca's *de Beneficiis*, which is composed of a series of prescriptions. Chapter 3 examines more particularly Rousseau's analyses of the functioning or malfunctioning of beneficence. Chapter 4 is devoted to an examination of Rousseau's explicit theory of human nature and of interpersonal relationships, presenting the argument that there is a clear contradiction between his theory about men (in general) and his theory about men and women. Chapters 5 and 6 provide close textual analysis to show the way in which sexual difference disrupts Rousseau's writing. The last chapter draws particularly from non-canonical texts which present situations (transgressions of pudicity) related to those of the major texts, but which are more unusual or extreme. By their very excessive nature they furnish new insights into the gaps in Rousseau's thinking about non-equals.

Rousseau is the writer who above all straddles the divide between ancient and modern, a writer who engages formidably with most moral and political issues, and a writer whose acute sensitivity made him the first truly introspective autobiographer. It is because of their Enlightenment rationality and yet almost pathological and obsessive sensibilities that his writings are a highly suitable scene in which to expect an enactment of the conflictual play between the two moral codes. The pits into which Rousseau falls are by no means peculiar to him. Indeed his work would be a useful starting point for a more general analysis of the inevitable failings of any moral or political thinking which does not pay sufficient attention to difference.

CHAPTER I

The problem: the intersection of beneficence and pudicity

This book seeks to draw together two apparently separate areas of interest in the works of Rousseau: beneficence and pudicity. These two social codes are points of reference for Rousseau in this analyses of relations between unequals, respectively relations between men and relations between men and women. The thorny question of inequality is one to which Rousseau constantly returns in all his works. In *Du contrat social* he seeks to define the principles which would underpin a just state – a state in which inequality between men would be reduced to a minimal level, getting as close as possible to the vestigial inequality of the hypothetical state of nature which Rousseau imagines in *Le Discours sur l'inégalité*. In most of Rousseau's other works inequality is a fact of social existence, and he devotes considerable energy both to analysing the evils of extremes of inequality and to suggesting how inequality could be attenuated in interpersonal relations.

In this book I argue that Rousseau's thinking on inequality is to a large degree unified, but breaks down on one point, that of sexual difference. The consistent thrust of Rousseau's work is to reduce inequality because it is the root of moral and political evil – that is to say, both bad relations between individuals and bad relations between individuals and the state. However, he insists that there should be a rigid demarcation between men's and women's roles of a kind which has traditionally implied a hierarchy. Inequality is, I shall suggest, the fruit of such oppositions, and the worst kind of inequality is that which is produced by an apparently fixed and unchanging difference.[1] Rousseau's proposals for moral or political improvements on the status quo which he himself experienced all involve artifice: the *construction* of a rational social self in harmony with natural emotion or intuition. However, sexual difference and amorous passion disrupt this project and Rousseau's writings about such projects. In this book I focus on Rousseau's theories concerning the possibility of good social relations between individuals, and suggest how these theories are problematised if attention is paid to the question of sexual difference.

In his desire to find a model for relations between individuals which works towards the reduction of inequality Rousseau draws on the code of *beneficence*.[2] That code may appear to impinge primarily on the economic domain, but cannot be confined to that domain due to the variousness of acts of beneficence (including, for example, education) as well as the interpenetration of the economic with other spheres. In Rousseau's fictional history, social inequality is first of all economic (possessing more or fewer goods, notably land), and then becomes political. In the modern (eighteenth-century) state the economic and the political had largely become mutually dependent and appeared inextricable – although with the benefit of hindsight the modern reader can see class divisions relating to certain strains in that union. Rousseau is sometimes assumed to represent in some way one of the key classes in the forthcoming struggle.[3] And yet, in his references to beneficence, on the one hand, he rejects Aristotelian aristocratic magnanimity, which I shall refer to as *false beneficence*; on the other hand, he also rejects what was to become the dominant ideology of the western world – *the law of the market*. False beneficence maintains and relishes hierarchies; the law of the market assumes homogeneity (if only for the sake of the argument), that is it assumes that hierarchies do not exist and so permits them to grow silently and unchecked. Beneficence, on the other hand, is a dynamic relationship which accepts *difference* and a real hierarchy in the short term; the benefactor and the beneficiary are different in that the one has something which the other lacks, whereas market agents are assumed uniform – exchanging commodities of equal value. Beneficence works to minimise the hierarchy both by a kind of emotional fiction in the short term and by real change in the long term: the benefactor's supreme gift to the beneficiary is that the latter is enabled eventually to become a benefactor.

However, Rousseau's moral and political sources, such as Seneca or Cicero, and his own writing, concern themselves with *man* in all the ambiguity of the term. In the case of some source texts it seems clear that women are excluded from the discussion, and this is not surprising given the societies in which the code was formulated.[4] On a metaphorical level, where thinkers, such as Aristotle, tend towards a more aristocratic conception of beneficence beneficiaries tend to be feminised – as innately weaker, inferior, passive recipients. Where beneficiaries are perceived as potential benefactors they are (metaphorically and sometimes literally) boys who will become men. Rousseau explicitly values classical notions of virtue because they are (he argues) *manly* unlike some versions of Christianity and unlike contemporary Parisian mores. In Rousseau's own writing 'man' and its avatars sometimes appear to refer to all human individuals – a kind of sexual homogeneity which can mask real inequality, a strategy of which Rousseau is only too aware when men are assumed to be homogeneous for the purpose of masking, say, economic inequality. The strategy is to some extent made plain when, as in *Emile*, women as a distinct category enter the scene belatedly (Book v) and Rousseau's outline of the code of pudicity, which he wants to structure feminine identity, disrupts the fine moral scheme laid down. Adherence to inegalitarian theories concerning women has long been perceived as a major flaw in Rousseau's otherwise coherent proposals for more just and equal relations between men.[5] I want to suggest that as well as a clear contradiction on the level of theory, which has unsurprisingly often been seen in a very negative light by feminists, there is a kind of feminine textual disruption that reoccurs in Rousseau's writing which may in fact be viewed in a more positive light.

BENEFICENCE

If relationships could function according to the code of
beneficence then it would be possible to live a just and virtuous
life within society, a possibility which Rousseau does not take as
given. Although Rousseau's work includes a powerful and
poetic image of man in a solitary state, it is the question of life
within society and its potential superiority as well as inevitable
degeneration with respect to a hypothetical state of nature
which interests him. Social relations, unlike encounters in the
state of nature, are to be judged according to the standards of
justice and morality. *Du contrat social* presents a set of principles
against which a state can be judged to see to what extent it fulfils
the criteria of liberty and equality. Similarly, on the scale of the
individual, moral codes provide a standard against which an
individual's behaviour can be measured to see if it meets their
criteria. The behaviour of an individual within any society
becomes of paramount importance when, as Emile discovers to
be the case, no contemporary state can be found which adheres
to the principles of political justice drawn up. Emile has to be
content with moral liberty, with his own self-mastery, which
will not be safeguarded by that particular political liberty
described in *Du contrat social*, although the very fact that he is a
member of a community at all means that he is, in Rousseau's
view, obliged to live as virtuously as possible within it.
Beneficence – the possibility of virtuous action and of mitigating
inequality – is all the more important in a society of non-equals,
founded on an unjust social pact, even though it is inevitably
more difficult to do good in such a society.

As regards both political and moral philosophy Rousseau's
conclusion is the same: market relations are pernicious. In this
he stands out from the more optimistic Enlightenment *philosophes*
with whom he often shares common cause when it comes to
attacking hide-bound royal, aristocratic or ecclesiastical privi-
leges. The law of the market, and the general outcome of a
multitude of particular transactions dictated by rational self-
interest, are becoming of increasing interest in the eighteenth
century; the appearance of *The Wealth of Nations* is the best

example of this growing interest.[6] Rousseau is convinced that the doctrine of the virtue of self-interest is dangerous as is any practice founded upon it, whereas many of the 'new men' of the time were convinced that the free market could liberate everyone from the static hierarchy of the *ancien régime* and furthermore that free competition is essentially egalitarian in character. Rousseau proposes a different dynamic model which would allow men of good character to evade the fixed relationship of master and underling. This is beneficence, a disinterested exchange of gifts which demands emotion and reason whereas market exchange is presumed to require reason alone.

The code of beneficence is, for Rousseau, the best possible way of regulating relations between unequals – not only unequals in the economic sense, but also in a moral sense, such as teacher and pupil, legislator and subjects, writer and reader. Beneficence is a vital factor in the attempt to be successful at living within society 'toutes les vertus sociales se rapportant à la bienfaisance' (*Lettre à d'Alembert*, p. 49); it is a cohesive force working to bind people together, both emotionally and materially. The code, which Rousseau inherits from classical antiquity and which is a point of reference for many eighteenth-century writers, is outlined in Chapter 2 of this book.

THEORETICAL CONTRADICTIONS

According to Rousseau, social existence is inevitably a condition of interdependence which may be so finely balanced that an individual can enjoy a measure of moral, and even political, liberty, or may, on the other hand, involve such a struggle to dominate that no one can be free. Relations between the sexes follow this general rule; and, indeed, they are a significant factor in influencing the modalities of social and political existence. However, Rousseau does not treat relations between the sexes as merely a prime example of a more general tendency of human relationships to fall into a 'master–slave' cycle. He finds a special solution to the problem of dominance in relations between the sexes, which is completely at odds with his general solution to the problems of interpersonal relationships. This special solution is women's adherence to the code of *pudeur*, a code of strict moral reserve; the code structures feminine identity in Rousseau's theoretical and fictional writings, providing a standard by which to measure feminine virtue.

Relations between the sexes are, for Rousseau, inaugurated with amorous passion and unthinkable without amorous passion. Only a shield (pudicity) can prevent the dire consequences of passion unleashed, amongst which perhaps the worst consequence is the death of passion and hence of sexual relations. Pudicity seeks to repeat, with regard to men and women, the original dispersion of humans: it keeps men and women apart. But it allows sociability amongst men (such as Emile and his tutor), and amongst women within their families. It does not entail the complete isolation of each individual as in nature; the danger that 'the other man' might represent (which lends him the figure of a giant) in the state of nature becomes the danger which the other sex really represents for Rousseau. One could say that Rousseau figures the impudic woman as a giantess – a devourer of men.

Rousseau discusses *pudeur* at some length in *Emile* (pp. 694–5), challenging those devious philosophers who simply brand it as unnatural:

Si les femelles des animaux n'ont pas la même honte, que s'ensuit-il? Ont-elles comme les femmes les désirs illimités auxquels cette honte sert de frein? Le désir ne vient pour elles qu'avec le besoin; le besoin satisfait, le désir cesse…l'instinct les pousse et l'instinct les arrête; où sera le supplément de cet instinct négatif dans les femmes quand vous leur aurez ôté la pudeur? Attendre qu'elles ne se soucient plus des hommes, c'est attendre qu'ils ne soient plus bons à rien.

It is in the nature of women to have unlimited desires. However, in the solitary state of nature, female desire could not have the pernicious consequences that it would have in society if it were unchecked. Female animals are governed by a 'negative instinct' which prevents them from being in a constant state of desire in which they could exhaust male animals to the point of death. Animals have no choice in the matter, for they do not have free will, whereas humanity is defined in the *Discours sur l'inégalité* by the possession of the quality of inner liberty; human beings, unlike animals, do not have to follow their instincts (pp. 141–2). Thus woman's lack of, or capacity to disobey, this 'negative instinct' is one of the marks of humanity, of liberty or perfectibility. One could perversely conclude that women are more fully human than men, more perfected and more degenerate.

Although Rousseau maintains that the appearance of pudicity cannot be sustained without inner assent, and Saint-Preux claims that 'on ne joue point la pudeur' (*La Nouvelle Héloïse*, p. 296), pudicity is a matter of appearances both in the sense of personal appearance and of opinion. Julie says of the virtuous wife: 'les apparences mêmes sont au nombre de ses devoirs' (p. 257). She describes marriage as having the following consequences for a woman:

elle doit compte de sa conduite à un autre; elle n'a pas seulement engagé sa foi, elle a aliéné sa liberté. Dépositaire en même temps de l'honneur de deux personnes, il ne lui suffit pas d'être honnête, il faut encore qu'elle soit honorée; il ne lui suffit pas de ne rien faire que de bien, il faut encore qu'elle ne fasse rien qui ne soit approuvé. (p. 257)

In *Emile*, Rousseau warns mothers that their daughters 'seront toute leur vie asservies à la gêne la plus continuelle et la plus sévère, qui est celle des bienséances' (p. 709). Women must be held within strict confines: those of pudic clothing, of the family circle and of public opinion.

Rousseau adds to the classical code of beneficence a theorisation of its passionate source – pity. Pity becomes fully human thanks to the imagination which allows us to relate the suffering of the other to our own past and future experiences. Jacques Derrida has shown the transgressive role of imagination with regard to nature, which Rousseau represents as a *reserve*.[7] Natural reservedness is the model for pudicity. Pity is a maternal voice but is also inextricably bound up with amorous passion, hence the possible transgression of pudicity. Beneficence is transformed in Rousseau's works from a stoical code dispassionately governing virtuous relations between men perceived as soldiers and statesmen, into a codification and universalisation of the generosity of maternal love as something to which men, too, should have access. That love is not, however, of a radically different order from amorous passion, and it has a lethal as well as a life-giving side to it – if we pursue a close analysis of Rousseau's texts.

Rousseau advocates that the code of pudicity should rule women's lives because it attempts to contain female passion, to treat it economically as something which should be stored up, held in reserve, and distributed as if a rather special scarce resource so that it retains its proper value. In fact, he tells us, female amorous passion (unlike female animals' sexual capacity) is boundless and hence highly dangerous. Here Rousseau falls into a certain tradition; in many writers feminine or maternal gifts are characterised as superabundant supply, something which is quite terrifying as well as exciting.[8] The imaginary economy of female passion does threaten beneficence by its irrational excess, and yet where the solution to that fantasised uncontrolled supply and demand is the strict reservedness of pudicity, the solution is even more inimical to beneficence than the problem was. Thus although there should be no conflict, according to Rousseau, between the moral aims and practice of pudicity and of beneficence, on a conceptual level one may be shown to exist. And in Rousseau's marginal texts the opposition between pudic reserve and beneficent expansion comes into even sharper focus.

TEXTUAL DISRUPTIONS

Rousseau's writing constantly undermines the very oppositions, such as those of the code of pudicity, which the theory sets up. On the level of representation Rousseau presents us with a number of ambiguous figures. The autobiographical texts are a major locus of such ambiguity: Rousseau himself often appears as an utterly androgynous creature supported by impudic female benefactors or by feminised male benefactors, such as Lord Keith. I shall explore a number of these representations in the sections ' *The Confessions*: the identification of the self with the weaker party ' and ' *The Confessions*: Rousseau as benefactor ' in Chapter 3 of this book. The argument could be made that Rousseau considers himself and the other characters in the *Confessions* to be the poor victims of an unjust and oppressive social system which emasculates men and encourages women to attempt to take on masculine roles. However, I would argue that in other major works of theory and fiction (*Du contrat social*, *Emile* and *La Nouvelle Héloïse*) the model male benefactors are not human individuals, they are no more than models, the conditions of possibility of their beneficiaries achieving virtue. The one human benefactor is Julie whose death appears as the inevitable result of the tension between her role as a major benefactor and her role as a pudic woman.[9] These figures are discussed in Chapter 3, in the sections 'Model beneficence: Wolmar, Emile's tutor and the legislator' and 'Model beneficence: Julie'.

One short piece of writing, the *6^e Promenade* of the *Rêveries du promeneur solitaire*, is a key example of textual disruption; it is, I would suggest, the pivot on which the questions of beneficence and pudicity can be turned. In Rousseau's earlier autobiographical writing it is largely the beneficiary who is identified with the privileged perspective of the self, and failures of beneficence are blamed on circumstances particular to the historical moment and the individuals concerned. In this *Promenade* Rousseau uses the device of the daydream to liberate himself from contingent factors: he imagines himself to be the perfect benefactor who has transparent vision of others while being himself invisible, thanks to the magic of Gyges' ring. This apparently unspoilable situation is nevertheless disrupted, and the breaking of the spell is an enigma to which the answer can only be sexual difference. The Gyges' ring daydream opens up an intertextual chain of illuminating associations concerning the transgression of pudicity by the benefactor. It is the reader, beneficiary of Rousseau's lesson, who must set to work and make a return gift, growing into a kind of writer or benefactor by teasing out the associations.

The problematic nature of the opposition set up between pudic reserve and beneficent expansion is made clearest in those of Rousseau's marginal texts on which I have focussed. This may be precisely because they engage less directly with contemporary reality or with abstract moral and political principles. Where Rousseau is closest to direct description of contemporary reality (say, in the *Confessions*) his prescriptions regarding relations between the sexes are far less clearly defined: Mme de Warens, for example, is praised in the highest terms in spite of her impudicity. Where Rousseau lays down general rules for man, femininity is evaded, and where he moves to precepts concerning women, say on women's education in *Emile*, it is assumed that pudicity can function without deleterious results – indeed must function to prevent deleterious results. However, in those of Rousseau's works which are more divorced from what is generally regarded as reality or from abstract prescription – such as *La Mort de Lucrèce, Les Amours de Milord Edouard, Le Lévite d'Ephraïm* and *Les Solitaires* – repressed contradictions, painful emotions and violence erupt at the surface. In each of these texts a desirable and ultimately virtuous woman is a victim, in fact a double victim. First of all she is violated: Lucretia is raped by a guest, Laure is a prostitute, the Levite's concubine is raped as a guest, and Sophie is either seduced or raped. Second, she (and her substitute in the case of the Levite's concubine) is a victim to virtue, dying, retreating to a nunnery, sacrificing the chance of marriage to the man she loves or in some other way effacing herself. In each case it is clear that the code of beneficence and the code of pudicity somehow fail in and of themselves or in conjunction with each other.

These works are generally fragmentary, supplementary or unfinished, less homogeneous, less harmonious and in some cases less tightly constructed than the major works. The major works, more closed and rounded, can give the impression that the reader has either to swallow them whole or spit them out. The fragments and supplements are easier for the reader to play with, their fantastical qualities inviting the imagination to wander a little.

WRITER–READER RELATIONS

One other area of interest on which I shall touch briefly is indeed that of the relationship between writer and reader. Rousseau theorises this relationship in terms of the code of beneficence: he presents his own works as benefits and those of some other writers as false gifts. However, his engagement with his imagined or real readers is far less simple than such a pronouncement would suggest. It has often been pointed out that Rousseau can be extremely hostile and aggressive towards his readers. While this can be theorised up to a point as a benefactor's response to his beneficiaries' hostility or to their 'grapple-hooks', their attempts to trap him into a greater commitment than he ever intended, his passionate outbursts seem to go well beyond the precepts of the code. A clue may lie in another side of his relationship with his readers, that of amorous passion solicited and offered. Many of Rousseau's readers have fallen in love with him just as many of them seem to hate him passionately.[10]

The creative reader needs space for her or his own construction and will often reject the suffocation of excessive nourishment or the sense of completion on the part of the writer. Rousseau, like many great readers, has a highly ambiguous attitude towards his precursors.[11] He does battle with them, and his weapons include subtle praise as well as fierce blame. The switching between the role of reader and the role of writer which all writers must constantly accomplish and reaccomplish may be compared to the switching between the role of recipient and that of donor, and between a feminine role and a masculine one. While Rousseau's prescriptions for social existence assert that femininity should be confined to females and masculinity to males, his texts represent a much more complicated pattern and his textual self oscillates between each possible combination of traits: femininity, masculinity, giving, receiving, reading, writing, loving, being loved, hating and being hated. This would not refute Rousseau's self-presentation as a benefactor, but would rather refine and enrich his portrait of the benefactor.

CHAPTER 2

The code of beneficence

Avant d'observer, il faut se faire des règles pour ses observations: il faut se faire une échelle pour y rapporter les mesures qu'on prend.   (*Emile*, p. 837)

Many centuries of moral and political philosophers have maintained that the question of beneficence is of crucial importance for the analysis of virtuous relations, relations which go beyond the call of justice, in a society of non-equals. Study of the discussion or the description of beneficence in different writers makes it possible to detect elements of a code, a set of prescriptions which seem to be presupposed by a large number of those who enter the debate.[1] This chapter will briefly outline and analyse some key elements of the code of beneficence based on eighteenth-century writing, and on some of the authorities who influenced the eighteenth century in general and Rousseau in particular. Even in this primary analysis it will start to become clear that many aspects of the code impinge on questions of sexual difference – if only in that elements of the definition of the true benefactor implicitly exclude the pudic woman.

Speaking of *the* code of beneficence might suggest something monolithic and inflexible; in fact, as the sociologist Jean Baudrillard has pointed out, individuals or groups use 'n'importe code moral ou institutionnel... à leur façon: ils en jouent, y trichent, ils le parlent dans leur dialecte de classe'.[2] While still being schematic, it is possible to distil three particular tendencies within the code of beneficence which can, partly for neatness but with some justification, be attached to the names of three classical thinkers. These three tendencies – Aristotelian magnanimity, Ciceronian calculation and Senecan 'sensibility' –

each have particular resonance in eighteenth-century society on account of the need of various groups to express class or (cross-class) preferences in a moral discourse.

Aristotle's *Nicomachean Ethics* (written in the fourth century B.C.) deals with magnanimity amongst other ways of achieving happiness through 'an activity of soul in accordance with virtue' (1, 7).[3] Aristotle presents a persuasive argument in favour of according greater prestige to the benefactor who is, of course, in the position of power, than to the beneficiary. It is an argument which was (unsurprisingly) widely adopted, and one which it is necessary to understand in order to comprehend Rousseau's stance in opposition to it. Aristotle provides a discourse of *nobility* which is easily appropriated by, for example, a hereditary aristocracy. The practice of beneficence in the eighteenth century may often have been closest to the theory expounded by Aristotle. He also had enormous influence, perhaps in part because he said what the most powerful in society wanted to hear, in political debates concerning tyranny and slavery and in discussion over the respective roles of men and women.

Cicero's *de Officiis* (44 B.C.) is a work which combines high moral sentiment with a pragmatism that makes his version of beneficence sometimes uncomfortably close to (profitable) investment.[4] For instance, a politician is advised to cultivate a reputation for virtue and generosity. The fine calculation which he encourages is particularly attractive to a class that wants to oppose profligacy both on the part of the spendthrift aristocracy and also – at least potentially – on the part of feckless underlings.

Out of those works which were available to Rousseau, the one coming closest to spelling out a code of beneficence in some detail and closest to Rousseau's own moral conclusions is Seneca's *de Beneficiis* (A.D. 62–4).[5] Seneca is a useful guide to fill in a number of the details Rousseau assumes will be familiar to his reader steeped in the moral teaching of the day which was influenced by classical antiquity as much as by Christianity.[6] Rousseau is able to use implicit reference to Seneca or to a Senecan tradition in order to construct a discourse of emotional identification with the weaker party in a transaction which would be comprehensible to his readers. That Rousseauian sensibility often approaches a feminine identification, but none of the classical writers approve this nor does Rousseau approve it in his prescriptive statements.

In this chapter, I shall first consider how beneficence is valued by classical and Enlightenment thinkers with quite different political preferences because it is believed to reinforce the social bond; all these thinkers place high value on that bond even though they may imagine the best possible social relations in various dissimilar ways. Then I shall turn to the elements of rational calculation and emotional intuition which must both be present in an act of beneficence, but which are differently emphasised by different writers. Finally I shall consider the hierarchical elements within beneficence, and that most extreme hierarchy which is represented by slavery.

SOCIAL BOND

Beneficence is generally presented by classical writers, however they understand the relationship between the benefactor and the beneficiary, as the cement which holds society together. Seneca refers to it as 'a practice that constitutes the chief bond of human society'. This notion is attractive to most Enlightenment thinkers, and Voltaire goes so far as to claim that beneficence *is* virtue because of its social function, whereas the cardinal or theological 'virtues' are no more than goodness since they can be practised in solitude and benefit only the self.[7] Voltaire's preference for public rather than private virtues is often contrasted, first of all by himself, with Rousseau's alleged rejection of society. That neat opposition can only be sustained by a caricatural presentation of Rousseau, who withdraws from society because he is, in his opinion, unfortunate enough to have become a public figure in a corrupt and hierarchical environment. While that decision to withdraw, and his appreciation of the private pleasures of solitude, make an important distinction between himself and many other writers of the period, it must be remembered that his expressed general preference is for life inside not outside a community. In fact, Rousseau shares with the *philosophes* a fundamental concern with social virtues at least on a theoretical level. Whether explicit or not, such a preference for beneficence is ranking it above Christianity as retreat from the world, even while retreat is presented as preferable to the kind of active engagement of, for example, the Society of Jesus.

The hierarchical opposition of public to private, or social to solitary, is not without interest for the question of sexual difference and of the code of pudicity. The public sphere has long been a masculine sphere both literally in many instances and in terms of its characterisation.[8] Rousseau allies himself with selected classical precedents in praising masculine public *virtu* and feminine confinement to the private domain. And yet in his own life – and hence the charge that he rejects society – he withdraws progressively; from Môtiers he writes to one of his female correspondents: 'J'ai pris l'habit long, et je fais des lacets: me voilà plus d' à moitié femme; que ne l'ai-je toujours été.'[9] Rousseau's withdrawals, and his exploration of the pains and pleasures of his feminine (greater) half, do not fail to leave their traces on what could otherwise be a simple and hierarchical division of roles between the sexes.

While I have argued that thinkers with quite different political positions all advocate the practice of beneficence, there are particular kinds of desired or actual states which are much less favourable to that practice. It is generally argued that beneficence is a feature only of those societies where private property is recognised since if all property is held in common no one can make a gift to another. This can be used as a point against beneficence (dependent on private property and probably inequality) or against communism (inhibiting individual virtue) depending on the prejudices of the thinker. Aristotle argues, in his *Politics*, that the communism of Plato's Guardians precisely prevents the exercise of generosity. Of course, beneficence can involve 'goods' other than material possessions, but then equally the community can take over responsibility for many services such as education or the provision of food and lodging – as it does for the Guardians in Plato's *Republic*.[10]

Beneficence, a positive virtue, is subordinated by the classical authorities to justice, which is a duty or negative virtue. Thus respecting the property of others comes before offering them something of your own. The particular act of beneficence must be subordinated to the universal consideration of society as a whole; for instance, conferring benefits on someone who is liable to use his advantages against others would be an unjust act, and therefore it might be generous, but it would not be truly beneficent. Chamfort remarks, towards the end of the eighteenth century: 'Il faut être juste avant d'être généreux, comme on a des chemises avant d'avoir des dentelles.'[11]

Justice defines and divides; beneficence begins at a point where two distinct and different parties can be identified so that one can offer a benefit to the other. However, the act of beneficence is the concrete expression of an emotional *rapprochement*. The benefactor must make an imaginative identification with the situation of the beneficiary (pity) before he will be inspired to act. The action should practically, as well as emotionally, narrow the gap between the two men as it is a transfer from the one with more to the one with less. Thus it is different from, on the one hand, false beneficence where the donor gives in order to emphasise his superiority and, on the other hand, a market transaction where in theory two commodities of equal value are exchanged.

The claim that the social bond is cemented by beneficence is often supported by an analogy with friendship between individuals, which both encourages and is reinforced by an exchange of benefits. Gifts are most often exchanged between friends, that is, according to the classical concept of friendship, people of like disposition. Examples of the ideal of friendship can be found in almost every classical text which influenced the Enlightenment, from Homer onwards. Homer's *Iliad* provides the example of Achilles and Patroclus; Plato's *Dialogues* provide numerous instances; Aristotle discusses friendship in Book VIII of the *Ethics* ('The kinds of friendship') and in Book IX ('The grounds of friendship') – he considers friendship to be the most common occasion for an exchange of benefits and 'the bond that holds communities together' (*Ethics*, VIII, I). Rousseau particularly acknowledges the influence which Plutarch had on him in terms of providing a model for friendship. That classical ideal friendship is very important in the centuries preceding Rousseau. One of the most famous examples is the friendship between Montaigne and La Boëtie celebrated in Montaigne's essay 'De l'amitié', which argues that true friendship should be valued far above blood ties or sexual love. However, that particular friendship is described as such a perfect union that beneficence becomes impossible since there is not the necessary difference between the two men. Friendship which does not go so far as a merging into one, but is nevertheless a powerful social bond is admired by many eighteenth-century thinkers. Voltaire, for example, mentions Cicero and explicitly cites Greek, Roman and Arab, rather than French, examples in his article 'Amitié' in the *Dictionnaire philosophique*. He suggests that the number of services exchanged is one measure of the degree of friendship. Later Chamfort writes:

On fait quelquefois dans le monde un raisonnement bien étrange. On dit à un homme, en voulant récuser son témoignage en faveur d'un autre homme: c'est votre ami. Eh! morbleu, c'est mon ami, parce que le bien que j'en dirai est vrai, parce qu'il est tel que je le peins. Vous prenez la cause pour l'effet et l'effet pour la cause. (*Maximes et pensées*, XIII)

This example in its combative spirit suggests, in conformity with the tradition, that such friendship, which is not based on self-interest, is known only to some men and not to all. That exclusiveness can be appropriated by any existing or would-be elite. For Rousseau it is a virtuous and emotional elite – 'les âmes sensibles'.

One consequence of the classical preference for beneficence between those of a like disposition is that it tends to exclude women in so far as they are regarded as essentially different from men. Indeed, while women may, exceptionally, be cited benefactors or beneficiaries, the classical model of beneficence is specifically between 'good men of congenial character'.[12] Women most often appear in Seneca's treatise as 'harlots' (female slaves) or 'promiscuous wives'. Women are often represented as incapable of the kind of friendships to which men have access. Montaigne, for example, writes of women and friendship: 'ce sexe par nul exemple n'y est encore peu arriver, et par le commun consentement des escholes anciennes en est rejetté' ('De l'amitié'). In 'De trois commerces' (III, 3), Montaigne juxtaposes friendships between men, amorous passion between men and women, and the relationship between men and books (representing the great men of the past).

In eighteenth-century worldly novels or comedies the language of beneficence employed by men to women is most frequently a mask for erotic love. Rousseau's *Confessions* contain traces of that duality of meaning. It is striking in, for example, Marivaux's *Le Paysan parvenu* where the beneficiary, Jacques, often speaks of his gratitude and affection for his succession of benefactors. If his benefactor is a woman then his words are understood in an erotic sense whereas if his benefactor is a man then the same words conform to the sense of the code of beneficence. Jacques has considerable mastery over the various linguistic codes and can successfully enter into relationships which are more like market transactions than beneficence with his female 'benefactors'. It is interesting to contrast his situation with that of the female beneficiary in Marivaux's novel of sensibility, *La Vie de Marianne*. Marianne at first takes Climal to be, as he describes himself, a benefactor; only when he offers her luxurious underwear does she realise that his apparent gifts are really *bait* and would become *payment*. She rejects that dangerous option and instead seeks and finds benefactors of her own sex. Giving presents to the beloved was so commonly understood as an erotic gesture that only the simplest individual could misunderstand; in *Les Liaisons dangereuses* Laclos gives an example of (false) beneficence manipulated far more subtly. Valmont takes care to be observed by La Présidente's servant while engaged in a 'secret' act of generosity; this proves far more successful in melting her heart than any direct gift (rightly suspected as self-interested) could have been.

The representation of female–female beneficence on a mother–daughter model in Marivaux's *La Vie de Marianne* is something which is rather less common in eighteenth-century writing than male–male beneficence, but more common than many of the theoretical accounts of beneficence or indeed friendship given by male writers would suggest. Sarah Scott's *Millenium Hall* (1762) describes a utopic all-female community sustained by friendship. Her characters Miss Melvyn and Miss Mancel both believe that 'the boundaries and barriers raised by those two watchful and suspicious enemies, Meum and Tuum, were... broke down by true friendship; and all property laid in one undistinguished common'.[13] Such 'communism' is, however, only to be experienced by those who are in some way equals. *Millenium Hall* also contains descriptions of many acts of beneficence carried out by the ladies who form the community, such as adopting and educating 'every child after the fifth of every poor person' (p. 15) in the vicinity.

The three Graces were evoked as a vivid illustration of the circulation of benefits holding society together in a tradition which stretches back at least as far as Hesiod. It is a particularly interesting image since it conjures up some kind of association between the exchange of benefits (Aristotle's *Ethics*, v, 5) and erotic love. The use of women (or goddesses) to represent a virtue traditionally associated with masculinity is not unusual, nor is it unusual that they should barely be clad – Seneca suggests that this might be because 'benefits desire to be seen' (1, 3). However, Edgar Wind has traced a quite specific shift in the meaning ascribed to the three Graces from that of charity to erotic love.[14] In general, Platonic communism, beneficence and the market economy all appear to expel eros in so far as they are rationalisations of human conduct. That expulsion is, however, impossible – although eros may not return via the difference between the sexes but via libidinally charged friendship.

According to Aristotle, the three Graces would remind men of the importance of gratitude. The question of gratitude does have a different resonance according to the politics underlying the writers' ethical positions. When the importance of the social bond is very firmly emphasised this can be part of an argument condemning ingrates as those who destroy the fabric of society. Cicero is useful for this purpose, claiming that 'all men detest ingratitude and look upon the sin of it as a wrong committed against themselves also, because it discourages generosity' (*de Officiis* II, 18). Rousseau (and others) will borrow certain tenets from Seneca in order to argue a much more complicated case. The more complicated case suggests both that ingratitude, like gratitude, is often the product of the benefactor's behaviour, and that giving is so pleasurable that the recipient necessarily confers a benefit on the donor.[15] Obviously such arguments promote much greater suppleness in the relationship between benefactor and beneficiary – undermining any case for a fixed hierarchy.

RATIONAL CALCULATION AND EMOTIONAL INTUITION

Beneficence should combine spontaneous emotion (nature) and learnt reasoned conduct (artifice).[16] The emotion involved is a blend of pity at the beneficiary's need and pleasure in the action; this will be discussed further in Chapter 4. By virtue of its combination of emotion and reason, beneficence should straddle many of the oppositions set up between the gift and the economic, such as those made often in the twentieth century by social anthropologists contrasting 'primitive peoples' with 'ourselves'. Here is an example of the chain of concepts which sustain each side of that opposition:

We have on the one hand, imagination, synthetic thought, gift-exchange, use-value and gift-increase, all of which are linked by a common element of *eros*, or relationship, bonding, 'shaping into one'. And we have, on the other hand, analytic or dialectical thought, self-reflection, logic, market exchange, exchange value and interest on loans, all of which share a touch of *logos*, of differentiating into parts.[17]

Such oppositional series frequently add 'feminine' to the erotic column and 'masculine' to the logical one.[18] The code of beneficence represents an attempt to use logical, analytical thought to govern a gift which is neither shadow market exchange nor erotic merging into one.[19]

The balance of calculation and sensibility is a difficult one, and while both Cicero and Seneca allow for both, Cicero certainly is more ready to emphasise calculation which includes some self-interest, whereas Seneca is more insistent on the need to identify emotionally with your beneficiary. Beneficence, as a three-part movement of gift, gratitude and repayment, can of course be taken over by those market values from which Rousseau, like Seneca, is determined to distinguish it. But if it becomes an interested act at any stage then, they would claim, it is no longer beneficence but something else. La Rochefoucauld is famous for encapsulating in his maxims a competitive society dominated by *amour-propre*; Rousseau describes his work as a 'livre triste et désolant, principalement dans la jeunesse où l'on n'aime pas à voir l'homme comme il est' (*Confessions*, p. 112). La Rochefoucauld observes of gratitude, for example: 'Il est de la reconnaissance comme de la bonne foi des marchands: elle entretient le commerce; et nous ne payons pas parce qu'il est juste de nous acquitter, mais pour trouver plus facilement des gens qui nous prêtent.'[20] There is already an attempted refutation of that argument in Seneca's treatise: if gratitude were motivated by the desire for further benefits, then ingrates would be regarded as disinterested, whereas in fact they are universally condemned and believed to be lacking in justice. Of course, a cynical observer of society might reply that ingrates are castigated only because they spoil social exchange for everyone else; or, as La Rochefoucauld puts it, echoing Glaucon in Book II of Plato's *Republic*: 'L'amour de la justice n'est en la plupart des hommes que la crainte de souffrir l'injustice' (no. 78). Rousseau is only too well aware – as his correspondence and autobiographical texts show – that the vocabulary of beneficence, of affection and disinterest, had long been used to mask a reality of obligation between patrons and clients inherited and adapted from feudalism.[21]

Seneca's *de Beneficiis* is an attempt at codification of a complex and multi-faceted human practice. It is, as Aristotle points out concerning the general study of ethics, 'arguing about what is for the most part so from premises which are for the most part true' (*Ethics*, I, 3). In an attempt at precision and comprehensiveness, Seneca sometimes goes into great detail about the smallest points; this helps to emphasise that beneficence is an art which cannot be learnt overnight. However, the learning must build upon and refine a certain sensibility. Seneca defines a benefit, not as the outer material form of a gift, but as the emotion which prompts the gift and the action of giving:

> That which falls beneath the eye is not a benefit – it is but the trace and mark of a benefit.
>
> What then is a benefit? It is the act of a well wisher who bestows joy and derives joy from the bestowal of it and is inclined to do what he does from the prompting of his own will. And so what counts is not what is done or given, but the spirit of the action because a benefit consists not in what is done or given, but in the intention of the giver or doer. (*de Beneficiis*, I, 5–6)

Rousseau is in complete agreement on this point: 'il n'y a que l'intention qui oblige' (*La Nouvelle Héloïse*, p. 446). Many of Seneca's specific precepts concerning beneficence follow logically from his definition of a benefit. For example, he suggests that you should bestow a benefit before your beneficiary has reached the point of actually asking you for it, because 'it is unpleasant... to have to say, "I ask,"'... A friend and everyone whom you hope to make a friend, by doing him a service must be excused from saying these words' (*de Beneficiis*, II, 2).

Cicero discusses at some length the question of who has the most claim on a person's beneficence. He proposes as a general rule that debts of gratitude should be repaid before we give to those who have never given to us. This underlines the circular nature of beneficence which was exemplified by the three Graces. The largest gifts must be repaid first, which means that it is necessary to discriminate between the quality of the different benefits which are received; a well-considered gift, for instance, is more valuable than one given on impulse.

Another method of ranking is to give more to those who need it most. But Cicero concludes that one should actually judge on merit (rather than on need), which makes classical beneficence rather different from *charité*, which is generally defined as 'bienfait *envers les pauvres*' (Paul Robert, *Dictionnaire de la langue française*, 1976, my emphasis). Charity may be offered to those who are, in different senses, very far from the donor and it does not attempt to break down boundaries but preserves the hierarchy between donor and recipient, who is defined as essentially needy. The benefactor, according to Cicero, gives to those who are close to, or like himself; in extreme circumstances he owes help first to his country, then to his parents, and then to his own family and dependants (*de Officiis*, 1, 17). In normal circumstances, however, Cicero rules that ties of friendship – assumedly male–male friendship – may be stronger than those of blood or matrimony.

Another general rule is that benefactors do not remind their beneficiaries that they have helped them.[22] Like many of the regulations of the code this general rule can have an aristocratic inflection. Indeed it is one of the themes, inspired by the classics, which recur in many of the plays which Rousseau so often went to see. In *Iphigénie* (IV, 6), for example, Racine borrows from Terence the line:

Un bienfait reproché tint toujours lieu d'offense.

The *rapprochement* of benefit and insult in that line is unsurprising since any beneficence in seventeenth- and eighteenth-century French theatre is usually a form of Aristotelian aristocratic magnanimity. This means that beneficiaries are often too eager to repay since they are unwilling to be obliged to anyone.

Where true beneficence is concerned the urge to repay should be fired by any need on the part of the benefactor not by the beneficiary's discomfort at being indebted – which rebuffs the benefactor's generosity: 'to put it briefly, he who is too eager to pay his debt is unwilling to be indebted, and he who is unwilling to be indebted is ungrateful' (*de Beneficiis*, IV, 40). It is crucial not to hope for your benefactor to experience need so that you can repay him; Seneca compares such a barbarous hope to the most misguided and selfish love (VI, 25). It may even stem from a secret desire to humiliate your benefactor. The beneficiary should wish that his benefactor will always be in a position to be generous himself, and that he need never ask for help on his own behalf. Rousseau takes this representation of the good beneficiary, as someone who enables the benefactor's virtue, a stage further, suggesting that even the expression of gratitude may be

magn] = *false bfscience*

insulting to the benefactor because it implies that he desired these formulas. He writes to François Coindet on 13 April 1759, 'j'aurais peur de grâter par mes remerciements le prix de vos soins, ainsi je ne vous dis rien' (*Correspondance complète*, VI, p. 70).

MAGNANIMITY AND SLAVERY

I am using Aristotle's term 'magnanimity' here to refer to what may also be termed – in accordance with Rousseau's interpretation – *false beneficence*. A great deal of contemporary gift exchange was, by Rousseau's lights, false beneficence, in other words, gifts or services which were rendered in a spirit of self-interest. Material self-interest would largely be excluded by Aristotle's definition of magnanimity and is a rather simpler case to dismiss. However, the kind of self-interest which lies in the sense that giving maintains the giver in a position of superiority relative to the recipient is far more difficult to pin down.[23] A long tradition has held that it is morally better to give than to receive; this can easily be appropriated by the aristocratic code of honour. Because of that social appropriation a moral reversal can occur making it possible to argue that paradoxically it is morally superior to receive than to give. La Bruyère, who is clearly influenced by *de Beneficiis*, writes 'Quelque désintéressement qu'on ait à l'égard de ceux qu'on aime, il faut quelquefois se contraindre pour eux, et avoir la générosité de recevoir' (*Du cœur*). Rousseau remarks in his *Confessions* (p. 112) that he would read and discuss La Bruyère with Mme de Warens, who preferred La Bruyère to the unhappy vision of La Rochefoucauld. Rousseau himself makes one of the most unequivocal statements on behalf of the beneficiary, in keeping with his constant protest against power. He writes on 17 December 1757 in a letter to Sophie d'Houdetot, 'entre deux amis, celui qui donne est sans contredit fort obligé à celui qui reçoit' (*Correspondance complète*, IV, p. 395).

Aristotle's argument that giving is superior because it is active, and that receiving is inferior because it is passive (an argument which Rousseau does not accept) must remind the reader of traditional oppositions between masculinity and femininity. An interpretation of biology, as perceived by a male-dominated society, presents men as naturally active and women as naturally passive. Aristotle's erroneous theory of repro-duction in which women provided the passive matter and men the active form of the foetus was enormously popular for centuries in which it coincided with the ideological needs of the dominant group.[24]

Aristotle compares the benefactor to an artist on the grounds that a benefactor creates his beneficiary as a poet creates his poem. This arises in answer to the question: 'Why are benefactors more loving than beneficiaries?' (*Ethics*, IX, 7). Aristotle answers this query as follows:

Every craftsman loves the work of his own hands more than it would love him if it came to life. Probably this happens most of all with poets, because they are exceedingly fond of their own poems, loving them as if they were their children. Well, the case of the benefactor is much the same. What he benefits is his own handiwork; so he loves it more than the work loves its maker.

Rousseau seems to reaffirm the first point in this quotation from Aristotle in his 'scène lyrique', *Pygmalion*, which is a version of the myth of the sculptor who falls in love with his own creation – a marble statue of a woman, Galathea. The marble statue is a concrete figure for the unresponsiveness of the created object. According to the myth, the statue is divinely accorded life and returns the love of her creator. However, in Rousseau's 'scène lyrique' the ending is ambivalent, for the statue having touched herself and uttered the word 'moi' and then touched a marble stone and recognised that it no longer resembles her, touches Pygmalion and pronounces with a sigh 'Ah! encore moi' (p. 1231). As Paul de Man points out 'the separation between Galathea's coldness and Pygmalion's impetuousness could not be greater'.[25] This representation appears to fall into the traditional pattern of opposition with regard to the sexes: man, the benefactor and quasi-divine creator, bestows form; woman is matter, creature, passive recipient. Rousseau's text, however, goes a long way in undoing these very oppositions: Galathea is not simply other, but a configuration of sameness and otherness.

Her stony coldness is also a reflection of the figural coldness of Pygmalion's condition, frozen before its own sublimity (de Man, *Allegories of Reading*, p. 178). Pygmalion's desire has self-erotic elements – as does that of Narcisse in Rousseau's play of that name. The initial polarities enter into a typically Rousseauian play of substitutions and reversals.

As long as the beneficiary is incapable of being a benefactor in his own turn, like the case of the young Emile in *Emile*, it may indeed be that the benefactor is the more loving, as is the artist towards his creation. However, when the beneficiary can respond and has the capacity to repay, then the creative act of the benefactor is able to function at its most sublime, that is, as a model which the beneficiary imitates, becoming active, creative and loving in his turn. This is where the dynamic model of beneficence is rather different from the more static model of male–female relations.

Beneficence indeed shares many characteristics with artistic creation; both may set themselves apart from any suggestion of a venal motive by seeing the act as its own recompense, and in both cases this motivation may slide into what is ultimately desire for recognition. That is all the more the case for Rousseau who sees himself as a creative artist only in order to be a benefactor thanks to the moral and political content of his writings.

Another scheme of comparison between the benefactor and the artist is that which takes a divine source of abundance (such as the sun, God or nature) as its model; this would appear to preclude any kind of self-interest. These comparisons to the sun or to a God the Father can be regarded as an attempt to virilise what might otherwise be compared to motherhood and to the imaginary superabundant maternal gifts. The rhetoric of analogy or of opposition is rarely innocent. Jacques Derrida has suggested that in the fictitious history of man in Rousseau's *Discours sur l'inégalité* there is a polarisation within man of animality and humanity.[26] Elsewhere he suggests that a similar polarisation occurs in accounts of artistic creation which oppose the disinterested artist to the craftsman, who is associated with wage-earning and hence venal (animal) motivation.[27] The

disinterested artist is metaphorically linked to divine beneficence. Derrida's analysis (which refutes the absolute opposition)
provokes the thought that the attempt to escape what is
characterised as the animal (material or venal) side of humanity
by a metaphorical leap into divine qualities is nevertheless
encompassed within the desire for some kind of recognition or
recompense, however rarefied. This makes the safeguard of
precise codification all the more important, for the lofty
inspiration is insufficient to prevent a slide into self-interest.[28]

Seneca advises his reader to follow the example set by the
immortal gods: 'let us follow these as our guides in so far as
human weakness permits; let us make our benefits, not
investments, but gifts' (*de Beneficiis*, I, I). This model of 'lavish
and unceasing kindness' must be set slightly apart from the
model of a circulation of benefits which strengthens the social
bond; for example, it involves the reversal of attitudes towards
ingrates: 'For they [the gods] follow their own nature, and in
their universal bounty include even those who are ill interpreters
of their gifts' (*de Beneficiis*, I, I). Whereas, from the standpoint of
circulation of benefits within society (the rational consideration), it is vital that the flow should not be interrupted by
ingrates, from the (emotional) standpoint of the bountiful
donor it is most important to give rather than to receive any
return. 'This is the mark of a soul that is truly great and good.'
For Seneca, the immediate fruit of a benefit for the donor is
delight in having done good; it is moral pleasure. This is
experienced by benefactors in Rousseau's texts; Julie, for
example, 'Jouit du bien qu'elle fait...cette âme si peu sensible
à l'amour-propre apprend à s'aimer dans ses bienfaits' (*La
Nouvelle Héloïse*, p. 532).

That moral pleasure is not of course to be equated with the
aristocratic sense of mastery described by Aristotle (or by
Mauss). But in many eighteenth-century texts it is a fine line
between the two. In *La Vie de Marianne*, Marivaux returns over
and over again to the problems of beneficence, false beneficence
and ingratitude. He deplores the 'unjust delicacy' which makes
people dislike to feel indebted; his solution to this apparently
widespread failing is to manipulate it to promote repayment:

Vous dites que celui qui vous oblige a de l'avantage sur vous. Eh bien! Voulez-vous lui conserver cet avantage, n'être qu'un atome auprès de lui, vous n'avez qu'à être ingrat. Voulez-vous redevenir son égal, vous n'avez qu'à être reconnaissant; il n'y a que cela qui puisse vous donner votre revanche. S'enorgueillit-il du service qu'il vous a rendu, humiliez-le à son tour et mettez-vous modestement au-dessus de lui par votre reconnaissance.[29]

In this quotation the slippage from beneficence into Aristotelian magnanimity is clear in the way that, for example, the correct Senecan adverb 'modestement' (how the action should indeed be done) is voided of its primary meaning by the imperative verbs 'humiliez-le' and 'mettez-vous . . . au-dessus de lui'. The self-effacing manner perversely becomes one more means of establishing the hierarchy.

Clarissa, in the novel of that name which Rousseau much admired, wishes for her benefactors on her deathbed 'that it may be in the power of you and yours, to the end of time, to *confer* benefits rather than to be obliged to *receive* them'.[30] She refers to conferring benefits as 'a goldlike power'. Such a sense of superiority as that cherished by Aristotle's magnanimous man might indeed create ingrates. Seneca's and Rousseau's identification with the beneficiary incites them to treat in some detail the question of an apparent benefactor to whom one does not owe gratitude, because he made 'an offering not to me, but to his pride' (*de Beneficiis*, 1, 7).

Rousseau's substitution of constructed moral bonds for naturally developing relationships – a feature of all his theoretical works – is, in general, designed to promote liberty and equality. In the case of the marital contract (another artificial alliance), however, Rousseau decides to institute inequality on pragmatic grounds. He therefore appeals to what he elsewhere denounces as an ideologically constructed nature (*préjugé* in eighteenth-century terms). This interesting aberration, and its effect on an otherwise coherent pattern of rejection of aristocratic theories of natural hierarchies, will be studied later.

Rousseau does nevertheless – and importantly – claim that interpersonal relations between men and women, like those between men and men, are political in nature and consequently subject to reversals.[31] Here he differs from Aristotle who argues that while the relation between husband and wife is one of political rule (whereas it is despotic rule between master and slave, and royal rule between father and child) it is not subject to reversals.[32] In any other kind of political rule the ruler may become the ruled, but, for Aristotle, the husband will always be the ruler of the wife on account of his natural superiority, just as free men have natural superiority over slaves.

It is interesting to relate the position of slaves and that of women with regard to beneficence. Rousseau addresses women as 'Sexe toujours esclave ou tyran' in *Le Lévite d'Ephraïm* (p. 1221) – that example is discussed further in Chapter 6. Sometimes Rousseau describes women as slaves without using the term 'slave'. In *Sur les femmes*, for example, he writes: 'Considérons d'abord les femmes privées de leur liberté par la tyrannie des hommes' (p. 1255). In *Emile* (p. 710), the lot of women has much in common with enslavement:

elles ont ou doivent avoir peu de liberté... elles ne cessent jamais d'être assujeties ou à un homme ou aux jugements des hommes, et... il ne leur est jamais permis de se mettre au-dessus de ces jugements... faites pour obéir à un être aussi imparfait que l'homme, souvent si plein de vices, et toujours si plein de défauts [la femme] doit apprendre de bonne heure à souffrir même l'injustice.

Rousseau claims, in *Emile*, that were it not for feminine ruse, women would indeed be the slaves of men; because of their cleverness they only appear to be slaves (p. 712). Yet the same might be said of any wily slave who secretly learns to dominate his master.

In the classical treatises under discussion it is implicitly assumed that both donor and recipient are male (and free). When Seneca gives an example of a man bestowing a dowry on a girl, the man does so in order to confer a benefit on her (dead) father. Like any other property, slaves could be gifts, and could be held in common. This possibility is more problematic with regard to wives. Plato's suggestion, in the *Republic*, that spouses should be held in common is rejected by Aristotle (and by Rousseau) on the grounds that this would weaken family affection and that this would be detrimental to the state. Such an argument supposes that the family bond has more influence on the larger social bond than vice versa, a position which Rousseau does not hold consistently. Furthermore, writes Aristotle in the *Politics*, holding spouses in common removes an exercise in virtue, that of self-restraint with regard to other men's wives.

Sparta is a state which Aristotle praises because it allows private property, but men may freely use other men's possessions. Rousseau bestows even more extensive praise on Sparta; his vision of Sparta as a site of civic virtue is largely taken from Plutarch's *Vie de Lycurgue* which proffers a positive moral account of the early days of the Republic.[33] The brief account of the education and role of women in Sparta bears certain resemblances to Rousseau's dictates on the education of women even though Rousseau is much less extreme, as befitting a writer for more corrupt times. Rousseau is noted for his banishing of jealousy from love; the Spartans are reported to carry this to the point where husbands invite worthy young men to sleep with their wives. Plutarch writes, 'la raison voulait que l'on permît à ceux qui en étaient dignes engendrer des enfants en commun' (*Vie de Lycurgue*, XXIX). The use of women was thus shared like the use of slaves or other possessions.

Slavery is defended by Aristotle on the grounds that there are natural slaves; in *Du contrat social* (p. 353), Rousseau makes a subtle attack on the defenders of this thesis:

Aristote avait raison, mais il prenait l'effet pour la cause. Tout homme né dans l'esclavage naît pour l'esclavage, rien n'est plus certain. Les esclaves perdent tout dans leurs fers, jusqu'au désir d'en sortir...s'il y a donc des esclaves par nature, c'est qu'il y a eu des esclaves contre nature.

It may be deduced from Aristotle's descriptions of magnanimity that the limited amount of virtue which he allows to the slave (such as the diligence necessary to prevent him from neglecting his work) would not be sufficient to allow a slave to be a benefactor. Neither would he be able to be a beneficiary in the full sense of the word (experiencing gratitude and the will to repay) for he benefits from his master only in the sense that

can slaves be bfactors?

domestic animals do. The Greek word for 'generosity' which Aristotle employs is *eleutheriotes*, that for 'meanness' is *aneleutheria*. As the term *eleutheria* means 'freedom', the very word brings together the concepts of generosity and freedom. *Eleutheriotes* is often translated by 'liberality', which is derived from the Latin *liberalis* or *liberalitas* (generosity) both related to *liber*, meaning 'free'.

Seneca's position is directly opposed to the tradition deriving from Aristotle and reflected in Roman law, which held the slave to be a *res* (thing), a status often compared with death. Seneca insists that the slave is a human being (*persona*) with respect to his ability to perform acts of beneficence, although he still appears to regard the slave as merely a piece of property with regard to benefits conferred upon him. Seneca gives, and then convincingly refutes, the arguments which deny that a slave may be his master's benefactor; for example, the argument that a slave saving his master's life is doing no more than what he is obliged to do. Seneca maintains, in his *Epistulae* (for instance, no. XLVII) and in *de Beneficiis*, that a slave is a fully moral being, capable of being morally superior to a man who is a 'slave' to his appetites: 'You who are a slave of lust, of gluttony, of a harlot – nay who are the common property of harlots – do you call any other man a slave?' (*de Beneficiis*, III, 28). Rousseau, like Seneca, believes that moral freedom is the only freedom necessary to be a benefactor and that this is available to men in any social condition and even under physical constraints; in *Les Solitaires* (the sequel to *Emile*) Emile writes: 'le temps de ma servitude fut celui de mon règne, et jamais je n'eus tant d'autorité sur moi que quand je portai les fers des barbares' (p. 917).

Rousseau's firm conviction is that a man can never be *res*, that men are born with an inalienable inner liberty and that this is what distinguishes them from other animals who are obliged to follow natural law through their instincts. Men always have a choice, and have the capacity for substitution which enables change; they are not obliged to keep to one particular diet, means of communication or way of life – as Rousseau points out in the *Discours sur l'inégalité*. In *Du contrat social*, Rousseau affirms that, despite the claims of Grotius, Hobbes and others, a man can never contract away his liberty, that 'renoncer à sa liberté, c'est renoncer à sa qualité d'homme, aux droits de l'humanité, même à ses devoirs' (p. 356). Man cannot renounce his duties any more than his rights, and this must include the duty to be grateful to that which has the intention of doing us good. In the *Dialogues*, Jean-Jacques is unable to perform any acts of beneficence because every opportunity which presents itself is a trap for him, or else it will only result in harm for his beneficiary. He is thus more effectively enslaved to the will of others than Emile is when literally in bondage. However, even in this situation, Jean-Jacques can retain a desire to do good, should the possibility ever arise. It is the men who tyrannise him who are truly moral slaves, enslaved to their will to destroy another human being.

True beneficence is a bond between individuals which should allow them both to experience true liberty; it is because both parties are subject to an unwritten contract that both can be free, as all are free if all join in the social contract, according to Rousseau. The marriage contract is another matter. The bond of beneficence requires, and creates, moral liberty or *maîtrise de soi*, the desire to *be* (and therefore do) what is both good for oneself and right for others, and also to be free from the wish to *appear* good or noble in the eyes of others. Wives must, however, not only be but also appear virtuous in the view of the world. They are not free in the same way that husbands are. Aristocratic magnanimity may appear to increase the sense of freedom of the donor by diminishing his recipient; in fact, it not only humiliates the recipient but also makes the donor dependent on the forced recognition of his victim or of society. A reciprocal tie, on the other hand, promotes mutual liberation – for men – whereas one-sided obligation engenders the oppressive reversals of mastery and enslavement.

CHAPTER 3

The practice of beneficence and model benefactors in the major works

In this chapter I am going to analyse a number of representations of the relationship between benefactor and beneficiary in Rousseau's work. I consider these first of all on
Rousseau's terms to see how he uses the moral code as a
standard against which interpersonal relationships can be
judged. Second, I analyse them 'against the grain' in terms of
sexual difference. It is not too much of an exaggeration to say
that wherever there is a hierarchy the tradition of western
thought has somewhere added femininity to the characteristics
loosely associated with the inferior party. Aristotle is – as I have
indicated in Chapter 2 – a source for such oppositions; he
associates activity with the strong and powerful benefactor, and
passivity with the weak and lacking recipient. In the Aristotelian tradition it is clear that the beneficiary is less of a man
than the benefactor – even though real women are usually not
even considered as potential beneficiaries.

In Rousseau's confessional works, however, the situation is
more complex: the young Rousseau is a feminised figure in a
series of engagements with male and female individuals who
variously act as benefactors, false benefactors, malefactors and
lovers. He plays the coquette with the Curé de Pontverre who,
an experienced seducer, makes him keep his promise to convert
to Catholicism. He is the more or less helpless victim of sexual
advances from older men and women. He exposes himself
physically, in narrative, and emotionally – wanting to arouse
(maternal) pity, (maternal) discipline and love in men and
women. While masculinity in a woman (as in certain traits of
Mme d'Epinay) and feminine elegance in a man (as in Grimm's

37

fingernails) may be represented negatively – and this is not
surprising given Rousseau's stated preferences in, say, *Emile* –
the corollary of the shifting sexual roles of Jean-Jacques is the
sexual role-shifting of his partners. The 'androgyny' of Jean-
Jacques is not something which is uniquely associated with
youth, helplessness and economic dependency; Lord Keith, for
example, combines 'seriousness' with the whimsy of 'a pretty
woman'. Rousseau's female benefactors are not only economically and socially dominant, but also, in the case of Mme de
Warens, an educational influence. Commentators have more
often focused on Mme de Warens's role as a sexual initiator, but
she is also, and perhaps more importantly, an intellectual
initiator. I would argue that, contrary to our preconceptions –
set up by Rousseau's own pronouncements – the feminisation of
not only victims and malefactors, but also beneficiaries and
even benefactors, is not necessarily pejorative. In fact, where
benefactors lack the characteristics associated with femininity
then those benefactors are indeed lacking.

Do Rousseau's model male benefactors (Wolmar, the tutor
and the legislator) lack feminine qualities? I would argue that
there are in fact feminine, maternal aspects to their characterisation, but that there is a textual tension, a constant
attempt to present their generosity and self-sacrifice in a virile
light. This is achieved by a certain dehumanising of the male
models, who all err on the side of the divine. Their creative
activity (creating virtuous human beings) which could, like that
of Mme de Warens, be presented as maternal is instead
compared to that of a god. They all use benign fictions as part
of the educative process – a suppleness which is often worrying
to those readers who are intent on fetishising monologic
indivisible Truth.

Thus, there is a shift in focus and emphasis as we move from
the classical treatises dealing with the code of beneficence to the
works of Rousseau. The authors of the classical treatises are first
and foremost concerned to examine, and to draw up, a set of
precepts for the right conduct of the benefactor; the benefactor
and the beneficiary are both abstractions, although anecdotal
illustrations are sometimes used. In contrast, the autobio-

graphical works of Rousseau (like certain eighteenth-century novels) offer a compelling portrait of a beneficiary, one particular individual who, throughout his life, is in need of assistance of various kinds. Although his other writings precede the autobiographical texts, they may be viewed as the responses to needs and demands experienced by the author first, but only later relived in writing. For this reason, I shall first concentrate on the striking self-portrait of Rousseau, and his innovatory representation of benefactors from the standpoint of the beneficiary. Then I shall turn to the model benefactors in *La Nouvelle Héloïse* and *Emile* and to the just society of *Du contrat social*, which are differing attempts to resolve the problem of maintaining justice with generosity in this relationship between non-equals. Rousseau's theoretical treatment of the motivation for beneficence in the *Discours sur l'inégalité* and *Emile* will be discussed in Chapter 4.

The traditional reading of the opposition between theory, philosophy or truth (moral codes) and fiction, story-telling or embroidery is yet another variant on the opposition (under the aegis of the masculine) between the masculine and the feminine. This is sometimes expressed by a link made between fiction and amorous passion (located by eighteenth-century convention in the warm climates of the South or the Orient).[1] As *Emile* shifts from a treatise into a novel, Sophie, the woman, and love enter the scene. Within his autobiographical writings, Rousseau himself is sometimes 'feminised', as a teller of fictions, especially in relation to certain father figures. As an autobiographer Rousseau claims to be telling the truth, and thus far his task is a virile and virtuous one, even though the verb 'tell' has a somewhat ambiguous ring. Rousseau's exposure of his self to our gaze renders the exposed self a passive (feminine) object even while the exposer may be a masculine truth-teller. In this kind of way the strict relating of qualities to genders, and the strict oppositions set up between qualities or genders, begin to break down in Rousseau's texts. The oppositions which he, and many others, protest their eagerness to sustain prove ultimately (or, perhaps, from the very beginning) unsustainable.

Rousseau's autobiographical writings have the task of telling

R 1Dpès w) weaker party

the truth about his experiences in an unjust and severely hierarchical society.[2] It is a society governed by the law of the strongest – the law which is an amoral fact in the hypothetical state of nature and which can become an immoral reality in society. This is recognised by Rousseau when he leaves the service of the French Ambassador in Venice and, seeking justice, is confronted by 'une des grandes maximes de la société qui est d'immoler toujours le plus faible au plus puissant' (*Confessions*, p. 325). In the first seven books of the *Confessions*, the young Rousseau intends to make his way in the world; he is at the bottom of the ladder and he wants help not only to survive but also to prosper. I shall refer to that young Rousseau, not yet the writer, as Jean-Jacques. After the success of his *Discours sur les sciences et les arts*, he undergoes a moral reform (*Confessions*, p. 362), and it is by conscious decision that he remains, not only spiritually but in the manner of his life, on the side of the poor and weak. There is a particular kind of public beneficence involved in his writings which is closely bound up with his simple and would-be independent life. This moral stance attracts false benefactors who wish to tame the 'bear'.

The *Confessions* relate a large number of interpersonal encounters and transactions; a great many of these are classified in terms of beneficence, failed beneficence, false beneficence or naked maleficence. Rather than attempting to list them all, this chapter will focus on certain examples where Rousseau's analysis of the functioning or malfunctioning of the code is particularly interesting.[3] His analysis creates a *perspective of the self* which retrospectively casts light on his elaboration of the model benefactors in his fictional and theoretical texts. These are formulated with the needs and interests of the weaker party (to an extent identified with the self) to the fore. This is in direct contrast to Aristotle's figure of the magnanimous man, who represents the self-interest of the strong. In spite of Rousseau's prescriptions concerning the clear demarcation of sexual roles, the self which is foregrounded is at least as much a feminine self (as traditionally conceived) as it is a masculine self.

Wherever he finds inequality, Rousseau tends to identify with the weaker party and to speculate on the possibility of a just strength (such as that of Wolmar, of Emile's tutor, or of the legislator) which would encourage the weak to grow just and strong themselves (as do Saint-Preux, Emile and the citizens of the just state). In the *Confessions*, Rousseau's identification with the weak extends to a frequent sympathetic identification with the position of women in a man's world. Yet the hierarchy of masculine and feminine is the one which Rousseau's theoretical writings appear to retain intact when he has displaced almost all other hierarchies. A beneficiary should be able to become a benefactor in his turn. But Rousseau does not suggest that men should exercise their power over women in such a way as to enable women to become more like men, that is to say, to exercise power in their turn.

THE *CONFESSIONS*: THE IDENTIFICATION OF THE SELF WITH THE WEAKER PARTY

Book 1 of the *Confessions* covers Jean-Jacques's almost idyllic Genevan childhood, his first experience of injustice and then his early taste of servitude and the moral degradation to which it leads. While he is a child, his benefactors are so conspicuously *in loco parentis*, or indeed financially rewarded for their care of him, that the relationships are not strictly analysed in terms of the code of beneficence. Furthermore, the child innocently accepts the generosity of adults as the natural order of things until he has experienced ungenerous treatment. The first experience of injustice, of which Jean-Jacques is aware both emotionally and intellectually, is the episode of the broken comb.[4] In this incident, entirely benevolent action on the part of the stronger party towards his charge is suddenly replaced by the exercise of force. This arbitrary event foreshadows the institutionalised and long-term mastery which is exercised over Jean-Jacques when he becomes an apprentice. The 'esclavage servile' of his apprenticeship (p. 31) leads him with inexorable logic into petty theft. The hierarchical relationship between Jean-Jacques and his master is the antithesis of beneficence: his master hands out blows rather than gifts, and Jean-Jacques, receiving nothing which is agreeable to him, takes what pleases him without permission.

Once Jean-Jacques has left Geneva, he is prematurely thrust into the adult world, into a world in which nobody owes him anything other than those acts of common humanity which are owed to any fellow being. His relationships begin to be more clearly structured in terms of beneficence; he has to rely on benefactors for he is penniless, homeless and has few marketable skills. The theme of hospitality in particular runs through Book II: there is a genuine hospitality, but also lodging for which the host seizes repayment without the consent of his guest.

In Book II of the *Confessions*, hospitality is associated with salvation; it saves Jean-Jacques physically from hunger and homelessness, and it is also associated with spiritual salvation. As a Genevan Protestant entering the Catholic world outside Geneva, Jean-Jacques is a natural target for those who make the conversion of heretics their business. Jean-Jacques mentally links Catholicism with food because the priests who live just outside Geneva are accustomed to offering hospitality to young Genevans. This specifically religious salvation is far from being presented as an unmitigated benefit; but more fruitful salvation is also connected with hospitality – a secular moral salvation through the love of women.[5]

The first instance of hospitality in Book II is the straight-forward and unambivalent welcome offered by peasants to the young boy. In this example the hierarchical aspect of benefi-cence is reduced until it is almost negligible. Rousseau describes this heartwarming phenomenon with an ironic reference to the aristocratic belief in the necessity for the charitable benefactor to assume a position of superiority: 'Ils m'accueillaient, me logeaient, me nourrissaient trop bonnement pour en avoir le mérite. Cela ne pouvait pas s'appeler faire l'aumône; ils n'y mettaient pas assez l'air de la supériorité' (p. 46). There are indeed relatively few cases of such uncomplicated generosity in the *Confessions*, but Rousseau celebrates the possibility where he finds it.[6]

The next instance of hospitality, that of the Curé de Pontverre, merits quite a close examination. Rousseau portrays in a subtle and delicate manner the conflicting emotions of a beneficiary who is spontaneously grateful for the good food and wine bestowed upon him, and does not want to hurt the feelings of his host, but who realises that he will be asked to pay a price (namely conversion to Catholicism) that is not acceptable to him. Throughout the narrative there is a shifting play of superiority and inferiority. The Curé de Pontverre, Jean-Jacques's host, is at an advantage as host, as older man, as social superior. His duty towards the young runaway, from this position of responsibility, would be (from Rousseau's moral standpoint, which is based on secular moral codes) to send him back to his family, his homeland and his religion. However, by the Curé's own lights, which are those of the established Roman Catholic Church, his task is to save Jean-Jacques's soul by separating him from his family and from Protestant Geneva, even though 'il y avait tout à parier qu'il m'envoyait périr de misère ou devenir un vaurien' (p. 47). His misguided conception of duty and his abuse of his position of power inevitably place him in a position of inferiority in Rousseau's narrative. Furthermore, he is not only morally inferior to the narrating self, but intellectually inferior even to the narrated self, Jean-Jacques. Rousseau informs the reader: 'J'étais certainement plus savant que M. Pontverre, tout gentilhomme qu'i était' (p. 46). Jean-Jacques's inferiority lies more on the conventional, social side, whereas his advantages are due to his natural ability. That analysis suggests to Rousseau an analogy with a feminine position for, in Rousseau's view, women should accept a conventional subordinate role (as chief minister to the husband king) on account of their natural advantages in a naked power struggle. Thus, with the Curé Jean-Jacques employs something like 'la coquetterie des honnêtes femmes, qui quelquefois pour parvenir à leurs fins, savent, sans rien permettre ni rien promettre, faire espérer plus qu'elles ne veulent tenir' (p. 47).

Jean-Jacques is 'touché de reconnaissance et de respect pour le bon prêtre. Je sentais ma supériorité: je ne voulais pas l'en accabler pour prix de son hospitalité' (p. 46). He implies an acquiescence in the Curé's plans for him, which in his heart he rejects. However, the material outcome, mediated by Mme de Warens and M. and Mme Sabran, is Jean-Jacques's conversion. By not rebelling openly against the yoke of apparent obligation he will be used, despite himself, in accordance with his benefactor's ill-advised wishes.

The scene with the Curé de Pontverre prefigures the more violent episode at the Catechumens' Hospice. There it is quite plain that the mask of charity covers a market transaction: Jean-Jacques receives hospitality only in exchange for his religious conversion. Again he attempts to maintain his integrity by relying on his natural intellectual superiority and powers of argumentation, without openly rebelling against his self-styled benefactors. His textual feminisation is heightened still further: in the Hospice he suffers a double homosexual assault – the first a physical approach, the second a verbal explanation of the first, which had been incomprehensible to the innocent Jean-Jacques. That he experiences the man's desire as if he were a woman, rather than as a boy, is made explicit in his subsequent statement concerning women: 'Il me semblait que je leur devais en tendresse de sentiments, en hommage de ma personne, la réparation des offenses de mon sexe, et la plus laide guenon devenait à mes yeux un objet adorable par le souvenir de ce faux Africain' (p. 69). He knows what men owe to women because he has experienced masculine desire, and 'si nous sommes ainsi dans nos transports près des femmes il faut qu'elles aient les yeux bien fascinés pour ne pas nous prendre en horreur' (p. 67). Unlike Tiresias Rousseau does not experience both masculine and feminine sexual pleasure, but rather achieves the 'androgyny' of the victim, and therefore learns, he says, never to abuse power. The 'Moor' who makes advances to Jean-Jacques is not a duped beneficiary like Jean-Jacques; he collaborates in the debased exchange (as do most of the *catechumens*) and is ready to sell his soul for his keep. He is a willing slave for he is hoping to exploit those who tyrannise him. It is one of the 'tyrants' who more than adds insult to injury in his explanation of the assault to Jean-Jacques. His arguments are reminiscent of those which could be addressed to a woman who has fended off a sexual aggressor and is now 'making a great fuss about nothing'. He explains that Jean-Jacques should feel flattered by the compliment to his attractiveness, and that he should not have been afraid as the experience would not have been such a bad one after all. Certainly there is no cause for scandal.

Although Jean-Jacques receives help from a considerable number of people in the *Confessions*, only a few of these offer the kind of help, in the right kind of spirit, that Rousseau can present as true beneficence in the moral sense. Far more offer material aid which is rightly praised for its usefulness, but will always come lower on the scale than the spiritual or emotional support which Jean-Jacques at many times in his life needs so urgently. His few true benefactors vary from the Abbé Gaime and Claude Anet, who conform to the type of Wolmar or Emile's tutor, to Mme de Warens, whose rational principles may err, but whose heart never fails to react in the right way. Once Jean-Jacques has undergone his moral reform, he has less need of receiving lessons on right conduct and is more in a position to give them himself. From then on he is most grateful to friends who offer emotional support at the same time as their concrete assistance, and he obtains this from M. de Luxembourg and Lord Keith.

The Abbé Gaime receives a brief but warm description in Book III of the *Confessions*. He cannot help financially, unlike Jean-Jacques's aristocratic patrons who sometimes prove so disappointing in friendship, but as Rousseau explains 'je trouvai près de lui des advantages plus précieux qui m'ont profité toute ma vie; les leçons de la saine morale, et les maximes de la droite raison' (pp. 90-1). Rousseau confesses that it is the Abbé Gaime who is the model for the Savoyard vicar in *Emile*, the source of the account of natural religion. The Abbé Gaime's lessons moved Jean-Jacques above all on account of 'un certain intérêt de cœur dont je sentais qu'ils étaient pleins'. He explains: 'j'ai l'âme aimante, et je me suis toujours attaché aux gens, moins à proportion du bien qu'ils m'ont fait que de celui qu'ils m'ont voulu' (p. 92).

Claude Anet becomes 'une espèce de gouverneur' (p. 177) to Jean-Jacques; by his sober good sense he is the most effective counterbalance to the emotional warmth provided by Mme de

Warens. Yet any suggestion that these characters match masculine and feminine stereotypes should be discounted; Anet's cool rationality is combined with 'passions d'une impétuosité qu'il ne laissait jamais paraître, mais qui le dévorait en dedans' (p. 177). Jean-Jacques is like Saint-Preux between Wolmar and Julie, except that in the historical situation Mme de Warens sees no philosophical objection to sharing her favours with both men, being married to neither. Her benign influence over those around her is such that, as at Clarens, the men can only feel affection for each other. Anet is a true benefactor in that, as Rousseau puts it: 'Sans affecter avec moi l'autorité que son poste le mettait en droit de prendre, il prit naturellement celle que son jugement lui donnait sur le mien. Je n'osais rien faire qu'il parût désapprouver, et il ne désapprouvait que ce qui était mal' (p. 178). Jean-Jacques experiences perfect freedom from the outset in his relationship with Anet and with Mme de Warens; despite the social hierarchy which exists he always feels a potential equal. He is never asked to repay, and always spontaneously desires to do so. There is, however, a mystery associated with his relationship with Anet, which is Rousseau's reason for giving his name to one of the few reprehensible figures in *La Nouvelle Héloïse*, a gesture which is at odds with his explicit tribute to him when he describes his early death: 'le plus solide ami que j'eus en toute ma vie, homme estimable et rare' (p. 205) and with his implicit tribute in his description of the relationship between Wolmar, Julie and Saint-Preux. In the *Confessions*, the name 'Claude Anet', the humble social position and the upright character and behaviour are indissolubly connected. In *La Nouvelle Héloïse*, which might be seen in some ways as Rousseau's rearrangement of reality in accordance with his dreams, the name and the character are separated as if repressed jealousy had returned. It is like a reversal of the disjunction between the name 'father', which is given to those who have the character of a benefactor, and actual paternal behaviour.

Mme de Warens is the most important of all the benefactors who occur in the narrative of the *Confessions*. Rousseau writes concerning his time living with her, 'cette époque de ma vie a décidé de mon caractère' (p. 48). And yet Mme de Warens does not resemble the model of feminine virtue which Rousseau prescribes in *Emile*, Book v. She is rather an individual of such talents that Rousseau claims, under different circumstances, she could have played an important role in affairs of state. As a benefactor she is impeccable on the emotional and intuitive side; Rousseau pays tribute to her repeatedly, writing for example 'Elle fut pour moi la plus tendre des mères qui jamais ne chercha son plaisir mais toujours mon bien' (p. 106). She plans for Jean-Jacques's future, as a benefactor should do, after carefully observing him and studying his character and talents. She supports him financially, emotionally and intellectually. Rousseau writes of their conversations: 'Jamais toute la morale d'un pédagogue ne vaudra le bavardage affectueux et tendre d'une femme sensée pour qui l'on a de l'attachement.' It is these useful conversations which are the most valued fruit of the sexual relationship initiated between them by Mme de Warens – not out of desire, but out of pity and a desire to preserve her beneficiary from the perils of other women. Finally, Mme de Warens saves Jean-Jacques's life by her devoted nursing – 'A force de soins, de vigilance et d'incroyables peines elle me sauva, et il est certain qu'elle seule pouvait me sauver' (p. 222) he claims.

However, it is also Rousseau's representation of his relationship with Mme de Warens which illustrates the error of a mode of beneficence which is not in strict accordance with the claims of justice and prudence. Mme de Warens is described as insufficiently discriminating in the distribution of her benefits, not only overstepping her means but wasting gifts on unworthy and unscrupulous supplicants. When Rousseau is in a position to repay in some small measure all that she has given him, he feels that it is pointless to send her money, despite her great need for it, because she will squander it on rapacious parasites. In this way her unthinking generosity robs her more careful beneficiaries of the inclination to repay her. It means that Rousseau feels guilty on account of his ungrateful conduct, although he claims that his feelings towards her have always been those of the deepest gratitude. When she dies he addresses her as follows:

'Allez, âme douce et bienfaisante auprès des Fénelon, des Bernex, des Catinat, et de ceux qui dans un état plus humble ont ouvert comme eux leurs cœurs à la charité véritable, allez goûter le fruit de la vôtre et préparer à votre élève la place qu'il espère un jour occuper près de vous' (p. 620). The last piece that Rousseau writes, the *10ᵉ Promenade* of the *Rêveries*, is concerned with happy memories of Mme de Warens.

From the perspective of the classical code of beneficence, Rousseau's representation of Mme de Warens's indiscriminate generosity can be treated as a moral portrait illustrating the error of not modifying your response to a spontaneous emotional impulse in accordance with rational precepts. However, from the standpoint of those anxieties which lead Rousseau to formulate the code of pudicity, the portrayal of this liberal woman may appear to include contradictions in the form of sexual metaphors. As already indicated, Rousseau's prescribed sexual economy is not like that of beneficence; it is an attempt to restrict unbounded feminine capacity (and Mme de Warens has '*inépuisable* bonté de cœur', p. 262, my emphasis) to the point where women would be more or less excluded from public life. Rousseau claims that Mme de Warens had unusually limited sexual desires, and that her sexual generosity is in fact part of a more general beneficence. His occasional moments of criticising her general beneficence may well be a synecdochal return to a repressed criticism of her sexual activity. This might be less surprising than the claim – from a man who argued forcefully for feminine pudicity – that he barely suffered from jealousy. The general moral argument that unconsidered generosity is not beneficence nevertheless remains a valid one.

However, while Rousseau's analysis of Mme de Warens's conduct is of interest as an application of the classical code of beneficence, the reader could be struck by any implied criticism on Rousseau's part of his great benefactor. Reading an autobiography is an experience which is significantly displaced from that of reading a work designated as fiction or philosophy. The referent of the latter kinds of text is usually assumed to be a general, if not universal, one – such as 'man' – even if one might be concerned to destabilise such 'universal' concepts. But

R is Mme de W's creation

autobiographical texts have particular referential moments explicitly built in to their range of significations. Hence criticism of the figure of the profligate benefactor will not be simply and happily mapped on to Rousseau's comments about Mme de Warens. Although I generally leave such referential questions aside, the reader's uneasiness about the author's 'use' of his real benefactors may generate embarrassment or even hostility as a reading response – and could therefore be relevant in so far as it affects writer–reader relations.

In the *10ᵉ Promenade*, Rousseau reiterates a sentiment which he first expresses in the *Confessions*; namely, that he is Mme de Warens's creation. After she brings him back from the brink of death he claims 'je devenais tout à fait son œuvre'. When, fifty years later, he recalls the day when he first met her, he writes 'ce premier moment décida de moi pour toute ma vie, et produisit par un enchaînement inévitable le destin du reste de mes jours' (*Rêveries*, p. 1098). This reflects the Aristotelian theory that a benefactor creates his beneficiary following the model of artistic creation (and, inevitably, of divine creation). In the case of Mme de Warens, Rousseau's feeling of being her creation is obviously reinforced by his passion for her. He first encounters her at the time in his life (puberty) when, according to his theory of human development expounded in *Emile*, his moral and his emotional capacities are ready to be formed. Rousseau advises, in *Emile*, that childhood should be a time of physical development, but that those faculties associated with the imagination should be allowed to lie dormant in order to hold back the passions. It is at puberty that both sentimental and intellectual education should begin. In his own case, this education began very prematurely through his avid reading of novels, encouraged by his father. However, in other respects his early life is simple and sheltered, and so he can still assert that his moral character was not really shaped when he met Mme de Warens – that this is another and decisive new beginning with a benefactor-parent replacing the natural parent. The *Confessions* are marked by a rhythm of decisive events which are new beginnings – usually beginnings of a process of degeneration. The years with Mme de Warens are different, in that it is

Rousseau's wish to be her creature, and her role in making him what he is is entirely beneficial, because she makes him what he is; she does not fashion him into something else: 'je fus moi pleinement sans mélange et sans obstacle' (*Rêveries*, pp. 1098–9). This paradoxical act of creation is possible because it occurs within an equally paradoxical structure of freedom: 'j'étais parfaitement libre, et mieux que libre, car assujetti par mes seuls attachements, je ne faisais que ce que je voulais faire' (*Rêveries*, p. 1099).

Jean-Jacques calls Mme de Warens 'Maman', and she calls him 'Petit'. It is a recurrent feature of relations between benefactor and beneficiary, not only in Rousseau's writing, that the former is referred to as a parent and the beneficiary as a child. These names might seem naturally inspired in the case of Mme de Warens and Jean-Jacques, for he is no more than sixteen and she is twenty-eight, only a few years younger than his mother could have been. However, much later in Rousseau's life, when he is fifty, he calls Lord Keith 'father' and accepts the name 'child' from him – which is an expression of the bond between them, and could not be a reflection of biological facts. The first reference to Lord Keith in the *Confessions*, in which Rousseau indeed names him 'father', occurs when Rousseau mentions one of his chief moral precepts, which is that you should avoid situations in which duty comes into conflict with self-interest. This statement arises in connection with Jean-Jacques's father's failure fully to perform his duty towards his errant son. Thus it is his natural father's shortcomings which are the occasion for Rousseau to cite a father-benefactor's generosity and also his own right conduct as a beneficiary-son, exemplified in his refusal to be included in Lord Keith's will.

Between Mme de Warens and Lord Keith many of Rousseau's patrons are ultimately unsatisfactory in the light of the code of beneficence, and so he becomes very suspicious of all attempts to place him under an obligation. However, in Books X and XI, he finds himself, to his surprise, able to accept help from the Maréchal de Luxembourg and Madame la Maréchale. The relationship is particularly precious in that the difference in social circumstances between Rousseau, the self-proclaimed enemy of privilege, and these members of the highest aristocracy would seem to prohibit genuine friendship. Yet almost immediately M. de Luxembourg and Rousseau are 'sur le pied d'égalité' (p. 519), a situation which contrasts strikingly with earlier painful experiences with men of considerably lower rank, such as the Baron d'Holbach and Melchior Grimm. Rousseau is able to accept hospitality and other benefits from M. and Mme de Luxembourg, although he has become accustomed to refusing all offers; in this case, however, they are proffered in the context of reciprocated friendship and consequent equality, and so Rousseau feels relatively free. M. and Mme de Luxembourg do not press him to accept continual favours which are not of his choosing, nor do they try to make radical changes in his way of life.

In Book XII Rousseau meets his final benefactor, a man with whom there are not so many social barriers as there are with M. and Mme de Luxembourg, but nevertheless a man in an important position: Lord Keith. Lord Keith, like Mme de Warens, is not always a model benefactor from the standpoint of plain reason, but Rousseau writes: 'Ces petites bizarreries semblables aux caprices d'une jolie femme, ne me rendaient Milord Maréchal que plus intéressant. J'étais bien sûr et j'ai bien éprouvé dans la suite qu'elles n'influaient pas sur les sentiments ni sur les soins que lui prescrit l'amitié dans les occasions sérieuses' (p. 598). Lord Keith's heart is irreproachable, which is consistently the first consideration for Rousseau, even though the behaviour of the Maréchal could be eccentric. It is not uncommon, in Rousseau's writing, for the beneficiary figure to be presented as feminine as well as child-like. Certainly Rousseau assumes certain traditionally feminine characteristics during his friendship with Lord Keith.[7] The above comparison of Lord Keith's behaviour with that of a pretty woman suggests the mutuality of their esteem and affection if not of their status and means. It also suggests that there is flexibility in Rousseau's sometimes apparently unyielding distinctions between the sexes.

Many people are mentioned in the *Confessions* because they give some kind of material help to Rousseau. The question of power relations and of the precarious liberty of the beneficiary arises even in fleeting exchanges. Simple country folk who perform some small service are valued for their unassuming manner, a point which Rousseau makes with reference to an innkeeper near Lausanne: 'Des services plus importants sans doute, mais rendus avec plus d'ostentation, ne m'ont paru si dignes de reconnaissance que l'humanité simple et sans éclat de cet honnête homme' (p. 147). At the other end of the scale, Rousseau acquires a number of aristocratic patrons who find him jobs, supplement his income, give him hospitality, send him their doctors when he is ill and so on. Soon after he leaves Mme de Warens and goes to live in Paris, he is invited to the house of Mme de Beuzenval who displays an extraordinary lack of tact in arranging for Jean-Jacques to dine with her servants. She repents of this arrogance when it is pointed out to her by her daughter; however, the incident is simply a gross example of the underlying attitude of a number of Rousseau's aristocratic benefactors who do regard him as a kind of servant, albeit a superior one. In the big cities which he visits there are also a number of wealthy people to whom he is introduced, who make promises of assistance but do nothing. In particular during his first period in Paris, Jean-Jacques was 'beaucoup flatté et peu servi'. Indeed Rousseau finds it a general characteristic of Parisians to appear interested and affectionate while offering little concrete help, and so cheating the hopes which they have raised.

The most significant of Rousseau's Parisian benefactors from the point of view of elucidating the functioning of the code of beneficence is Mme d'Epinay. She gives him considerable material assistance but fails as a true benefactor by exacting repayment on her own terms; when she is thwarted in her expectations she becomes, in Rousseau's eyes, an implacable enemy. Her conduct represents, for Rousseau, the epitome of aristocratic beneficence – she is a benefactor who enjoys the sense of her superior position, a position which is inevitably superior socially and financially, and which leads her to feel that it is also morally superior. In Rousseau's eyes, such benefactors believe that they have a right to gratitude and to repayment in the form of flattery, courtship, assiduous visits and protestations of affection. They erode the freedom of their beneficiaries by incessant demands, moral homilies and emotional blackmail. Mme d'Epinay is very generous to Rousseau in her own way and, at the outset, he is touched and pleased by her spontaneous demonstrations of affection. Rousseau admires the beautiful location of a ruined cottage on her country estate, and Mme d'Epinay, acting on his word, has it repaired and made into a home for him. Rousseau is moved by this emotionally powerful appeal; he writes: 'Je mouillai de pleurs la main bienfaisante de mon amie' (p. 396). However, his previous plan had been to move to Geneva; although there are now factors which make Geneva a less appealing proposition, Rousseau does not enjoy being forced into a decision about where to live. Later, when he accepts the offer of a small house in the grounds of the Maréchal de Luxembourg's mansion, he is completely free to accept or refuse, and without having been first placed under an obligation as he is by Mme d'Epinay's having rebuilt and furnished the Hermitage for him. Thus, from the very beginning of their relationship, Mme d'Epinay acts with a certain authority and a lack of sensitivity concerning the paramount requirement that her beneficiary should feel free to do as he pleases. However, at this stage, Rousseau is swayed by her kindness; he states: 'La main qui avait donné ses soins à cet ameublement le rendait à mes yeux d'un prix inestimable, et je trouvais délicieux d'être l'hôte de mon amie dans une maison de mon choix qu'elle avait bâtie exprès pour moi' (p. 403).

Rousseau at first expresses his gratitude and visits Mme d'Epinay regularly, considering it not a duty but a pleasure. As time passes he is made aware of the concern aroused by his missing an opportunity to visit; concern on the grounds that he would only miss a chance to visit if he were seriously ill. He recognises that keeping Mme d'Epinay company when she is bored or lonely is his duty, and that he is bound to fulfil it. In contrast to the freedom he experiences with Mme de Warens, he discovers 'que cette liberté qu'elle m'avait tant promise ne m'était donnée qu'à condition de ne m'en prévaloir jamais' (p. 411). At first he accepts this as 'un assujettissement nécessaire' and yet the situation is clearly untenable, for he is a

bfr → tyrant

man who has resolved to live 'sans assujettissement personnel' (p. 362). Rousseau prefers those gifts which are pure reflections of affectionate feelings – of all Mme d'Epinay's gifts, he is most touched by her sending him a piece of her flannel petticoat to keep him warm in winter. He feels less gratitude for her giving him a home when it becomes clear that her motive is, at least in part, to have someone available to amuse her when other friends cannot be there. Rousseau's feeling of being in servitude is accompanied by a sensation of nullity, the belief that he is regarded as no more than a meagre supplement. He wishes to feel that he, in his turn, is a benefactor. In fact, he devotes hours, when he could be writing or earning money, to entertaining this lady of leisure, and even to listening to her reading aloud what she has written, which, furthermore, he considers of little merit. But Mme d'Epinay subtly refuses to allow him to be her equal in beneficence. When they finally quarrel, she is most unwilling to permit him to pay the wages of her gardener; this may be due to her spirit of generosity or may more likely, in the light of Rousseau's presentation, be due to a refusal to accept any measure of repayment except on her own terms.

For a time Rousseau, while recognising that he is caught in a chain of obligation, is willing to continue performing his duty out of a sense of gratitude and of friendship. However, there are two factors which wear him down: the first being the increasing demands and possessiveness of Mme d'Epinay; the second, the moral commentary on his actions and intentions which his friends provide for him. Mme d'Epinay gradually becomes less like a benefactor and more like a tyrant. Benefactors wish to see into the hearts of their beneficiaries, and to know and understand them. However, this moral penetration may easily be abused, for knowledge is power which may serve the beneficiary but can also serve the interests of the benefactor. There is a certain sexual role reversal in this episode where Rousseau's privacy is infringed by the phallic gaze of the masterful (and, Rousseau informs us, almost breast-less) Mme d'Epinay. The significance of the tyranny of the gaze will be unfolded through analysis of Rousseau's loaded reference to Gyges' ring in the *6ᵉ Promenade*. Mme d'Epinay becomes fascinated by Rousseau's friendship with her sister-in-law, Mme d'Houdetot, who is not a material benefactor to him and therefore might have a claim on his time, which in Mme d'Epinay's opinion is less legitimate than her own. Rousseau feels that her gaze follows Sophie d'Houdetot and himself during their walks together; he describes her as 'ne cessant de nous examiner'. This visual infringement of his privacy goes a stage further when she secretly attempts to get hold of the correspondence between them. This infringement of his freedom is barely tolerable, especially since he is constantly made to feel that he is in the wrong, by his friends' moral commentary on his actions.[8] On the one hand Rousseau feels trapped by what is actually happening, on the other he is caught by the verbal reformulation of events in which moral codes are misused to distort the truth. Thus he is falsely accused of ingratitude, when he himself has suspicions about the genuineness of his benefactor which, if founded, would render his obligation null and void.

This relationship culminates in the strange episode of Mme d'Epinay's trip to Geneva. This journey, ostensibly for the purpose of consulting Dr Tronchin about her chest complaint, has a secret purpose which Rousseau only discovers by the servants' gossip. He is generous enough not to reveal this purpose to his readers even though he is not entrusted it as a secret. His benefactor's constant secrecy concerning her own affairs, combined with her furtive inquiry into his own, is bound to infuriate him and increase his feeling of servitude. The pattern conforms to classical models of tyranny as elucidated by Aristotle or Herodotus, for example. The self-effacement of the just benefactor has turned to the concealment of the illegitimate master, just as observation had turned into Gygean spying. Rousseau then receives a letter from his friend Diderot, advising him: 'Mon ami, content de Mme d'Epinay il faut partir avec elle: mécontent il faut partir beaucoup plus vite. Etes-vous surchargé du poids des obligations que vous lui avez; voilà une occasion de vous acquitter en partie et de vous soulager. Trouverez-vous une autre occasion dans votre vie de lui témoigner votre reconnaissance?' He spells out the threat: 'On vous soupçonnera ou d'ingratitude ou d'un autre motif secret'

(p. 476). Rousseau reproduces the text of the actual letters pertaining to this crisis in his life: his desire *to be seen* to be telling the truth is more fervent than at any other moment. The secret motive to which Diderot refers is believed by Rousseau to mean friendship with Mme d'Houdetot; he already suspects that Mme d'Epinay or Grimm have informed Sophie d'Houdetot's lover that his friend, the honest 'citizen', is paying court to her in his absence. After a series of letters and visits, Mme d'Epinay departs without Rousseau, having induced her husband to accompany her. Soon afterwards, with no real explanation, first Grimm and then Mme d'Epinay break off their friendship with Rousseau, and he is made to feel that he should immediately, in the middle of winter, find somewhere else to live.

This unhappy episode is characterised by incidents which Rousseau categorises as false beneficence. At one extreme there are Diderot's interventions, which Rousseau considers well-meaning but wrong-headed and impertinent; the disagreement represented in the *Confessions* is paralleled in the writings of the two men. In the *Entretiens sur le fils naturel*, Diderot puts these words into the mouth of Constance: 'Ne vaut-il pas mieux encore... faire des ingrats, que de manquer à faire le bien?' Rousseau would answer a resounding 'no!' How can doing good create ingrates? At the other extreme, however, is Grimm's behaviour which Rousseau castigates in far stronger terms. Even before Mme d'Epinay's proposed trip to Geneva, Rousseau writes concerning Grimm's behaviour in her house:

Il ne me traitait pas précisément comme son inférieur; il me regardait comme nul. J'avais peine à reconnaître là l'ancien cuistre qui chez le Prince de Saxe-Gotha se tenait honoré de mes regards. J'en avais encore plus à concilier ce profond silence et cette morgue insultante avec la tendre amitié qu'il se vantait d'avoir pour moi près de ceux qu'il savait en avoir eux-mêmes. Il est vrai qu'il ne la témoignait guère que pour me plaindre de ma fortune dont je ne me plaignais point... et pour se lamenter de me voir me refuser durement aux soins bienfaisants qu'il disait vouloir me rendre. C'était avec cet art qu'il faisait admirer sa tendre générosité, blâmer mon ingrate misanthropie, et qu'il accoûtumait insensiblement tout le monde à n'imaginer entre un protecteur tel que lui et un malheureux tel que moi que des liaisons de bienfaits d'une part et d'obligations de l'autre, sans y supposer même dans les possibles, une amitié d'égal. Pour moi j'ai cherché vainement en quoi je pourrais être obligé à ce nouveau patron. (p. 466)

Grimm is culpable as Rousseau's former beneficiary (he shows no gratitude); also as friend (they should be equals); and as self-proclaimed benefactor – something which is a contradiction in terms, and particularly false when no benefaction has in fact been bestowed. Mme d'Epinay is a slightly different case, and Rousseau writes to her at the end of their friendship: 'Je n'ai point oublié vos bontés pour moi, et vous pouvez compter de ma part sur toute la reconnaissance qu'on peut avoir pour quelqu'un qu'on ne doit plus aimer' (p. 485). If judged as referring to an empirical situation then, of course, Rousseau's conduct and commentary, as well as that of others, can be verified against other available evidence, and analysed in terms of a number of different ethical criteria. However, I am only concerned here to read the episodes as if they were *examples* relating to the classical code of beneficence.

After Rousseau has left the Hermitage and ended relations with his former hostess, the false beneficence which he describes as Grimm's constant practice becomes, in his opinion, a systematised campaign against him by his enemies. In the *Confessions* he says of Grimm 'sa grande adresse est de paraître me ménager en me diffamant, et de donner encore à sa perfidie l'air de la générosité'. In the *Dialogues* this hypocrisy and malevolence is represented at its most extreme.

THE *CONFESSIONS*: ROUSSEAU AS BENEFACTOR

It is interesting to consider Rousseau's presentation of himself in the *Confessions* as a benefactor. Although he was more often in a position of needing help than of being able to offer it, he does mention certain occasions when he takes on the role of the giver. These give the reader some insight into the difficulties of the benefactor, and into the points where he is most vulnerable to exploitation. Rousseau is always willing to be generous in circumstances where he is not entering into a commitment which it may later prove difficult to meet. He is known for his readiness to distribute alms to the poor – he writes, with reference to the people of Neuchâtel, 'je devais, j'ose le dire être aimé du peuple dans ce pays-là, comme je l'ai été dans tous ceux où j'ai vécu, versant les aumônes à pleines mains, ne laissant sans assistance aucun indigent autour de moi, ne refusant à personne aucun service que je pusse rendre et qui fût dans la justice...' (p. 624).

It is important that this kind of generosity has a transitory, contingent nature, and Rousseau is infuriated when it is suggested that he is culpable for moving from Paris and leaving the Parisian poor without his assistance in times of need.[9] Rousseau regards this kind of beneficence as something which stems from a common humanity and does not involve a special and lasting bond between individuals. It is beneficence which is, in a sense, appropriate for anyone, just because anyone is human; it is not a mark of particular virtue but a demonstration of the goodness natural to a human heart. Rousseau's position is a condemnation of the unhealthy self-interest and philosophical reasoning which hardens the heart against suffering by recourse to specious arguments.[10] Rousseau directly attacks the apparent good sense of these arguments in *La Nouvelle Héloïse* (v, 2) in which Saint-Preux reports his discussion with Julie on this subject. Julie repeats Wolmar's comparison of beggars with actors: both may move you to pity, but the one promotes active and the other sterile pity. It seems ridiculous to pay and praise the latter rather than the former; the representation of misfortune should not be valued over and above what may be genuine misfortune. The editor (Rousseau) counsels, in a footnote, against driving the very poor into crime by making them despair of receiving help from their fellow men. The experiences of the young Jean-Jacques, narrated in the early books of the *Confessions*, show how easily a boy or man who is treated as worthless may be brought to dishonesty. Julie declares that the blame for the very existence of beggars rests in the end on the social system; it is the task of the state to remove the need for men to be in such a condition, rather than the task of citizens to try to discourage them by constant refusals. This suggests the ultimate need for a just state.

Rousseau's experiences of acting as a benefactor to individuals known to him are on the whole less happy than the casual and sometimes anonymous beneficence he bestows on strangers. The two most important women in the *Confessions*, Mme de Warens and Thérèse Levasseur, constantly frustrate his attempts to help them by what he considers to be their fecklessness over money matters and their own ill-considered generosity. Rousseau writes, 'tandis que Maman était en proie à ses croquants, Thérèse était en proie à sa famille, et je ne pouvais rien faire d'aucun côté qui profitât à celle pour qui je l'avais destiné' (p. 350). Both women are victims of their own kindness; they also sacrifice Rousseau and other would-be benefactors to the 'blood-suckers', as Rousseau calls them. Thérèse Levasseur allows her mother to take everything she can from Rousseau and, without his knowledge, from his friends. Rousseau is not strictly speaking in the position of a benefactor to Thérèse Levasseur; on the one hand, he feels that what he does for her he is doing for himself (p. 418), and, on the other hand, she does contribute to the maintenance of the household by acting as housekeeper. Most importantly, in Rousseau's eyes, she repays his devotion to her with affection and loyalty. However, his generosity to her family meets with little gratitude or trust. Mme Levasseur does do some work for Rousseau in return for her keep (for example, acting as secretary, p. 352). He tells the reader that he would have liked to be treated like a member of her family; instead she treats him more like an employer to be duped and exploited than either as a benefactor or as a son. Rousseau finds this lack of emotional reciprocity very painful. He presents Mme Levasseur to the reader as perhaps the epitome of an ungrateful beneficiary: she lies to him and plots against him behind his back while making all the profit she can from him. She complains about him to his friends, with the result that they try to use her as a lever to persuade him to live a less independent life. In this way Rousseau's difficulties as benefactor are increased by his wish to remain independent of patronage, a wish which provokes others to attempt to conquer his resistance. His own dependants are an obvious means of access to his needs; it is difficult for Rousseau to refuse a gift which is ostensibly offered to Mme or Mlle Levasseur.

Rousseau's self-sufficient and modest life is bound up with the way in which he perceives his role as a writer. It is a common claim in the eighteenth century that you are writing for the good of your fellow men; beneficence is often the justification for literature and the source of pleasure in writing. Rousseau's writing is by far the most important area of his active beneficence, and that which, to an extent, precludes his being a benefactor in other ways. Where Rousseau differs from many of his contemporaries is that he believes he can only write as he wishes if he is free, and that means poor. He makes a deliberate decision against writing in order to earn money, a path which was open to him after his first success. Although he is content to receive payment for his books, he does not write for that reason, and he continues to work at copying music in order to support himself. Rousseau believes that it is only if he is independent, both of individual patrons and of the public, that he is able to write what he knows to be important both to individuals and to society, and strictly according to the truth as he understands it.[11] However, his attempt to be a moral example to his age in his life as well as in his works attracts the attention of those who would like to prove him wrong.

Rousseau writes in the *Confessions*: 'Il est trop difficile de penser noblement quand on ne pense que pour vivre. Pour pouvoir, pour oser dire de grandes vérités il ne faut pas dépendre de son succès. Je jetais mes livres dans le public avec la certitude d'avoir parlé pour le bien commun, sans aucun souci du reste' (p. 403). Rousseau may be considered a public benefactor in that the excellence of his writing is not motivated by literary aspirations, but by the importance of its subject-matter or message. For example, in *Du contrat social* he believes that he is asking important questions which could reveal truths that are vital for human happiness. In *La Nouvelle Héloïse* he wishes to make virtue lovable, and also to reconcile dogmatic atheists and Christians through the figures of Wolmar and Julie. In the *3e Promenade* of the *Rêveries du promeneur solitaire*, Rousseau explains that in the *Profession de foi du Vicaire Savoyard*, he intended to reveal the consoling truths of religion, which could do because he was not committed to any particular party position.

In the *Lettre à d'Alembert* (p. 8) he deals with a topic of immediate importance and 'une vérité de pratique importante à tout un peuple'. His own role in that instance is contrasted with that of d'Alembert, who is represented as a false benefactor. D'Alembert allures and deceives the people of Geneva with the most seductive proposition possible: by following his advice they themselves will benefit the whole of Europe by the example of their theatre. D'Alembert thus falsely imitates the benefactor who enables his beneficiary to become a benefactor in his turn. Rousseau writes of this 'voilà . . . le plus dangereux conseil qu'on pût nous donner' (*Lettre à d'Alembert*, p. 6). In the *Confessions*, disillusioned with the response to his philosophical writings, he has a new project. In *Mon portrait*, a collection of fragments apparently written between 1756 and 1762, he explains it thus:

J'approche du terme de la vie et je n'ai fait aucun bien sur la terre. J'ai les intentions bonnes, mais il n'est pas toujours si facile de bien faire qu'on pense. Je conçois un nouveau genre de service à rendre aux hommes: c'est de leur offrir l'image fidèle de l'un d'entre eux afin qu'ils apprennent à se connaître. (*Mon portrait*, p. 1120)

Rousseau takes up the classical position that self-knowledge is the source of wisdom and virtue; in helping men to know themselves he is giving them the only knowledge which it is really important to acquire. But it is a novel route to self-knowledge which he is offering: no longer a philosophical treatise on human nature, but a portrait of an individual, an introspective narrative, the story of his own life.

Rousseau's view of worthwhile literature is analogous to a view of beneficence. He puts his position clearly in his description, in the *Dialogues*, of an enchanted world of his imagination; when the inhabitants of this world write books,

il faut qu'ils y soient forcés par un stimulant plus fort que l'intérêt et même que la gloire. Ce stimulant, difficile à contenir; impossible à contrefaire, se fait sentir dans tout ce qu'il produit. Quelque heureuse découverte à publier, quelque belle et grande vérité à répandre, quelque erreur générale et pernicieuse à combattre, enfin quelque point d'utilité publique à établir; voilà les seuls motifs qui puissent leur mettre la plume à la main. (*Dialogues*, p. 673)

The writer, like the benefactor and in order to be a benefactor, must be entirely disinterested, caring only for the good that he will bring about. His motive must be generous, but guided by reason.

If the writer is a benefactor, this implies that he has a beneficiary. The beneficiary is, in the first place, the reader; in the second place, all those with whom the reader, an improved man, comes into contact; and thus finally, society even humanity at large. Even the first of these categories, the reader, is not easy to determine – there is, for example, the reader inscribed in the text, the reader imagined by Rousseau, the reader created by his writing. Then there is the empirical public, which is encountered by Rousseau on occasion, for instance when he reads sections from the *Confessions* aloud, and this encounter is then described in writing which creates the effect of embedding.

Rousseau's reader/beneficiary enters into a moral contract with him by reading his work, accepting the gift. This is one of the most tenuous of moral contracts, and one of the easiest for the person put under an obligation to break. Rousseau lays out the terms of the contract in the *Confessions* as follows: 'C'est à moi d'être vrai, c'est au lecteur d'être juste' (p. 359). The reader should show his gratitude, repay Rousseau for his gift of truth, by judging his case fairly. However, this exchange is not quite what it seems, for the judge's verdict, in order to be just, must be one of 'Not guilty'. Rousseau informs the reader that anyone who condemns him is himself 'un homme à étouffer' (p. 656). However, even this moral sanction has no real force; a history of the reader's response to the *Confessions* would reveal many who are ready to suspect Rousseau of dishonesty, and also to judge with the utmost severity those 'crimes' which he confesses. Yet the contract and the sanction have a certain linguistic or textual force, despite their failure to affect many of the empirical reading public. It is the relationship with the reader/beneficiary which Rousseau, as author, sets up within the text which structures the text.[12]

THE *DIALOGUES*: FALSE BENEFICENCE

The *Dialogues* may be called autobiographical for they share with the *Confessions* the subject-matter of Rousseau himself, yet the mode of presentation is fictional and Rousseau's experiences are magnified to the point where the false beneficence which he encounters is represented as a systematic and deliberate attempt to humiliate and degrade him. Michel Foucault refers to them as '*anti-Confessions*' written in a voice which is already stifled as opposed to the voice which speaks aloud in the *Confessions*.[13] The *Dialogues* give the most extreme representation of false beneficence to be found in any of Rousseau's texts; there is both a conspiracy involving material gifts and a shroud of secrecy which is proclaimed benevolent. At the same time the *Dialogues* show how tyrannical false benefactors may reduce a man to a state like slavery, that is, a state where he is not permitted to exercise virtue in the smallest degree, unable even to perform the acts of common humanity owed to a stranger. In such a situation, Jean-Jacques's major benefactions, his books, are perverted, or else they are denied him.

The terms 'bienfaisance', 'bienfait' and 'bienfaiteur' are all reversed or polluted in the system of signification evoked by the *Dialogues*.[14] These terms occur roughly four times as often in the *Dialogues* as in the *Confessions*[15] but their meanings are perverted: 'beneficence' means discrediting the unwilling recipient, the 'benefit' is an unwelcome gift which makes him unhappy and humiliated, the 'benefactor' is the secret enemy. In the *Dialogues*, language is undermined as a vehicle for truth or as a means of communication in the normal sense. However, it is effective, it works rather as a magic charm or a ritual incantation might be thought to work: repetition of the sounds has a certain effect, it changes people's minds as if they were bewitched. Rousseau rarely shows this kind of use of language outside his autobiographical writings; one significant exception occurs in *La Mort de Lucrèce*, in which the tyrant Sextus learns from his slave how to employ such language in an attempt to seduce, seduction which becomes deadly rape.

The secrecy and mystery which surround Jean-Jacques are

represented by his enemies as the result of their generous desire
to save him from ignominy or even physical injury and death.

They wish to know every small detail concerning him, and so
they spy on his every move: 'ils gagnèrent tout ce qui l'entourait
et parvinrent ainsi par degrés à être instruits de ce qui le
regardait aussi bien et mieux que lui-même' (p. 701). They
claim that this is for his own good, and to prevent him from
committing further crimes which would necessitate his imprisonment. However, it is demonstrated that their actions
cannot be true beneficence:

quand ils comptent pour un bienfait le mal mérité dont ils disent
exempter sa personne ils en imposent et mentent, puisqu'ils ne l'ont
convaincu d'aucun acte punissable, qu'un innocent ne méritant
aucun châtiment n'a pas besoin de grâce et qu'un pareil mot n'est
qu'un outrage pour lui. Ils sont donc doublement injustes, en ce qu'ils
se font un mérite envers lui d'une générosité qu'ils n'ont point, et en ce
qu'ils ne feignent d'épargner sa personne qu'afin d'outrager impunément son honneur. (*Dialogues*, p. 743)

The false benefactors are archetypal tyrants in that they work
under a cloak of invisibility so that no information about
themselves can be used against them; at the same time they
have a network of spies so that they can reinterpret in an
unfavourable light the body of information gathered about
their victim.

The most important point about this alleged beneficence is
that the beneficiary's consent is not sought. Rousseau declares:
'Tout don fait par force n'est pas un don, c'est un vol; il n'y a
point de plus maligne tyrannie que de forcer un homme de nous
être obligé malgré lui' (p. 746). This clear and incontrovertible
rule is transgressed in every act of so-called beneficence
bestowed on Jean-Jacques. Therefore the accusation that he is
an ingrate is rendered null and void, although it is repeated so
often that it appears to the unsuspecting populace to be true.
Jean-Jacques is portrayed in these terms: 'ce monstre d'ingratitude ne sent rien, ne sait gré de rien, et tous les ménagements
qu'on a pour lui loin de le toucher ne font qu'irriter sa férocité'
(p. 710), despite the fact that, as the Frenchman later testifies

bfit ← int^ 26   R prevented fr.
exercising   bfee
Beneficence and benefactors in the major works   65   ///

for himself, 'ce que sur leur parole j'avais pris pour bienfaisance
et générosité ne fut l'ouvrage d'une animosité cruelle, masquée
avec art par un extérieur de bonté' (p. 929). The intention of
the 'benefactors' is to demonstrate Jean-Jacques's ingratitude
to the general public; Rousseau points out that the intention to
humiliate cannot merit gratitude. He is referring to the classical
code which lays down that the benefit lies in the intention, and
not in the material gift. The Frenchman reveals that he, for his
part, has been building his argument on unsure foundation;
when he claims that money itself deserves gratitude this proves
to all those familiar with the code of beneficence that he has
been misled. The false portrait of Jean-Jacques which results
from the false beneficence inflicted on him is made concrete in
Ramsay's portrait painting of him which is commissioned by
Hume, whom Rousseau names 'le bienfaiteur à toute outrance'
(p. 779), which is a contradiction in terms. According to Jean-
Jacques this portrait is a deliberately disfiguring one, which
would mislead any naive spectator. It is the complete opposite
of the gift he offers the world: his own true self-portrait which
should help his readers to know themselves. On this occasion
words (Rousseau's autobiographical texts) are more true than a
concrete image.

The major evil perpetrated by Jean-Jacques's enemies 'est de
lui avoir ôté la douceur d'être utile aux hommes et secourable
aux malheureux' (p. 906). The Frenchman reports that 'l'un
de nos Messieurs m'a même assuré avoir eu le sensible plaisir de
voir des mendiants lui rejeter au nez son aumône' (p. 714).
These anonymous gentlemen actually take pleasure in having
deprived Jean-Jacques of the power to offer a coin to a beggar
– in this case the pettiness of the tyranny implies its labyrinthine
ramifications, like the hundreds of tiny threads with which the
Lilliputians bind Gulliver. Jean-Jacques is rendered, to all
intents and purposes, immobile, because he is surrounded by
potential traps; the treacherous suppliants who approach him
aim to 'l'enlacer par ses propres bienfaits' (p. 963). This is a
horrible parody of the moral bonds of obligation, which between
benefactor and beneficiary are formed as if naturally. Jean-
Jacques is caught in a 'double bind'; if he gives something he is

branded a hypocrite, if he refuses to give he is deemed uncharitable.

This scheme extends into the past as well as the present and the future: Jean-Jacques's previous acts of beneficence are denied, and alleged acts of maleficence replace them. This has particular reference to his writing, which has the intention of influencing men to lead more virtuous lives. Such a moral achievement cannot be accredited to him if his false benefactors are to gain their purpose of making him despised by everyone. Their very tales of his criminal activities would, in Rousseau's opinion, preclude the possibility that he has also written his books.

Rousseau, the independent observer, says that *Emile*, the *Discours sur l'inégalité* and *Du contrat social* 'm'échauffent, me touchent, m'attendrissent, me donnent la volonté sincère d'être meilleur' (p. 686).[16] The author cannot be a debauched criminal, for such a man would not create so many new obstacles in his path 'dans tous les prosélytes que ses livres feraient à la vertu' (p. 687). A man who regarded women as he regards chamber pots could not have written *La Nouvelle Héloïse*. In other words, the author of the alleged crimes cannot be the author of the books – the author of the books is a benefactor and cannot simultaneously be a malefactor. Rousseau therefore suggests that Jean-Jacques is attributing to himself books written by another. The Frenchman follows a different chain of reasoning. He believes that the author of the crimes is indeed the author of the books, and therefore the books must contain a hidden poison, they must be criminal books 'nuisibles et dangereux' (p. 697) which, for example, encourage their readers to commit murders.[17] Both of these hypotheses are refuted by empirical observation and concrete evidence. Rousseau then meets Jean-Jacques and realises that he is not a man to attribute to himself books that were written by another. The Frenchman reads the books and can discover no hidden poison, simply a disinterestedness which will inevitably attract powerful enemies. The *Dialogues* are a written text, purporting to record spoken words (dialogues) and thus doubly verbal. Yet Rousseau appears to be appealing to concrete, material, physical contact, to emotional recognition and empirical evidence. Words, the repetition of words, have been discredited, and yet the body of Rousseau's writing is, we learn, evidently sincere to the reader.

At the conclusion of the *Dialogues* another hypothesis is found to be correct: that the books are an inspiration to virtue, and that their author, who is Jean-Jacques, is therefore a good man. This is satisfying to some extent, and it restores the past. However, the solution to Jean-Jacques's situation, a solution which is reaffirmed by Rousseau in the *Rêveries*, is found to be inaction; for any deed he does will be turned against him or against his beneficiary. This 'negative virtue' becomes progressively more important in Rousseau's work. It is present as a possibility from the beginning, but in the clarion call to virtue of *La Nouvelle Héloïse*, *Emile* and *Du contrat social* it is of secondary importance. However, in the *Dialogues* and the *Rêveries* it is the only remaining possibility; god-like beneficence is present only in the magical daydreams of the enchanted world or of Gyges' ring. Negative virtue is achieved at some cost in a corrupt world, and is not to be belittled, although it may sound a subdued note in comparison with the activities of those classical heroes of Rousseau's boyhood and indeed manhood.[18]

Negative virtue in Rousseau's sense would not traditionally be accepted as beneficence, nor perhaps as a social virtue of any kind. Rousseau makes it appear such because he is not dealing in abstract philosophical terms with absolute virtue, but rather speaks as an observer of society. The negative benefit of not having harmed anyone is to be compared with the harmful actions of most other individuals in society. Rousseau presents inaction in the face of what appears to be an invitation to do good as the result of a struggle against one's inclinations (and hence, as virtue). That can only be the case if we assume the existence of natural passions, encouraged by social intercourse, which drive men to do good. This is what emerges in Rousseau's account of humanity and of the natural passions of *amour de soi* and pity, which he adds to the stoical theories of reasoned beneficence.

MODEL BENEFICENCE: JULIE

In Rousseau's fictional and theoretical writing, the positive alternatives to negative virtue are forcefully put forward. The relationships which may fall within the domain of the code of beneficence are both moral (between individuals within society) and political (between the sovereign and the people). *La Nouvelle Héloïse*, *Emile* and *Du contrat social* provide four models of justice combined with generosity: Julie, Wolmar, Emile's tutor and the legislator.[19] These works provide a pattern of right conduct on an interpersonal and on a political level, and contribute to the standard provided by the code of beneficence against which Rousseau can measure contemporary situations. All four models are benefactors of the highest kind in that they bestow the benefit of benign moral influence, an influence which transforms the recipients enabling them to attain self-mastery or moral liberty on the one hand, and, in the case of the legislator, political liberty on the other hand. Julie, the feminine benefactor, is the most human of the models in that she is passionate and sensual, and has to struggle to achieve virtue in an imperfect world. Wolmar is also a specific character, and a benefactor to specific individuals, although he is closer to the abstract models of Emile's tutor, who creates justice for one individual, and the legislator, who creates justice for a whole society. Saint-Preux, Emile and the society moved by the general will are the beneficiaries whose needs are answered by these benefactors, and who, because of this, may grow to be benefactors in their turn. In the *Confessions* we gather that this was not possible for Rousseau; he did not meet the right models or the right society which would have enabled him to become a material benefactor himself. Instead he becomes an author; he turns to what he describes as the 'supplément' of writing.

Julie presents quite a different pattern from the one which will be identified with Wolmar, Emile's tutor and the legislator. Julie's strength is not simply the cool and rational observation of human passions in which she does not share; her power lies in the very intensity of her own passions and in her passionate identification with others. In a sense this gives her access to

J : struggle vs inclinations   J's God the god father

greater virtue than the three superhuman masculine models, for virtue is, by definition, struggle against one's inclinations. Wolmar never has to struggle, and, as he frankly admits, on the sole occasion when he experiences temptation (when he first sees Julie) he succumbs to it. From the beginning to the end of *La Nouvelle Héloïse*, Julie carries on an inner battle against her emotions – and she is truly virtuous.[20]

She is a practical benefactor to all around her, or rather to all who merit it, for, although she hates to refuse a request, she is governed, like Wolmar, by the code of beneficence rather than by irrational generosity; she shows 'un discernement exquis dans la distribution de ses bienfaits'. In this respect she differs from Rousseau's memories of Mme de Warens, the most influential of his female benefactors. According to Saint-Preux, 'Toutes les maisons où elle [Julie] entre offrent bientôt un tableau de la sienne; l'aisance et le bien-être y sont une de ses moindres influences, la concorde et les mœurs la suivent de ménage en ménage' (p. 533). Claire also pays tribute to her: 'ton cœur vivifie tous ceux qui l'environnent et leur donne pour ainsi dire un nouvel être dont ils sont forcés de lui faire hommage, puisqu'ils ne l'auraient point eu sans lui' (p. 409). Julie gives life, and that life is in her own image. She creates, and is like a moral parent to, her beneficiaries.

Julie's beneficence is supported by her belief in God the father/benefactor:

Partout elle aperçoit la bienfaisante main de la providence; ses enfants sont le cher dépôt qu'elle en a reçu; elle recueille ses dons dans les productions de la terre; elle voit sa table couverte par ses soins; elle s'endort sous sa protection; son paisible réveil lui vient d'elle; elle sent ses leçons dans les disgrâces, et ses faveurs dans les plaisirs, les biens dont jouït tout ce qui lui est cher sont autant de nouveaux sujets d'hommages; si le Dieu de l'univers échappe à ses faibles yeux, elle voit partout le père commun des hommes. (*La Nouvelle Héloïse*, p. 591)

In this description of Julie's faith, Rousseau suggests (as he reiterates elsewhere) that Julie's God is father and benefactor, and not the punitive tyrant who sends those who are ignorant of him to eternal torment. He is quite different from the earthly fathers portrayed in *La Nouvelle Héloïse*, who are characterised

by an abuse of power (the Baron d'Etange) or by dereliction of
duty (Claire's father). Scenes involving Julie's biological father
are the most negative passages in a work devoted to the
depiction of beneficent moral influence, which shows the real
incompatibility between *blood father* and *benefactor* in fullest
force. While benefactors are accurate observers, Julie's father is
full of blind prejudice caused by an inflexible inegalitarian
social code, which chooses to deny and negate a situation (of
reciprocal love) which it must not see. What is impossible must
not exist, or it would challenge the original cause of its non-
existence. The benefactor, on the other hand, must see
accurately and judge perceptively. The code of honour, of
respect for rank (birth), one formulation of the law of the
strongest and of paternal authority, is thus shown to be violently
at odds with the code of beneficence, allegedly an expression of
the honour of high rank. This is a crucial object of Rousseau's
social criticism as well as a vital dimension of the family drama
in *La Nouvelle Héloïse*.[21] Even those men who are models of
virtue, and should therefore fulfil the duties which might be
thought to arise from biological paternity, are shown not to do
so: Saint-Preux and Edouard decide not to marry nor to have
children; M. d'Orbe dies when his child is very young; Wolmar
asks Saint-Preux to educate his children instead of doing it
himself. The three men who live at Clarens after Julie's death
are all moral fathers, benefactors, like Julie's image of God. 'Le
"père de famille" devient alors semblable à Dieu, il est présent
dans tout ce qu'il possède et se suffit à lui même.'[22] This suggests
the extent to which art takes over from nature, creating a new
denatured nature in accordance with the spirit of nature, by
means of rational codes. It is like the art of the tutor who makes
his pupil into a virtuous man, or the art of the legislator who
creates citizens.

  Julie, unlike the male benefactors, is not directly inspired by
the classical texts which influenced Rousseau so much.[23]
Plutarch's *Lives* are all of famous men, and not of famous
women; indeed, the very idea of fame is contrary to the code of
feminine virtue to which, according to Rousseau's theoretical
writings, a virtuous woman must cling.[24] The masculine models

of beneficence seem almost like gods on earth; Julie only becomes divine in death. Jean Starobinski comments, 'la mort de Julie, qui est une accession à la transparence, représente aussi le triomphe de la voile' (*La Transparence et l'obstacle*, p. 146). Julie's divinisation occurs at the same time as, and as a result of, her final and absolute retreat. It is a retreat demanded by her code of feminine virtue, which cannot allow the possibility of her taking pity on Saint-Preux. Wolmar's divine beneficence makes him take this dangerous outsider into his house. Julie, however, is torn between beneficence and pudicity; she is therefore, up until her death, which represents a final choice, more human.

Wolmar, an atheist, is not dependent on a benefactor-God. Julie, however, a victim of her blood father's violence, actually named 'la force paternelle' in Rousseau's title to an engraving for *La Nouvelle Héloïse*, is too deeply wounded by that violence to be redeemed other than by miraculous intervention. This is an important point in Rousseau's critique of society, marked by his historical pessimism.[25] However much virtuous men, such as Wolmar or Lord Edouard, may attempt to right social wrongs through beneficence, once injustice in society has reached a certain pitch then it is, to all intents and purposes, impossible for men to reform it. Submitting to violence, Julie resolves to be an adulterous wife, as her father had been an adulterous husband – the perceptive Claire sees repressed guilt about this as the source of his unreasonable behaviour. This adultery would have been the moral downfall of Julie and Saint-Preux; happiness in adultery would not have been, in Rousseau's terms, very edifying for the reader, thus annulling his justification for writing a novel: the claim that it could act as an antidote, helping to cure a sick (unjust) society. Therefore Julie is saved from this crime by the grace of God bestowed on her during the wedding ceremony. Her eyes are opened to the duties of a virtuous wife and mother, and she makes her vows with both lips and heart; afterwards she experiences the joy and peace of virtue. In gratitude for these gifts Julie offers up her heart and mind to her heavenly Father, and lives until her death according to the precepts which come to her in that moment of exaltation.

There is the most complete contrast between Julie's punitive, unseeing and unwise earthly father and the merciful, omniscient Father of all. Julie turns more and more to the latter – her real father is not present at her death, but she says of her heavenly Father: 'Qui s'endort dans le sein d'un père n'est pas en souci du réveil' (*La Nouvelle Héloïse*, p. 716). She awoke after a blissful reconciliation in the bosom of her fleshly father only to learn that he was adamant in thwarting her dearest wish and excluding her lover from his mansion. Julie is confident that her other Father will be hospitable, and welcome both her former lover and her husband, Wolmar, as well as herself. Wolmar as individual is not changed by Julie's transfer of allegiance from her father to her beneficent heavenly Father; but if considered as a signifier for others, he may be seen as transformed from false benefit forced upon Julie by an aggressor (her father) into an almost perfect gift from God.

MODEL BENEFICENCE: WOLMAR, EMILE'S TUTOR AND THE LEGISLATOR

Each of the three masculine models of a benefactor is characterised by independence from the usual human passions and concerns. These benefactors are cold observers of their fellows. Rousseau writes of the legislator: 'Il faudrait une intelligence supérieure, qui vît toutes les passions des hommes et qui n'en éprouvât aucune' (*Du contrat social*, p. 381). Wolmar says of himself, 'J'ai naturellement l'âme tranquille et le cœur froid' (*La Nouvelle Héloïse*, p. 490) and also, 'Si j'ai quelque passion dominante c'est celle de l'observation' (*La Nouvelle Héloïse*, p. 491). In order for a man to be a successful moral example to others, he must know them and understand their motives. This point is made most clearly in *Emile*, in which the tutor's role for the first part of his pupil's life is largely that of invisible observer since 'il faut des observations plus fines qu'on ne pense pour s'assurer du vrai génie et du vrai goût d'un enfant' (*Emile*, p. 475).[26] When the pupil reaches the age of puberty and is being prepared to be an active benefactor in his turn the tutor must show him the spectacle of his fellow men, so that he can penetrate behind their appearances and see them as they really are. To this end he may not participate in the human comedy for fear that he would be drawn into the play of passions and self-interest and thus lose his impartiality. Rousseau suggests that he should study classical history so that he can look at humanity, as represented by the classical historians, as a 'simple spectateur, sans intérêt et sans passion, comme leur juge, non comme leur complice, ni comme leur accusateur' (*Emile*, p. 526).

In *La Nouvelle Héloïse*, Rousseau also presents this relationship from the point of view of the beneficiary, the one who is being coldly scrutinised. It is important to recall that the coldness is far from being a coldness of disdain or rejection; it is the cool clarity of reason and does not exclude affection for those who are seen to be good. It is Saint-Preux's respect for Wolmar which makes him write: 'Je commençai de connaître alors à quel homme j'avais à faire, et je résolus bien de tenir toujours mon cœur en état d'être vu de lui' (p. 425). When Saint-Preux recalls a moment of temptation, he writes: 'Je croyais voir son œil pénétrant et judicieux percer au fond de mon cœur et m'en faire rougir encore; je croyais entendre sortir de sa bouche des reproches trop mérités, et des leçons trop mal écoutées' (p. 487). Although Wolmar is not physically present, his gaze seems to be piercing his beneficiaries at all times; the visibility of the beneficiary contrasts with the effacement of the benefactor. In *Emile* and *Du contrat social*, both philosophical treatises although *Emile* has elements of a novel, no individual is characterised for the reader to any great degree. However, in *La Nouvelle Héloïse*, Wolmar who is morally dominant is also the least well known of the major figures both to the characters and to the reader. Emile is known through and through by his tutor, if not by the reader, from the earliest moment, whereas he does not know the tutor until he is old enough to become a benefactor in his turn. He is not aware of the extent to which the tutor controls the circumstances of his life – this is, of course, because he is too young to understand on the one hand; but, on the other hand, his unawareness also permits him to feel absolutely independent which is a feeling necessary to the beneficiary if he is to be truly grateful. The legislator, similarly, must know everything about his people so that he can devise appropriate laws for them. They, however, must be under a benign illusion about him, believing that he is instructed by the gods rather than by reason. 'Cette raison sublime qui s'élève au-dessus de la portée des hommes vulgaires est celle dont le législateur met les décisions dans la bouche des immortels, pour entraîner par l'autorité divine ceux que ne pourrait ébranler la prudence humaine' (*Du contrat social*, pp. 383–4).

It is the legislator's superhuman powers which both oblige and enable him to claim divine counsel. Rousseau makes a further rhetorical link between the true benefactor and a god, suggesting indeed that benefactors should be (like) gods: 'Il faudrait des dieux pour donner des lois aux hommes.'[27] The blindness of the citizens ('une multitude aveugle' *Du contrat social*, p. 380) means that the legislator's vision must substitute for their own. He must not only have insight into them, but for them, on their behalf; he must be their eyes so that they can see. 'De lui-même le peuple veut toujours le bien, mais de lui-même, il ne le voit pas toujours...Il faut lui faire voir les objects tels qu'ils sont' (*Du contrat social*, p. 380). Just as Mme de Warens makes Jean-Jacques what he truly *is*, so the legislator makes the people see things as they *are*.

Wolmar is a benefactor on two interdependent levels. As the owner of an estate he is a benefactor to his employees, their families, and those who live nearby. In addition to this important social role, he acts as moral benefactor to Julie and, more particularly, Saint-Preux – restoring him to himself and to the active virtuous life which Julie's father, the voice of aristocratic privilege, seemed to have ended for him. The first of these roles also falls upon Wolmar because of social inequality; and it has irked some readers that the Wolmar family, created by the egalitarian Rousseau, should have servants at all, however few or kindly treated. Rousseau is not advocating the social system in which men are forced to hire their labour, and indeed Saint-Preux remarks: 'La servitude est si peu naturelle à l'homme qu'il ne saurait exister sans quelque mécontentement' (*La Nouvelle Héloïse*, p. 460). However, Rousseau is, in this novel, concerned to show the most just and generous way of living in an unjust society, that is, the society which he himself experienced. These are benefactors whom he could imagine encountering, people from his less fantastic daydreams. In this society it would, he suggests, be wrong for landowners to turn their backs on their responsibility to be a source of employment and a fund of help and advice in times of need, even though they themselves dislike having servants and enjoy the times when they are free of their servants' supervision. At Clarens all relationships are structured by the code of beneficence, whereas at Etange (Julie's father's house) relationships are judged by the aristocratic code of honour.[28]

In their beneficence to their employees and neighbours M. *servants* and Mme Wolmar are as one; by the will of both 'tout se fait par attachement' (*La Nouvelle Héloïse*, p. 470). They aim to win the affection of their servants by their own genuine fondness for them, by their honesty and fairness, and by their generosity. The servants are treated as 'des membres de la famille', 'des enfants de la maison' (*La Nouvelle Héloïse*, p. 445) – terms which may sound suspicious to a twentieth-century ear accustomed to the abuse of paternalism. However, Rousseau, well aware of the potential abuses of paternal power, redefines 'father' when he associates it with benefactor. Saint-Preux regards himself as 'l'enfant de la maison' (*La Nouvelle Héloïse*, p. 527), as well as viewing the servants in that light. He asks rhetorically: 'Ai-je tort, Milord, de comparer des maîtres si chéris à des pères et leurs domestiques à leurs enfants? Vous voyez que c'est ainsi qu'ils se regardent eux-mêmes' (*La Nouvelle Héloïse*, p. 447). The result of the Wolmars' kindness is not only the material well-being of their servants, but also, and more importantly, the fact that the servants are encouraged to lead morally good lives, something which servitude in general discourages. 'L'on dirait qu'une partie des lumières du maître et des sentiments de la maîtresse ont passé dans chacun de leurs gens, tant on les trouve judicieux, bienfaisants, honnêtes et supérieurs à leur état' (*La Nouvelle Héloïse*, p. 470): according to Saint-Preux the benefi-cence of the Wolmars enables the servants to be benefactors in their turn, which is the greatest tribute to their system. The servants are encouraged to ask for favours on each others' behalf rather than on their own, and are discouraged from boasting of their disinterestedness. The moral resemblance between the Wolmars and their beneficiaries is a counterpart to the physical similarity between parents and children. In material terms the giving of benefits may be favourably compared to the inheritance children (especially sons) receive from their parents (especially fathers). Rousseau in general disapproved of systems of inheritance both in that they exaggerate or, at least, ossify inequalities, and in that they allow someone to profit from another's ill fortune, that is to say, death.

Wolmar's major gift of moral influence is his transformation of the relationship between Julie and Saint-Preux. Julie feels that she is restored in virtue, and thus to self-respect, by him; she writes: 'J'aurais peine à dire comment s'y prend cet homme incomparable; mais je ne sais plus rougir de moi devant lui. Malgré que j'en aie, il m'élève au-dessus de moi-même, et je sens qu'à force de confiance il m'apprend à la mériter' (*La Nouvelle Héloïse*, p. 431). He does not succeed in making her love for Saint-Preux entirely a thing of the past, as we learn in her last letter, but he does achieve a temporary respite for her, a moment when she can write to Saint-Preux:

Se voir, s'aimer, le sentir, s'en féliciter passer les jours ensemble dans la familiarité fraternelle et dans la paix de l'innocence, s'occuper l'un de l'autre, y penser sans remords, en parler sans rougir, et s'honorer à ses propres yeux du même attachement qu'on s'est si longtemps reproché; voilà le point où nous en sommes. (*La Nouvelle Héloïse*, p. 664)

She speaks of Wolmar's success as if he were a god, exclaiming 'Payons de nos vertus celles de notre bienfaiteur; voilà tout ce que nous lui devons' (*La Nouvelle Héloïse*, p. 665).

Saint-Preux is more in need of help than Julie is, for he does not enjoy her strength of character, nor her emotional outlets in, for example, maternal love. He benefits even more than she does from Wolmar's efforts, and writes to him in these ecstatic terms:

Jouissez, cher Wolmar, du fruit de vos soins. Recevez les hommages d'un cœur épuré, qu'avec tant de peine vous avez rendu digne de vous être offert. Jamais homme n'entreprît ce que vous avez entrepris, jamais homme ne tenta ce que vous avez exécuté; jamais âme reconnaissante et sensible ne sentît ce que vous m'avez inspiré. La mienne avait perdue son ressort, sa vigueur, son être; vous m'avez tout rendu. J'étais mort aux vertus ainsi qu'au bonheur; je vous dois cette vie morale à laquelle je me sens renaître. O mon bienfaiteur! O mon père! En me donnant à vous tout entier, je ne puis vous offrir, comme à Dieu même, que les dons que je tiens de vous. (*La Nouvelle Héloïse*, p. 611)

Wolmar's divine paternal gift is an illusion; their love is not a thing of the past; however, Rousseau presents it as a benign illusion like the political fiction in *Du contrat social* (the fiction that the legislator is only God's mouthpiece) and also like its precursor, the noble lie in Plato's *Republic*. In contrast to these political examples, the illusion of *La Nouvelle Héloïse* appears to deceive Wolmar also, although he is not shocked or even surprised by Julie's death-bed revelations. In any case it is an illusion which promotes freedom, happiness and moral growth for the beneficiaries. Wolmar's benefaction to Julie and Saint-Preux is an artifice; but the natural development of their feelings would be impossible or pernicious in a social situation. Indeed the relationship between Julie and Saint-Preux is the product of a highly artificial and unjust social hierarchy. A remedy has therefore to be found in art which is in conformity with nature, rather than in nature itself.

Emile's tutor is a benefactor to his pupil in every sense. First of all he selects his beneficiary with great care and consideration, as is recommended by the classical code. He devotes his life to doing what is best for his charge with no thought of personal recompense or demand for gratitude. His role is purely a function of the (self-)interest of the beneficiary; he does not have his own private concerns even to the minimal extent that Wolmar does. Like Wolmar, he is a practical benefactor to all around him, giving material things and also time and advice, so that he is loved and respected by all and sets a good example for the boy. Until Emile reaches puberty he is not permitted to imitate the tutor's beneficence for, according to Rousseau, this would be an empty gesture. The child will be more aware of the responsibilities of being a benefactor if he does not associate the form of it with childhood, with the mechanical aping of a gesture rather than with the conscious emulation of the spirit of generosity. In his days of weakness and dependence it is more appropriate for Emile to learn to be a good beneficiary. He learns how to ask a favour: 'Vous voyez à l'air dont il prie qu'il sent qu'on ne lui doit rien. Il sait que ce qu'il demande est une grâce, il sait aussi que l'humanité porte à l'accorder...'(*Emile*, p. 442). He accepts refusal with perfect equanimity; in the event of his wish being granted he will not discharge his obligation with polite formulas; rather 'il sentira qu'il a contracté une dette'.

Emile learns about the refinements of obligation because his tutor arranges situations which teach him naturally, such as the incident with the fairground conjuror whose trick is imitated by Emile, which discredits the conjuror to his audience. The conjuror has his revenge with a new trick, but then generously explains his method to Emile in the privacy of his home. He refuses a gift in return, which teaches Emile that repaying generosity in kind is an honour which you must merit; the conjuror tells them: 'Non, Messieurs, je n'ai pas assez à me louer de vous pour accepter vos dons; je vous laisse obligés à moi malgré vous, c'est ma seule vengeance' (*Emile*, p. 440). The initial social hierarchy is upturned, and a new moral hierarchy is established. This incident also illustrates the hidden beneficence of the tutor when he follows his charge in bad behaviour, like the general who turns and runs in front of his fleeing troops crying that they are not deserting but following their leader. While there are times for the tutor to set an example in good conduct, at other times he supports his charge in his misdeeds in the short term and thus, by winning his confidence, increases the chance of winning him to moral excellence in the long term.

Emile himself learns to be a benefactor when he reaches puberty and the passions which inspire generosity are awakened. The translation of these emotions into beneficent action prevents them from becoming selfish: 'l'exercice des vertus sociales porte au fond des cœurs l'amour de l'humanité' (*Emile*, p. 543); this disinterested concern for his fellow men also helps to form Emile's judgement. At the same time, Emile naturally becomes aware of his debt of gratitude to his tutor, for he is never made to feel that he has been unwittingly trapped into a commitment. 'L'ingratitude serait plus rare, si les bienfaits à usure étaient moins communs' (*Emile*, p. 521). Emile repays his tutor, as Saint-Preux repays Wolmar, by his virtuous way of life, and also by his deep affection and respect for him. His gratitude and love for the tutor make him do good, as do his gratitude and love for God; these emotions encourage him to 'faire le bien loin des regards des hommes' (*Emile*, p. 636). 'Il tire le bien qu'il fait de son cœur et non de sa bourse. Il donne aux malheureux son temps, ses soins, ses affections, sa personne...' (*Emile*, p. 786). He has learnt how to reduce the inevitable hierarchy between benefactor and beneficiary, because he is happy to receive as well as to give: 'Il prend souvent son repas chez les paysans qu'il assiste, il l'accepte aussi chez ceux qui n'ont pas besoin de lui; en devenant le bienfaiteur des uns et l'ami des autres il ne cesse point d'être leur égal' (*Emile*, p. 805). At this point of choosing his future way of life, Emile declares: 'Je ne connais point d'autre gloire que d'être bienfaisant et juste' (*Emile*, p. 834). He is attracted to his future wife because of her sensibility, each of them admires the virtue and kindness of the other.

Thus the tutor's excellent model of beneficence creates a model benefactor in his pupil Emile. Any doubts that Rousseau has, about the effects which the injustice and falseness of society in general will have on the miniature just society which Emile and Sophie create, are not expressed until he plans a sequel to his treatise on education, although Book v, in its account of feminine education, already jars in tone and content with what has preceded it. The unfinished sequel, *Emile et Sophie ou Les Solitaires*, is not a philosophical or pedagogical treatise; it is written in the novel form.[29] *Emile* itself reveals a pattern of successful right conduct which engenders more right conduct. This is a standard, and the imperfections of real (or realistic, as in *La Nouvelle Héloïse*) society can be measured in terms of their deviation from it.

The legislator also creates; indeed, he is the greatest creative artist of all the model benefactors and the ideal parent. He takes

the legistr

a collection of individuals and changes them so that they can become a people:

celui qui ose entreprendre d'instituer un peuple doit se sentir en état de changer, pour ainsi dire, la nature humaine; de transformer chaque individu, qui par lui-même est un tout parfait et solitaire, en partie d'un plus grand tout dont cet individu reçoive en quelque sorte sa vie et son être; d'altérer la constitution de l'homme pour la renforcer; de substituer une existence partielle et morale à l'existence physique et indépendante que nous avons tous reçue de la nature. (*Du contrat social*, p. 381)

Du contrat social is the most radical of Rousseau's attempts to find a solution to the problem of justice in society. The legislator creates the conditions in which all virtues, including beneficence, could flourish,[30] which involves removing the need for extensive material beneficence by preventing great inequalities in fortune (*Du contrat social*, pp. 391–2). If no man is rich enough to buy another, and no one poor enough to want to sell himself, then each can live independently of the other and no one need rely on charity. However, the occasions for beneficence will still arise even if the education of children is provided by the state and illness is less common because of healthy living. The legislator has a secret influence on the mores of the citizens, which Rousseau calls the fourth sort of law, 'la plus importante de toutes' (*Du contrat social*, p. 394). The offering of hospitality, the giving of advice, the exchange of gifts would presumably be common, and would enhance the social cohesion necessary so that individuals are responsive to the general will. It would indeed be the society of the three Graces. The legislator is the most self-sacrificing, the most self-effacing of all Rousseau's imaginary model benefactors.[31] He has enormous moral power, which some readers find disquieting, yet he is nothing but the answer to the needs and interests of the people and he abdicates all legislative or executive power (*Du contrat social*, pp. 382–3). Furthermore, the moral codes which he encourages are the fourth sort of law which 'substitue insensiblement la force de l'habitude à celle de l'autorité' (*Du contrat social*, p. 394). The people are those with whom Rousseau identifies in his constant protest against power. The highly visible self, to be revealed in the *Confessions*, the beneficiary, invents ever more self-effacing benefactors. This does not preclude identification with the benefactor as well, for the greatest gift which is bestowed is that of moral example. Behind this pattern is another particular kind of invisible beneficence : *writing*.

CHAPTER 4

The passion of pity in Rousseau's theory of man

According to Rousseau's theory of human nature, rational codes would be of little avail were man not in some way inspired by his passions to follow them. It is, therefore, crucial to look closely at the passion which prompts the true benefactor; this passion is pity, an extension of *amour de soi*. Pity works for the good of mankind not only by inspiring beneficence, but also by channelling energy away from amorous passion. Both pity and amorous passion are forms of self-love directed onto the other. Both are originally general emotions which, in society, have specific objects, and both should, in different ways, work to preserve humanity. Yet there is a violence in amorous passion which necessitates its being rigorously curbed in society by another social code, that is pudicity. Pudicity, according to Rousseau, serves to protect the social cohesion which beneficence promotes. Yet pity is closely related to amorous passion; both are awakened by the imagination, which is itself aroused by a spectacle, an object which could be either pathetic or erotic or, more dangerously, could evoke both pity and desire. This fact will clearly have implications for beneficence.

THE RELATION OF PASSIONS TO REASONED BEHAVIOUR

Rousseau does not simply import the classical code of beneficence into his thinking, and leave it unassimilated like a foreign body. He integrates what he has appropriated, reshaping it in terms of his account of human nature. For Rousseau, reason alone is not reliable as a spur to virtue, and so a rational code is a guide rather than a motor force – it is a pattern to follow but it does not supply in itself a reason why men will follow it. Unlike the Stoic philosophers, Rousseau does not believe that the passions are by definite pernicious; he holds rather that they may develop for the good as well as for the bad. In his *Dialogues*, Rousseau sums up why it is necessary to take the passions into account:

La sensibilité est le principe de toute action. Un être, quoique animé, qui ne sentirait rien, n'agirait point: car où serait pour lui le motif d'agir?...Il y a une sensibilité physique...Il y a une autre sensibilité que j'appelle active et morale qui n'est autre chose que la faculté d'attacher nos affections à des êtres qui nous sont étrangers. (p. 805)[1]

Although beneficence is an art, a product of society, Rousseau proposes that, in order to be useful to men, it must be in conformity with their *nature*, which he represents in the *Discours sur l'inégalité* in the form of his theory of the state of nature. Social codes should supplement or substitute for the law of nature which is written in men's hearts.[2] In the *Discours sur l'inégalité*, Rousseau states that there is one primary and innate passion, which is *amour de soi*. These general points concerning passion work to break down certain *topoi* of sexual differentiation since it appears that all human beings are passionate as well as having access to reason.

SELF-LOVE: *AMOUR DE SOI* AND *AMOUR-PROPRE*

Amour de soi originates in the instinct for self-preservation; it is a natural and *amoral* preference for oneself over all others. It is a form of self-love which, unlike *amour-propre*, is not directly harmful to others, except where there is a momentary conflict of interests. At the same time, *amour de soi* is not in itself beneficial to others, since it is not directed at them but at the self. It exists before man has begun to compare himself with others; comparisons are the result of regularly encountering others, and so do not occur in the state of nature. Comparison, which is a conceptual skill reliant on measurement, ideas of beauty and so on, engenders *amour-propre* – which can be judged by moral criteria. A man who nurtures this social self-love harbours the impossible desire that others should prefer him to themselves, impossible because each individual tends to prefer himself to all others. In society *amour-propre* can be channelled so that an individual acts in accordance with *amour de soi*, taking the path of justice and moral health, or he may deviate from this into an inordinately competitive *amour-propre*, which is, of course, encouraged by life in a society where there is great inequality.

Having established, in the *Deuxième Dialogue*, that *la sensibilité*, in general, is the motive of all action, Rousseau subdivides sensibility into a physical and a moral kind. He further subdivides moral sensibility, on the model of a magnet, into positive (attraction) and negative (repulsion). From the former, he claims, spring all loving emotions; from the latter spring hatred and cruelty. It is *amour de soi* which produces positive sensibility; *amour-propre* can produce negative sensibility.

La sensibilité positive dérive immédiatement de l'amour de soi. Il est très naturel que celui qui s'aime cherche à étendre son être et ses jouissances, et à s'approprier par l'attachement ce qu'il sent devoir être un bien pour lui: ceci est une affaire de sentiment où la réflexion n'entre pour rien. (*Dialogues*, pp. 805–6)[3]

It is because the benefactor acts on a natural passionate impulse (pity) that he acts immediately when his help is sought; equally the beneficiary responds spontaneously.[4] Yet this connection between impulse and action is established by reason, and Seneca, before Rousseau, feels the necessity to *urge* spontaneity on benefactors. This is, however, no more para-doxical than urging someone to act in accordance with his nature rather than to follow a degenerate social habit.

Disinterested beneficence is possible, according to Rousseau, because of the primary passion of *amour de soi* – in that it is a benign regard cast by me on myself,[5] which may be extended to the other in pity. It means that there is a possibility of looking on the other as another 'myself', emphasising similarity (although not identity) rather than difference. *Amour-propre* has the tendency to look upon the other as a rival; in an attenuated form this can be a useful encouragement to virtue: the desire to outdo someone in virtue, to be their rival in good deeds. However, it easily becomes pernicious and even violent. *Amour-*

propre is, in general, more concerned to mark differences (of a hierarchical nature) than similarity. In Rousseau's scheme of things Aristotelian magnanimity would be directly inspired by *amour-propre*. Emile moves from *amour de soi*, when his gaze focuses on himself, to *amour-propre*, when he compares himself to others, at puberty.

Mon Emile n'ayant jusqu'à présent regardé que lui-même, le premier regard qu'il jette sur ses semblables le porte à se comparer avec eux, et le premier sentiment qu'excite en lui cette comparaison, est de désirer la première place. Voilà le point où l'amour de soi se change en amour-propre. (*Emile*, p. 523)

Beneficence also involves a certain hierarchical difference (the one who has something to give is in a superior position to the one who needs to receive it) – but this does not derive entirely from a complicity with *amour-propre*. Even in *amour de soi*, in nature, a difference is already established *within* the self, in so far as there is an *I* (subject), who loves a *myself* (object). Social structures are typically held dormant, 'en creux', in this way in Rousseau's state of nature; it is an oversimplification to claim that Rousseau's philosophy is based on binary oppositions. Although there is a series of apparent antitheses which occur in his argumentation, such as that of art and nature, or that of *amour-propre* and *amour de soi* (and it would be wrong to try to annul these polarities), the relationship between the terms is characteristically far more complex than one of opposition.[6] The urge to be a benefactor, aroused by pity (an extension of *amour de soi*), should be nourished by those elements of *amour-propre* which are most closely related to *amour de soi*.

The structure which enables beneficence is thus one of proximity but not identity, one of differences which are not absolute or fixed. It is interesting to compare Rousseau's description with recent characterisations of femininity. Luce Irigaray claims that 'la femme resterait toujours plusieurs, mais gardée de la dispersion parce que l'autre est déjà en elle et lui est auto-érotiquement familier', which might remind us of Rousseau's *amour de soi*, and particularly of the pleasure he experiences dreaming by lakes or walking in the woods. Irigaray

a/soi ⟶ pity for Os ⟶ generosity = bfce
                   + Jice

goes on to explain that while property is foreign to the feminine, proximity is not, and that this prevents any kind of economy we know; at this point her proximity does seem closer to the merging and indistinction of that friendship which excludes beneficence: 'Elle s'échange elle-même sans cesse avec l'autre sans identification possible de l'un(e) ou l'autre' (*Ce sexe qui n'en est pas un*, p. 30).

THE THREE STAGES OF PITY

Amour de soi extended to others in pity is, then, the source and motive force for generosity, which, when regulated by justice, becomes beneficence. By combining Rousseau's account of pity in the *Discours sur l'inégalité* and in the *Essai sur l'origine des langues*, it is possible to separate the development of pity, from natural instinct to the social code, into three stages. The first moment, which is described most fully in the *Discours*, is the animal stage, at which pity is a 'répugnance innée à voir souffrir son semblable', a 'vertu d'autant plus universelle et d'autant plus utile à l'homme, qu'elle précède en lui l'usage de toute réflexion, et si naturelle que les bêtes mêmes en donnent quelquefois des signes sensibles' (*Discours*, p. 154). At this stage it is hardly necessary to separate the passion of pity from the instinct for self-preservation (the earliest moment of *amour de soi*) as pity is no more than this instinct extended to other sentient beings. This extension of the instinct for self-preservation to our own kind tempers the potentially aggressive aspect of a survival instinct. This early pity is 'le pur mouvement de la nature' (*Discours*, p. 155) which takes the place of instituted law during Rousseau's hypothetical solitary stage of humanity.

The second stage is what Jacques Derrida describes as the 'devenir-humain de la pitié'.[7] This development of pity into a specifically human quality occurs at the beginning of socialisation, during the Golden Age when man's imagination is awakened but not yet pernicious. This period, which might be termed the adolescence of humanity, is like the beginning of puberty for Emile. For the boy, Emile, and for mankind, the newly aroused imagination enables human pity. In the *Essai sur l'origine des langues* (p. 517), Rousseau says that we are moved to pity 'en nous transportant hors de nous-mêmes; en nous identifiant avec l'être souffrant'. This passionate expansion of the self is necessarily accompanied by reflection, because it involves a judgement of the suffering of the other; this is achieved by a comparison with the beholder's own personal experience of suffering. As Rousseau explains:

Nous ne souffrons qu'autant que nous jugeons qu'il souffre; ce n'est pas dans nous, c'est dans lui que nous souffrons. Qu'on songe combien ce transport suppose de connaissances acquises. Comment imaginerais-je des maux dont j'ai nulle idée? Comment souffrirais-je en voyant souffrir un autre, si je ne sais pas même qu'il souffre, si j'ignore ce qu'il y a de commun entre lui et moi? Celui qui n'a jamais réfléchi ne peut être ni clément, ni juste, ni pitoyable; il ne peut pas non plus être méchant et vindicatif. Celui qui n'imagine rien ne sent que lui-même; il est seul au milieu du genre humain. (*Essai*, p. 517)

In the *Discours*, Rousseau describes the becoming-human of pity in ambivalent terms: '[quoique] la pitié naturelle eût déjà souffert quelque altération, ce période...dut être l'époque la plus heureuse' (p. 171). The development of pity is part of the movement of *perfectibility* which characterises his imaginary human history, and which is at once progress and corruption. Imagination promotes tender emotions, but also opens the way for dissatisfaction with one's lot; the understanding of temporality which is necessary for pity (since pity entails memory of one's own past sufferings, and anticipation of the same in the future) makes it no longer possible to live entirely in the present, which is a mixed blessing.

The new faculty to compare and contrast, the basis of judgement and reasoning, is an essential attribute of full humanity, and a necessary part of subscribing to a moral code such as beneficence; yet it may be a sterile or even deathly quality as Rousseau points out in his critique of society.[8] Perfectibility is equivalent to liberty; while animals must obey their natural instincts, have no free will or power to substitute one way of life for another, and do not know progress or corruption, men are free to change for the better or for the worse.

pity ← spec.

Pity is aroused by a spectacle. When Rousseau introduces the subject of pity in the *Discours sur l'inégalité* he describes it as a 'répugnance innée à *voir* souffrir son semblable' (p. 154, my emphasis). I have emphasised the term *voir* on the grounds that, in the state of nature, it would be impossible to pity suffering that one did not see. The suffering must be of the most visible and clearly identifiable kind in order to affect natural man, whose imagination has been little exercised. Rousseau employs the terms *voir*, *image* and *spectacle* (and related terms) most frequently when discussing the arousal of pity. For example, he asks 'qui est-ce qui ne plaint pas le malheureux qu'il voit souffrir?' (*Emile*, p. 503); he emphasises the importance of showing an adolescent 'des spectacles de douleur et de misère' (*Emile*, p. 512). Sounds may also, of course, be an important part of the piteous spectacle; an adolescent boy will find that 'les plaintes et les cris commenceront d'agiter ses entrailles' (*Emile*, p. 505) at the same time as the sight of blood or of the convulsions of a dying animal will cause him pain.

In the *Discours sur l'inégalité*, images of suffering which arouse pity are described like scenes or spectacles. Rousseau speaks of 'l'horrible spectacle' of an abbatoir for cattle, and he gives Mandeville's example: 'la pathétique image d'un homme enfermé qui aperçoit au dehors une bête féroce, arrachant un enfant du sein de sa mère, brisant sous sa dent meurtrière les faibles membres, et déchirant de ses ongles les entrailles palpitantes de cet enfant' (*Discours*, p. 154). Rousseau even speaks of 'l'animal spectateur' who identifies with 'l'animal souffrant'. This is the predecessor of the perceptive benefactor who observes his beneficiary in order to act in his best interest.

The identification of the beholder with the sufferer has to be controlled, in accordance with the good of the beholder and with justice (the good of society). The identification goes only so far as is necessary in order to comprehend the suffering by a comparison with personal experience, and this allows room for the pleasurable awareness that one is no longer suffering oneself. In this way pity is contained within the bounds of self-love even as it acts as a restraint, a containing force upon self-love; each balances the other. This permits beneficence to be a hierarchical

pity → bfa
    fship

structure, yet one which will tend towards reciprocity. At the same time it renders it vulnerable, for excessive *amour-propre* may encourage the beholder to take too much pleasure in his own present good fortune (and hence capacity to aid) and in the sufferer's ill fortune (furnishing an occasion for aid). This could even degenerate into sadistic delight at the sight of suffering.

In *Emile* (p. 508) Rousseau states: 'La pitié qu'on a du mal d'autrui ne se mesure pas sur la quantité de ce mal, mais sur le sentiment qu'on prête à ceux qui le souffrent.' This is one of three maxims in an extended development on pity, which takes up the themes of the citation from the *Essai sur l'origine des langues* above. This maxim indicates that pity is based on a *perception* rather than an objective fact; a king will not pity the sufferings of the poor if he holds them in contempt, and believes that their emotions are not as his would be. For the same reason most people readily feel sorry at the sight of obvious physical suffering, but moral or psychological anguish touches only the sensitive. Rousseau tells us that once a human being has understood the meaning of mortality, then death will always move him to pity because he knows that he cannot hope to escape from it himself. This is also another way of saying that the benefactor and the beneficiary must have some common ground, must resemble each other in some way.

The third stage of pity is the fully social one. So that men will not enslave one another, moral codes and written laws have to replace the gentle voice of nature in regulating men's behaviour and providing the conditions for freedom. This role is played by, amongst other things, the code of beneficence. In the *Discours sur l'inégalité* (p. 155), Rousseau writes:

La bienveillance et l'amitié même sont, à le bien prendre, des productions d'une pitié constante, fixée sur un objet particulier: car désirer que quelqu'un ne souffre point, qu'est-ce autre chose que désirer qu'il soit heureux?

In this rhetorical question Rousseau affirms the continuity (from nature to society) of the emotion of pity, and suggests that the desire that someone should not suffer is equivalent to desiring that he should be happy. Pity thus implies feelings of benevolence and friendship which prompt acts of beneficence. In the preface to the *Discours*, Rousseau explains that this continuity of pity is not seamless. He says that from the two natural principles of *amour de soi* and pity

me paraissent découler toutes les règles du droit naturel; règles que la raison est ensuite forcée de rétablir sur d'autres fondements, quand par ses développements successifs elle est venue à bout d'étouffer la nature. (*Discours*, p. 126)

Outside the hypothetical state of nature the tenets of natural law must be re-established on another basis, that of rational, logical thought. Similarly, in the *Profession de foi*, Rousseau supplements the voice of conscience, the intuition of God, with logical enquiry. Reasoned beneficence is motivated by spontaneous pity, but also supplants it. Pity must not only be transformed from a passing emotion into something more lasting; a further crucial aspect of socialisation is that the effects on society at large are considered before the benefit to any one individual. This consideration of justice is strongly emphasised by the classical code. In *Emile* (p. 548) Rousseau writes, 'de toutes les vertus la justice est celle qui concourt le plus au bien commun des hommes. Il faut par raison, par amour pour nous, avoir pitié de notre espèce encore plus que de notre prochain, et c'est une très grande cruauté envers les hommes que la pitié pour les méchants.'

In the *Discours* (pp. 174–5) Rousseau describes the birth of society thus:

de libre et indépendant qu'était auparavant l'homme, le voilà par une multitude de nouveaux besoins assujetti, pour ainsi dire, à toute la nature, et surtout à ses semblables dont il devient l'esclave en un sens, même en devenant leur maître; riche il a besoin de leurs services; pauvre il a besoin de leurs secours, et la médiocrité ne le met point en état de se passer d'eux.

In the state of nature, man's relative strength and independence from other men makes mutual aid less necessary than in society where men are subject to more desires. Rousseau rejects the theory that society can exist happily with each member acting according to self-interest alone.

If pity does not develop into active virtue, as beneficence, then it becomes sterile self-indulgence. Rousseau gives as an example of this the pity experienced by a theatre audience for the characters on stage.[9] As spectators at a theatre we are easily moved to pity because our feelings are

pures et sans mélange d'inquiétude pour nous-mêmes. En donnant des pleurs à ces fictions, nous avons satisfait à tous les droits de l'humanité, sans avoir plus rien à mettre du nôtre; au lieu que les infortunés en personne exigeraient de nous des soins, des soulagements, des consolations, des travaux qui pourraient nous associer à leurs peines, qui coûteraient du moins à notre indulgence, et dont nous sommes bien aises d'être exemptés. (*Lettre à d'Alembert*, p. 33)

In *La Nouvelle Héloïse*, Rousseau attributes to Wolmar the suggestion that beggars are more socially useful than actors precisely because when they have moved us to pity (even if they are acting a part) we have the opportunity to succour them. If you choose to respond to a beggar, 'Dieu vous assiste' (*La Nouvelle Héloïse*, p. 540) instead of helping him, you are making the theatre spectator's response of facile and meaningless pity.

Rousseau claims that there is more real pleasure in active pity, in beneficence, than in what he calls 'cette pitié cruelle qui détourne les yeux d'autrui pour se dispenser de les soulager' (*Lettres morales*, p. 1118). He explains this not only by his theory of man's natural enjoyment of doing good, but also in terms of self-esteem, an explanation directed towards the priorities of social life:

L'exercice de la bienfaisance flatte naturellement l'amour-propre par une idée de supériorité; on s'en rappelle tous les actes comme autant de témoignages qu'au delà de ses propres besoins on a de la force encore pour soulager ceux d'autrui. Cet air de puissance fait qu'on prend plus de plaisir à exister et qu'on habite plus volontiers avec soi. (*Lettres morales*, p. 1116)

Pity itself includes an element of pleasure derived from relief at not being in the position of the sufferer oneself; beneficence adds to that the certainty that not only is the benefactor not enduring what his beneficiary endures, but that beyond that negative advantage, he has the positive one of being in a *pleasure of doing good*

position to help. This brings Rousseau to within a hair's breadth of the aristocratic, magnanimous account of generosity, but an important distinction remains. La Rochefoucauld claims that 'Ce qu'on nomme libéralité n'est le plus souvent que la vanité de donner, que nous aimons mieux que ce que nous donnons' (*Maximes*, no. 263). He is asserting that if one is liberal one clearly prefers the action of giving to the object given. A point with which few would differ. Yet his term 'la *vanité* de donner' suggests that the feeling of superiority experienced by the giver is an empty feeling not altogether justified, whereas the feeling of superiority which Rousseau's benefactor enjoys is justified as it is based on a simple matter of fact. The notion that it is pleasurable to do good is an eighteenth-century *topos*, to be found not only in sentimental novels, but also in worldly novels such as Duclos's *Les Confessions du Comte de* ***, (pp. 124–6). However, it is important to differentiate between the various ways in which the *topos* is presented – it can serve a number of different ideological positions.

While passions add force and intensity to the social code, they do also have a dangerous aspect. They have a logic of their own, which is apart from the rationality of the codes. Having established the links between beneficence and *amour de soi* and pity, we must examine the interrelationship between pity and amorous passion, between beneficence and pudicity, and between the passions and the social codes in order to have a theoretical background for analysing the detail of Rousseau's writing on beneficence.

THE RELATION BETWEEN PITY AND AMOROUS PASSION

Pity, the passionate source of beneficence, is also related to another passion: love between the sexes or *passion amoureuse*.[10] In society, pity not only works for the good of mankind in general, but is also supposed to work to preserve men from the ravages of amorous passion. The term 'men' here, as so often in Rousseau, is significantly ambiguous.

Amorous passion is sometimes presented as a perversion of natural pity, which could, unfettered, lead to a total perversion of natural order. Human pity is aroused by the faculty of imagination, and it is tied to sensual perception and to the emotion aroused by a perception. At puberty, Rousseau writes,

l'œil s'anime et parcourt les autres êtres; on comence à prendre intérêt à ceux qui nous environnent; on commence à sentir qu'on n'est pas fait pour vivre seul; c'est ainsi que le cœur s'ouvre aux affections humaines et devient capable d'attachement. (*Emile*, p. 502)

The awakening of the adolescent makes him susceptible on the one hand to feelings of pity, generosity and friendship, and, on the other hand, to amorous passion. It is essentially a spectacle (of suffering) which inspires pity, just as it is a spectacle (of women) which arouses desire. Interestingly, one example of a spectacle of suffering which is frequently cited involves a mother and child, and descriptions of horrendous scenes which inspire pity (such as Voltaire's poem on the Lisbon earthquake) usually invoke mothers and babes. As so often, the term 'woman' must be split in a manichean fashion into mothers and 'whores'. Pity works to preserve men from amorous passion by substituting one spectacle for another. Rousseau recommends:

Quand l'âge critique approche, offrez aux jeunes gens des spectacles qui les retiennent, et non des spectacles qui les excitent: donnez le change à leur imagination naissante par des objets, qui loin d'enflammer leurs sens, en repriment l'activité. Eloignez-les des grandes villes, où la parure et l'immodestie des femmes hâte et prévient les leçons de la nature... ne leur montrez que des tableaux touchants, mais modestes, qui les remuent sans les séduire, et qui nourrissent leur sensibilité sans émouvoir leurs sens... Il faut toucher votre élève à l'aspect des misères humaines. (*Emile*, p. 517)

Both pity and amorous passion are awakened at puberty by the nascent imagination; both are aroused by *images*, by *spectacles*, including theatrical spectacles which, according to the *Lettre à d'Alembert*, promote the worst side both of pity and amorous passion. It is the very affinity of pity with amorous passion which allows passion to deflect it, whereas *pudeur*, the other safeguard against amorous passion, the social code which governs the relations between the sexes, checks passion by opposing it.

love as social P   imag ——? love
(rp chron)   ↘ kn f   (M)
94   *Justice and difference in Rousseau*

In Rousseau's account of amorous passion, it is not natural, but 'un sentiment factice né de l'usage de la société' (*Discours sur l'inégalité*, p. 158). In a natural state there would be no contact between the sexes other than animal-like mating, which is outside the realm of morality, whereas *la passion amoureuse* is also designated, by Rousseau, *l'amour moral* – in other words it is subject to moral judgement. Rousseau says of natural man 'toute femme est bonne pour lui' (*Discours sur l'inégalité*, p. 158); there is no element of choice, preference, or recognition of difference between one individual and another. Amorous passion, on the other hand, involves recognition of difference; the eye must compare, measure and calculate on certain criteria, which are those governed by the imagination, such as aesthetic ones. In nature, attachments (which imply continuity) would not be formed; but social relations are more constant, and therefore lie in the sphere of morality. To this extent the development from (animal) sexual instinct to moral love is parallel to the development from animal pity (a vague instinct) to human pity.

However, amorous passion has the seeds of destruction within it, 'la jalousie s'éveille avec l'amour; la discorde triomphe, et la plus douce des passions reçoit des sacrifices de sang humain' (*Discours sur l'inégalité*, p. 169). As well as this practical link between jealous passion and violent death, man's *knowledge* of death is associated with amorous passion in the *Discours*. Both developments are the fruit of the imagination, and so divide man from the animals.[11] A mental relationship with death (fear) stands in the same relation to the fact of death as amorous passion does to the fact of sexual reproduction. The young Sophie learns about death through identifying the reproductive succession; it is man's knowledge of his inability to preserve the species other than by sexed reproduction which makes him realise that his individual death is inevitable.

In the state of nature no events, not even couplings and deaths, become images in the mind of animal man, because he has no imagination, he exists entirely in the present moment. Animality is represented by Rousseau as pre-reflexive and pre-passionate. Once the imagination is awakened man can have a

Love → rivalry, violence

mental image of and a mental relationship with anything. His knowledge will be accompanied by an affective charge, positive or negative, desire or aversion. Rousseau describes men in primitive southern society gathering around the waterhole, dancing and decorating themselves. Their first words, *aimez-moi*, imply some mental image of *amour* (*moral*) which goes beyond the sex instinct (*amour physique*). For Rousseau those words not only represent positive affection, but also a risking of the self and an exposure to (the fear of) death. It is interesting to contrast this account with Diderot's *Supplément au voyage de Bougainville* where he represents sexual relations in primitive society as completely untroubled and free of any possessive or jealous sentiment. Diderot's Tahiti is also an incestuous society. For Rousseau the moment of incest is pre-passion and pre-social in the strict sense of the term: the interdiction of incest arrives with the first primitive societies proper. According to Diderot it is only with the arrival of corrupt European society that the Tahitians begin to make a strange (for them) practical connection between love and death, between sexual relations and both murderous jealousy and venereal disease. Rousseau's version is closer to Freud's Oedipal accounts of primitive man and Lévi-Strauss's anthropology.

Amorous passion is thus related to death (or the fear of death) on a fundamental level, and also on the superficial level of arousing rivalries and hence murderous disputes. These arise because amorous passion involves comparison, not only of the beloved with others, but also of the self with others, as the self must be assured of being uniquely chosen by the beloved. This mechanism of *amour-propre* may prove fatal 'surtout dans les pays où les mœurs étant encore comptées pour quelque chose, la jalousie des amants et la vengeance des époux causent chaque jour des duels, des meurtres, et pis encore' (*Discours sur l'inégalité*, p. 157). In Rousseau's major theoretical and fictional works he warns against amorous rivalry and jealous passion; in *La Nouvelle Héloïse* a duel between Edouard and Saint-Preux is happily averted. In his 'minor' works he shows more clearly the bloody consequences of amorous passion; for instance, in *Les Amours d'Edouard*, Edouard is forced to fight a duel with his mistress's husband and kills him. The extreme of amorous passion which is dominated by jealousy is the state in which the desire for the beloved is superseded by the desire to be preferred to the rival; the rival replaces the beloved as the object of passion (jealousy) and is fearfully imagined as stronger and happier than the self.[12] Thus *amour moral* is paradoxically 'propre à détruire le genre humain qu'elle est destinée à conserver' (*Discours sur l'inégalité*, p. 157).

If adolescent boys are exposed to women too early they become cruel and inhuman; Rousseau writes that, in his experience, 'la fougue du tempérament les rendait impatients, vindicatifs, furieux: leur imagination pleine d'un seul objet se refusait à tout le reste, ils ne connaissaient ni pitié ni miséricorde; ils auraient sacrifié père, mère et l'univers entier au moindre de leurs plaisirs' (*Emile*, p. 502). It is the duty of whoever has the charge of their upbringing to delay their knowledge of, and exposure to, women (as objects of desire) until the last possible moment, so that their character may already be formed. This delay may be achieved by channelling all the nascent passion into pity and beneficent action, which will form the boy into a compassionate and virtuous man before he encounters the perils of amorous passion.

The passion of love is dangerous not only for the sanguinary effect it has on men, but also because of the power it bestows on women, a potentially deadly power, according to Rousseau. In the *Lettre à d'Alembert* (p. 63), Rousseau warns that 'l'amour est le règne des femmes', and that women will use men's passion as a means to enslave them. Women will attempt to keep men constantly in their company, and this excessive proximity, this mingling of what should be kept apart, is debilitating for both sexes, but particularly for men: 'elles n'y perdent que leurs mœurs, et nous y perdons à la fois nos mœurs et notre constitution' (*Lettre à d'Alembert*, p. 135). As they lose their health and strength, men also lose their masculinity through spending too much time indoors with women, engaged in idle womanly pursuits. The life-style of a harem, asserts Rousseau, turns men into eunuchs. Thus, in Rousseau's view, women's usurpation of men's necessary authority must inevitably lead to

women, actresses, prostitutes

the degeneration of the human race. Even women do not really benefit from their tyranny, in so far as enslaved men are not real men and cannot offer the truly masculine love which women desire. Rousseau says of a man in the sexual relationship that 'son mérite est dans sa puissance, il plaît par cela seul qu'il est fort' (*Emile*, p. 693). As an example of the emasculating power of the company of women, Rousseau suggests that it is the nature of a woman to be always sexually a woman, whereas men are only sometimes sexually men, therefore a man in a constant state of (imagined) desire is not a man. In *Emile*, Book v (p. 766), Rousseau suggests that a wife should govern her husband as a minister governs the king, 'en se faisant commander ce qu'elle veut faire'. Acknowledging women's ability to govern, Rousseau is horrified at the idea that they should also seize the right to command.

Even in the theatre, the sight and sound of women on the stage is liable to 'étendre l'empire de sexe... rendre des femmes et des jeunes filles les précepteurs du public, et... leur donner sur les spectateurs le même pouvoir qu'elles ont sur leurs amants' (*Lettre à d'Alembert*, p. 63). Rousseau's condemnation of the influence of actors is closely related to his condemnation of the influence of women. Actresses who are almost, if not exactly, prostitutes, are presented as the most pernicious of all. In *La Lettre à d'Alembert*, the condemnation is partly an economic one: (actors) actresses and prostitutes sell themselves, and they also increase the sale of goods, especially luxury goods. They, therefore, stand at the antithesis to gift-exchange, to the gift of self, and to the kind of barter of necessary goods which Rousseau prescribes in *Du contrat social*. Actresses and prostitutes offer a simulacrum of the gift: *se donner* (the gift of self) becomes *se donner pour* (representation) which becomes *se donner pour de l'argent* (sale).[13]

PUDICITY

In Rousseau's account of human history, the development and degeneration of passions which are dormant in the state of nature is balanced by the formation of a complementary system of checks and antidotes, often called 'suppléments'. This goes some way towards restoring the equilibrium which characterises the state of nature. Amorous passion is checked by the supplement of pudicity as detailed in Chapter 1.[14] Jacques Derrida emphasises that *pudeur* is at once a 'produit du raffinement social' (*De la grammatologie*, p. 255) and yet governed by a *natural* economy. Paul de Man proposes another way of interpreting Rousseau's manipulation of the categories of the natural and the social, which is pertinent to my treatment of pudicity. In *Allegories of Reading* (p. 249), de Man warns of

the danger of hypostasizing such concepts as 'nature', 'individual' or 'society' as if they were the designation of substantial entities. Rousseau can legitimately shift these terms around...because they designate relational properties, patterns of relational integration or disintegration...Rousseau calls natural any stage of relational integration that precedes in degree the stage presently under examination.

This leads to the conclusion that Sophie's pudicity may well be natural relative to the life of Parisian ladies in their salons or to actresses on the stage, but yet social relative to the state of nature. In this chapter, pudicity will be considered a social code because it is considered from the viewpoint of the state of nature, even though Rousseau occasionally qualifies it as 'natural' in order to give it priority over degenerate social behaviour.

Unlike the other marks of humanity (imagination, reason, writing and so on), which all have a positive as well as a negative side, women's unlimited sexual desire is, according to Rousseau, a benefit only in the moral pleasure gained from checking it by means of the supplementary code of *pudeur*. The other two divinely appointed supplements which Rousseau cites when he discusses *pudeur* in Book v of *Emile* are the law, which regulates man's intentions, bringing him liberty as self-mastery, and reason, which governs his immoderate passions:

L'Etre suprême a voulu faire en tout honneur à l'espèce humaine; en donnant à l'homme des penchants sans mesure il lui donne en même temps la loi qui les règle, afin qu'il soit libre et se commande à lui-même; en le livrant à des passions immodérées, il joint à ces passions la raison pour les gouverner: en livrant la femme à des désirs illimités, il joint à ces désirs la pudeur pour les contenir. Pour surcroît, il ajoute encore une récompense actuelle au bon usage de ses facultés, savoir le goût qu'on prend aux choses honnêtes lorsqu'on en fait la règle de ses actions. Tout cela vaut bien, ce me semble, l'instinct des bêtes. (*Emile*, p. 695)

The two supplements which apply to men (in general) are both forms of control which clearly increase true freedom, as opposed to anarchy or libertinage. Women in particular, on the other hand, are above all given the ability to contain themselves and a pleasure in, or taste for, self-containment. That is not so much a structure of freedom within bounds as a pleasure in bounds (which are recognised as being for the common good).

This passage introduces the complexity involved in designating mankind as *l'homme*. It is possible to read statements referring to *l'homme* as statements which apply to man in general. It would indeed be possible to read much of the first four books of *Emile* as if the general rules they contain apply to both sexes; this sometimes happens when the work is approached as a pedagogical treatise. Yet the fifth book of *Emile* insists on the specificity of women, and, in the remarks cited, the account of *l'homme* is followed by an account of *la femme*. The appended account of woman makes the reader question the generality of the statements concerning man. This is not to say that Rousseau claims that women are totally without reason, but rather that reason comes under the aegis of the masculine. It appears under the aegis of the masculine largely because of Rousseau's insistence on the specificity of women. Those qualities in mankind which are not specially feminine tend to fall to the lot of masculinity as if by default. That which is first is only so because something succeeds it. The first is dependent on the second as a master is upon a slave (who allows him to exist in the capacity of master). Likewise the benefactor exists *qua* benefactor because of the beneficiary, something about which Rousseau is explicit, and man acquires masculinity through the detailing of the traits of femininity, a reversal which is more implicit in the Rousseau texts. It is interesting to compare this conclusion to Rousseau's conclusion (quite differently reached) in the *Lettre à d'Alembert* (p. 110): 'Voulez-vous donc connaître les hommes? Etudiez les femmes.'

economics of publicity

A further reward follows women's willed holding back of their erotic power; it allows the possibility of pudic love, which Julie praises: 'je ne connais pas d'amour sans pudeur' (*La Nouvelle Héloïse*, p. 139). While 'la débauche' swiftly leads to satiety, pudic love can bring increased enjoyment, according to an Epicurean economy of reserve:

A l'égard de la pudeur du sexe en particulier, quelle arme plus douce eût pu donner cette même nature à celui qu'elle destinait à se défendre?... L'obstacle apparent qui semble éloigner cet objet est au fond ce qui le rapproche. Les désirs voilés par la honte n'en deviennent que plus séduisants; en les gênant la pudeur les enflamme. (*Lettre à d'Alembert*, pp. 112–13)

The principle that a limitation on, or rationing of, pleasure will in fact increase pleasure is also applied by Rousseau to food and drink, but not to healthy pleasures such as walking in the open air.[15] The economy of pudicity is intended to preserve men's health, virility and freedom. This protective function is also linked by Rousseau to the natural need of lovers to withdraw from the gaze of others, as a safeguard against attack in a state of post-coital weakness.[16] This protective modesty is displaced, as if by synecdoche, to become the responsibility of *the* sex (*le sexe*), that is, women.

Although pity and *pudeur* both act to modify amorous passion, for the good of men and of mankind, they are conceptually very different from each other. Derrida points out, in his analysis of the *Discours sur l'inégalité*, that Rousseau represents nature as a limit, like a moral reserve or a law, and as an impossible equilibrium of desires and powers.[17] Again, in *Emile*, Rousseau explains man's natural situation thus:

C'est ainsi que la nature, qui fait tout pour le mieux, a d'abord constitué [l'homme]. Elle ne lui donne immédiatement que les désirs nécessaires à sa conservation et les facultés suffisantes pour les satisfaire. Elle a mis toutes les autres comme *en réserve* au fond de son âme, pour s'y développer au besoin. Ce n'est que dans cet état primitif que *l'équilibre* du pouvoir et du désir se rencontre, et que l'homme n'est pas malheureux. Sitot que ces facultés *virtuelles* se mettent en action, l'imagination, la plus active de toutes, s'éveille et les devance. (*Emile*, p. 304, my emphasis)

In the state of nature man's virtual faculties are held in reserve, like a stock or provision. Once social development begins these reserved faculties can be released. The imagination is the faculty which inspires a breaking away from the reserve, and once man's powers are liberated so are his desires which easily outstrip his power to satisfy them. While pity is one of the passions which are innate yet virtual, only fully released by the imagination, pudicity mimics the natural holding in reserve; it is indeed a reinforcement of boundaries and a law. As nature holds perfectibility in reserve so pudicity holds women's desirability in reserve. It reserves women (as sexual beings) for their husbands. Pudic women are reserved in both senses of the word, since *reserve* can function as a synonym for modesty as well as conveying the meaning of *saved up*. A reserved woman does not give herself away, does not give her person up to someone else, where that gift would be inappropriate. Pudicity confirms the integrity and stability of the unbreached and static self, whereas pity is dynamic and expansive, a movement out of the self towards the other.

SPECTACLE

Pity is aroused by the spectacle of suffering; the benefactor must first be the pitying beholder. This is another of the aspects of beneficence which bring it into conflict with the code of pudicity unless women are strictly excluded from being beneficiaries. Rousseau says of the young Emile, 'il souffre quand il *voit* souffrir; c'est un sentiment naturel' (*Emile*, p. 545, my emphasis). Like the natural man, Emile is moved by the spectacle of suffering. Thanks to his education this pity is not sterile; it develops into beneficence:

S'il voit régner la discorde entre ses camarades il cherche à les réconcilier; s'il voit des affligés il s'informe du sujet de leurs peines; s'il voit deux hommes se haïr il veut connaître la cause de leur inimitié; s'il voit un opprimé gémir des vexations du puissant et du riche il cherche de quelles manœuvres se couvrent ces vexations, et dans l'intérêt qu'il prend à tous les misérables, les moyens de finir leurs maux ne sont jamais indifférents pour lui. (*Emile*, pp. 545–6)

Emile's good deeds are provoked by the sight of unhappiness, which makes him interested in the unhappy individuals he sees. In Chapter 3 it emerged that benefactors are observers of humanity in general and, more particularly, of their chosen beneficiaries, since they must know them, and 'pour connaître les hommes, il faut les voir agir' (*Emile*, p. 526). This is the reasoned development of the hypothetical image of the savage gazing on a pitiful sight. The code of beneficence adds, to that initial emotional response, rational comparisons and a weighing up of the situation in a wider context.

Although Rousseau asserts that the pity aroused at a theatrical performance is sterile, he repeatedly uses the theatre as an example or as a metaphor in his discussions of pity. When Emile's tutor wants to initiate him into the pleasure of pitying his fellow men, he shows him 'le spectacle du monde' (*Emile*, p. 525). When Emile reaches adolescence, the tutor's role is indeed to present him with a series of spectacles, which will each carry a moral lesson. Rousseau cites the example of a father who takes his son to a hospital for the treatment of venereal diseases in order to cure him of a tendency towards lechery. The tutor may also use words to convey his message but their sensual, emotional force must predominate over their intellectual content; the tutor's narrative must be like a theatrical performance:

Surtout n'allez pas lui dire tout cela froidement comme son caté-chisme; qu'il voie, qu'il sente les calamités humaines: ébranlez, effrayez son imagination des périls dont tout homme est sans cesse environné; qu'il voie autour de lui tous ces abîmes, et qu'à vous les entendre décrire il se presse contre vous de peur d'y tomber. (*Emile*, p. 508)

The spectacle of human suffering shares a further point of comparison with a theatrical spectacle. The reaction of the spectator is, in both cases, a mixture of pain and pleasure. The spectator identifies with the suffering he observes, but is also conscious that he is himself in a more fortunate position. Rousseau affirms: 'Si le premier spectacle qui le frappe est un objet de tristesse, le premier retour sur lui-même est un sentiment de plaisir' (*Emile*, p. 514). Observation from a distance, it is suggested, is preferable to participation in society at too early an age; one might become embittered after suffering personally from men's injustice.

Emile's tutor teaches him penetration of gaze, so that he may see not only the social mask which he despises, but also the natural man behind it whom he can respect and pity. Rousseau warns that there are dangers associated with being a spectator of society; it may, for example, make a young man cynical and inured to the sight of hardship; and so he suggests the more edifying spectacle of history as another possibility.

The link between beneficence and spectacle is also represented in the *Rêveries*. In the *9ᵉ Promenade*, Rousseau presents a series of examples of occasions when he acts as a benefactor. It has been suggested that one can consider these as a series of *petits tableaux* entitled, for instance, 'The Cooper's Son', 'The Wafer-Seller', 'Festivities at the Castle' and 'The Pensioner'. The episodes are indeed just like *tableaux vivants* with Rousseau as the anonymous beholder.[18] The whole *Promenade* is dominated by pleasure at the sight of others. The introductory paragraph, added after the composition of the *Promenade*, argues that 'contentement' is preferable to 'bonheur' because 'Le bonheur n'a point d'enseigne extérieure; pour le connaître il faudrait lire dans le cœur de l'homme heureux; mais le contentement se lit dans les yeux, dans le maintien, dans l'accent, dans la démarche, et semble se communiquer à celui qui l'aperçoit.' Contentment is visible. Rousseau asks rhetorically: 'Est-il une jouissance plus douce que de voir un peuple entier se livrer à la joie un jour de fête?'

The verb *voir* occurs over and over again in this *Promenade*. Apart from the crucial anecdote of reading which was the event which sparked off Rousseau's writing the *Promenade*, we find: 'voir de petits bambins folâtrer'; 'regarder leur espièglerie'; 'voir que ma vieille figure ne les avait pas rebutés'; 'je le vis partir'; 'le plaisir que j'avais à voir et observer les enfants'; all these instances occur on one single page of the Pléiade edition (p. 1087). Indeed, seeing takes precedence over beneficent action. Rousseau finds that to see happiness without beneficence is pleasurable; but to be beneficent without seeing happiness is not pleasurable.

Not only are Rousseau's beneficiaries in the 9e *Promenade* represented as a 'spectacle'; in addition, there is an effacement of Rousseau, the beholder, which is similar to that observed of benefactors in *La Nouvelle Héloïse* and *Emile*. An extreme moment of self-effacement occurs earlier in the 6e *Promenade*, when Rousseau imagines himself as a benefactor made invisible by a magic ring; the 9e *Promenade* presents an attenuated form of the same phenomenon. Rousseau initially proposes that this self-effacement is a sign of his true and selfless affection for children: he simply observes them rather than forcing himself on them as playmate, as Mme Geoffrin is presumed to do, regardless of children's antipathy for old faces. By these means, he represents as a moral gesture his art of turning a relationship of reciprocity (which may be forced and unnatural) into the relationship of a beholder to the object of his gaze. However, Rousseau's self-effacement is also his response to the injustice of society, which forces anonymity upon him. If he is recognised, his good works will come to nothing, because of the machinations of his enemies. Discovery may be perilously near; this is illustrated in the case of the child to whom Rousseau gives a few pence for Nanterre rolls: the child's father is immediately approached by a man who appears to provoke hostility against Rousseau in him. There are thus two sources for the anonymity, or even invisibility, of the benefactor: a contingent one (Rousseau's historical situation) and one which is suggested by the very nature of the 'spectacle' of beneficence, that the audience is not visible to the players, that Mandeville's imprisoned man is hidden from the mother whose child is attacked by a wild beast.

The spectacles of the 9^e *Promenade* are moral spectacles not only because of the morally necessary withdrawal of the benefactor/beholder, but also because of their content, which the beholder has, to some extent, stage-managed. The 'Festivities at the Castle' is a diptych in which the first immoral scene is redeemed by the second, which affords the beholder moral pleasure. These two scenes furnish a stark contrast: the first is an organised spectacle which is violent and undignified, humiliating to the actors and unedifying for the spectators, a scene in which Rousseau finds himself in a festive group of

fantasy of invisibility

aristocrats who throw gingerbread to the scrambling peasants; the second is actually a spectacle of beneficence, in which Rousseau pays for a little girl to distribute her apples amongst some small boys.[19] In the second half of the eighteenth century French art critics appeared to consider it admirable that a painting should create the effect of neutralising the beholder, of resisting his involvement in the situation depicted, by portraying characters who are utterly absorbed in their activity. This was believed to move the beholder and command his attention on a deeper level. Paintings such as Greuze's *Un père de famille qui lit la Bible à ses enfants* (exhibited in 1755) or Chardin's *Un philosophe occupé de sa lecture* (exhibited in 1753) were praised by contemporaries for their representation of intense absorption.[20] Similarly the fiction of Rousseau's absence (the fact that, having paid for the apples, he withdraws to let the girl distribute them) intensifies the beholder–spectacle relationship which has been established. The negation of the beholder as a presence is the condition of his being a perfect beholder. Likewise, in the *6ᵉ Promenade*, which is discussed in Chapter 5, Rousseau conjectures that he could only be a perfect benefactor if he were negated as a physical presence, that is to say, if he possessed a ring which made him invisible. As his *being* fades so he is able *to do* more. Only the invisible spectator can truly see (and hence be moved to do good) because only he is not in any way implicated in the action. The theatre audience are similarly able to see but, of course, their good intentions are sterile as what they see is only fiction. The omnipotent spectator of the world has both the privilege of the clear-sightedness of the theatre audience and the access to virtuous action offered by the real world. A further analogy may be made with the position of the writer, invisible to his reader, and in a position of power to do good if he is both an understanding observer and a detached one. Both observation and generosity have great moral value, and yet there are some spectacles of virtue which should not be offered to the gaze: this is the teaching of the code of pudicity.

All moral social codes should be able to function together in harmony, for example, the benefactor must act in conformity

with the principles of justice. It is not surprising, however, that
in an extremely degenerate and unjust environment, circumstances militate against the smooth functioning of moral codes,
whether independently or in unison. That is why it is necessary
to abstract from the environment, and to examine both the
conceptual elements of the codes and the passions which inspire
behaviour in accordance with, or in transgression of, those
codes. That examination has suggested that the two codes of
beneficence and pudicity, both of which are, according to
Rousseau, vital to social existence, are on a collision course. The
passion which inspires the benefactor (pity) is closely related to
amorous passion, which is directed towards the breaching of
pudicity. The first element of beneficence (penetrating observation) may arouse not only pity, but also amorous passion,
and is opposed to pudicity, which veils from the gaze. The
benefactor, in general, seeks to increase similarity and proximity
between himself and the beneficiary: he offers gifts (moving in
the direction of a more equitable distribution of goods between
the two), he is hospitable (bringing about a physical proximity),
he shares his wisdom and experience. Pudicity, on the other
hand, requires distance, separation, a strict enforcing of barriers
and the maintaining of (sexual) difference.

The easy slippage from pity to erotic desire may be illustrated
in responses to paintings of the period as well as within literary
texts. Where sentimental paintings portray men the reported
response is unequivocal; Greuze's *La Piété filiale* (exhibited in
1763) was reputed to have moved beholders in the Salon to tears
by its depiction of the emotionally charged moment when a
paralysed old man is fed by his son-in-law. However, Greuze's
paintings of tearful young women, such as *Une jeune fille qui a
cassé son miroir* (displayed 1763) or *Une jeune fille qui pleure son
oiseau mort* (displayed 1765), are not regarded with pity alone,
but are reinterpreted erotically. The spectacle of suffering
women arouses imaginary transgression; the power of the
spectator's gaze is no longer that of the invisible benefactor, but
that of the voyeur. Diderot first focusses on the pain and grief of
the young girl with the dead bird, but then comments that his
reaction is to cry '*délicieux! délicieux!*' (*Salons*, II, 145). He

fantasises a conversation with the girl, hints that her grief is the result of the loss of her virginity, and attempts to 'console' her. Thus, little by little he assumes a position of penetration into her sorrow and hence an erotic dominance. Diderot portrays observers of pathetic scenes shifting position in just such a way in his novel *La Religieuse*, with tragic results for the unfortunate heroine. Interestingly some readers respond to this by attempting to discover ways in which the heroine 'invites it' by mingling seductive wiles or at least dramatic exploitation of her plight with her appeals for pity. Thus the readers take up a similar position to Diderot in front of Greuze's pictures, speculating on a loss of innocence on the part of the female victim. *La Religieuse* is itself originally conceived by Diderot and Grimm as bait for a friend, a would-be benefactor. In spite of this Diderot claims that he was moved to tears while writing the story – we could compare him to Pygmalion falling in love with his statue or Rousseau writing *La Nouvelle Héloïse*. It is interesting to speculate whether Diderot could be considered a writer-benefactor in giving his intended reader, Le Marquis de Croismare, the pleasure of being a benefactor – perhaps only in the sense in which Baudelaire would be a benefactor in giving a false coin to a beggar.

The next two chapters consider some of the texts in which Rousseau represents, more or less explicitly, both beneficence and the transgression of pudicity. Rousseau does explore the dangers attendant upon the coincidence of the beholder/benefactor with spectacles (women) which should be shielded from the gaze and from the generous impulse. However, his exploration is itself couched in veiled terms or separated from the main body of his work.

CHAPTER 5

Gyges' ring: a reading of Rousseau's 6ᵉ Promenade

This chapter is an extended analysis of a short piece of writing, the *6ᵉ Promenade* of Rousseau's *Rêveries du promeneur solitaire*, a piece of writing which emerges as crucially important for this study. The *6ᵉ Promenade* may be seen as a history of Rousseau and of man: his natural goodness, his life in society fraught with difficulties and dangers, and his struggle to achieve virtue. It is, moreover, the history of man as benefactor.

Rousseau's identification with the perspective of the beneficiary in his *Confessions* does not preclude a wishful identification with the benefactor; every beneficiary must ultimately aim to be a benefactor in his turn. The *6ᵉ Promenade* contains one of Rousseau's rare discussions of the problem of beneficence from the point of view of the donor; it reveals important implications of Rousseau's portrayal of the perfect benefactor. It begins with an anecdotal example of failed beneficence, a failure which could be blamed on the socio-historical situation of the benefactor (Rousseau) and of his beneficiary. This example, as a real event, should be regulated by, and can be analysed according to, the classical code. But Rousseau proceeds to test his generosity by means of a magical daydream, allowing himself an exaggerated version of the characteristics which he attributes to his models in *La Nouvelle Héloïse* and *Emile*: self-effacement and penetrating vision.[1]

Rousseau's daydream has as its context a myth, the myth of Gyges; as a mythic daydream it is of a different order of human experience from that of the anecdote of everyday social exchange. In removing the socio-historical situation, Rousseau also removes the usual constraints on social codes; this heightens

certain tensions implicit in the relationship between benefactor
and beneficiary, and even allows a breakdown of that relationship, without it being possible to blame the breakdown on
external and contingent factors such as the malice of Rousseau's
persecutors, or the desire of any particular beneficiary to exploit
him. The tensions in the relationship between benefactor and
beneficiary have already been suggested in earlier chapters. The
first is the proximity of pity to amorous passion, the second is
that pity is related to the emotional response to a (theatrical)
spectacle, the third is the hierarchy between donor and
recipient. The factor of a magically literal invisibility, which is
afforded by Gyges' ring, increases these three tensions, and so
their consequences may be writ large. Rousseau does not,
however, do this; the daydream ends enigmatically with a gap
in the text, a point at which Rousseau's normally clear and
precise language becomes opaque. It is for the reader to fill this
gap by reference to other works by Rousseau, and, more
importantly, to the myth of Gyges' ring, which is the pretext
and context of Rousseau's daydream.

FAILED BENEFICENCE

The *6ᵉ Promenade* begins with the analysis of a 'mechanical'
response which Rousseau has observed in himself. The first
sentence of the *Promenade* is an aphoristic statement of confidence
in the potential extent of self-knowledge; it states that actions
which may seem indifferent and disinterested are often in fact
motivated, and that this motivation may ultimately be accessible to introspection. 'Nous n'avons guère de mouvement
machinal dont nous ne puissions trouver la cause dans notre
cœur, si nous savions bien l'y chercher' (*Rêveries*, p. 1050). This
maxim is illustrated by an anecdote, which is offered as a source
for the insight contained in the maxim; this is a mingling of
autobiography and philosophical thinking which is characteristic of the *Rêveries*.[2] The self-duplication of autobiography
(the 'I-who-writes' and the 'I-who-acted') is magnified by the
philosophical commentary which increases the distance to that
between the 'I-as-spectator' and the 'I-as-object-of-study'.

The action which Rousseau analyses in the *6ᵉ Promenade* is a detour which he has frequently made on one of his favourite walks. He explores various possible psychological or social reasons for the pattern which he has uncovered. He realises that he deviated from his route in order to avoid a crippled boy, to whom he had become accustomed to give alms every time he walked past the mother's stall. The boy showed his gratitude in innocent chatter, and so 'the triple rhythm of generosity, which consists of giving, accepting and returning'³ was accomplished. However, the routine became an unavowed burden, and therefore, without any element of conscious decision, Rousseau changed the route of his walk so that he did not have to pass the crippled boy. Rousseau uses the classical code of beneficence to set a standard against which he can measure his actions. He states accordingly 'le bienfaiteur s'engage...à conserver à l'autre, tant qu'il ne s'en rendra pas indigne, la même bonne volonté qu'il vient de lui témoigner, et à lui en renouveler les actes toutes les fois qu'il le pourra et qu'il en sera requis' (*Rêveries*, p. 1054). Rousseau's hidden motive for his literal deviation is to avoid a charitable gesture which he had been in the habit of performing; the detour in the walk is therefore also a moral departure from a habitual course of action and from the code of beneficence.

Rousseau writes that the experience of beneficence 'se trouva *je ne sais comment* transformé' (my emphasis). There has been a mysterious degeneration in social relations; what was pleasurable, characterised by mutual freedom and satisfaction, has become an embarrassing, and finally unbearable, burden for Rousseau, who feels enslaved. Why, he asks, does this change take place? Was it unavoidable? Was it the fault of others, of outside agents? Is it Rousseau's own nature which is at fault, and if so, is it criminally so? Or is it inherent in society or in the social code of beneficence itself? Rousseau sets out to explore these questions in the rest of the *Promenade*, but his acknowledgement of incomprehensible elements at the outset, 'je ne sais comment', suggests that there may be a point of insertion of a reading which goes beyond what Rousseau discovers by introspection.

Rousseau's mental path in the *Promenade* moves to the first
detectable influence on his actions (the sinister 'they'), the
outside agents who haunt the *Rêveries* from the very first
paragraph. 'Ils ont cherché dans les raffinements de leur haine
quel tourment pouvait être le plus cruel à mon âme sensible, et
ils ont brisé violemment tous les liens qui m'attachaient à eux'
(*Rêveries*, p. 995). 'They' are woven into the crippled boy
narrative as the devious instructors ('ceux qui l'avaient in-
struit', *Rêveries*, p. 1051). As he commences his analysis,
Rousseau laments that his enemies have immobilised him in
their web of intrigue as a spider does the hapless fly. They have
prevented him from being a benefactor: 'Il y a longtemps que ce
bonheur a été mis hors de ma portée, et ce n'est pas dans un
aussi misérable sort que le mien qu'on peut espérer de placer
avec choix et avec fruit une seule action réellement bonne. Le
plus grand soin de ceux qui règlent ma destinée...' (*Rêveries*, p.
1051). It is because social relations have deviated from the paths
of justice and honesty, under the influence of the anonymous
'them', that Rousseau himself is forced to turn away from the
sweet pleasures of social intercourse and become the 'solitary
walker'.

However, Rousseau's enemies are not the only factor governing this degeneration of beneficence. Rousseau looks back to
earlier, happier days when he was relatively unhindered by
exterior powers, and recalls 'cependant j'ai senti souvent le
poids de mes propres bienfaits par la chaîne des devoirs qu'ils
entraînaient à leur suite' (*Rêveries*, p. 1050). This is the problem
of the beneficiary's *grapple hook*, his expectation that a benefit
will always be the first of an indefinite series of benefits. This
problem is to some extent inherent in the code of beneficence
itself, as the benefactor does have the duty to continue to
provide for his beneficiary, although the latter should never
demand this as a right. The danger for the benefactor of being
chained by his obligations is not great until it is magnified by an
unjust society. Rousseau is confronted with a ridiculous and
disproportionate burden of apparent obligation when he
emerges in the public eye as a celebrated author: 'je devins le
bureau général d'adresse de tous les souffreteux ou soi-disants

tels' (*Rêveries*, p. 1052). At that point in his life he realised that the most laudable natural sentiments and practices can lead to great harm in a corrupt society, in which there is an inevitable deterioration in good social relations (in particular beneficence) because each individual is governed by an *amour-propre*, which is not in conformity with *amour de soi* and pity. The competitive impulse of self-interest is alien to the spirit of beneficence, and can only pervert its functioning, as it does in Rousseau's anecdote.

In addition to this, when Rousseau looks into his own heart he has to confess that his natural independence makes him disinclined to be bound by social duties.[4] 'Natural independence' is not simply an empirically verifiable condition, specific to Rousseau, but part of his theorisation of his self-portrait, as well as of his portrait of man. His choice of example to illustrate his natural independence will seem peculiarly significant in the light of the rest of the *Promenade*: 'j'eusse été chez les Turcs un mauvais mari à l'heure où le cri public les appelle à remplir les devoirs de l'état' (*Rêveries*, p. 1052). Rousseau finds the moral contract of beneficence, like enforced conjugal duty, too great a constraint on him. His hatred of being obliged to do something is indeed extreme; involved with it is his liking to be entirely independent of others, so that for instance, he would always carry a map: 'Je n'aime pas même à demander la rue où j'ai à faire, parce que je dépends en cela de celui qui va me répondre...' (*Mon portrait*, p. 1127). He writes that he can virtuously follow duty only in a negative way. This negative (inactive) tendency (both his sins and his virtues are usually of omission rather than commission, he tells us) governs much of the *Promenade*. The opening aphorism is expressed negatively; the anecdote is important because of a not-doing (not giving alms) and an evasive action (the detour) undertaken only to avoid another action (the encounter with the boy and its necessary consequences). The two positive passages are the remembered early exchanges with the boy and the dream of invisible beneficence wearing Gyges' ring; both memories suggest Rousseau's natural goodness rather than achieved virtue.

' have I been corrupted?'

Rousseau next wonders whether the severe degeneration in social relations which he has experienced – he names former friends who have profited from betraying him[5] – has changed him for the worse. He may have become too embittered, too suspicious, so that he abstains from action unnecessarily because 'je ne puis plus regarder une bonne œuvre qu'on me présente à faire que comme un piège qu'on me tend et sous lequel est caché quelque mal' (*Rêveries*, p. 1055). Rousseau wishes to discover whether a man such as he, who appears to shy away from beneficence in society, can, nevertheless, be shown to be a good man, essentially uncorrupted by his environment. The daydream to which Rousseau frequently has recourse, to reassure himself that he still loves justice and pities his fellow men with as much passion as ever before, is that of owning Gyges' ring.

THE GYGES' RING DAYDREAM, AND THE ORIGIN IN PLATO'S *REPUBLIC*

The apparently insignificant deviation in Rousseau's walk turns out to be the most important thing about it: it is the detour which engenders the written *Promenade*. It also engenders, within the *Promenade*, the daydream which serves the purpose of reassuring Rousseau that he would act as a benefactor if he had the opportunity. Gyges' ring makes him invisible and able to wander where he pleases: the ring of invisibility means that he need not mechanically deviate from his route. Marcel Raymond has suggested that the term *rêver* in Rousseau's *Rêveries*, must derive etymologically from a Vulgar Latin form *reexvagare* which would mean *to stray outside*.[6] He sees Rousseau's use of the term as a kind of unconscious return to the semantic source, since Rousseau's daydreams are always walks. Certainly the mental wanderings of Rousseau's daydreams do match his physical wanderings in nature. In this instance the deviation in the walk is reflected in a deviation from the course of his daydream of invisible beneficence as the possessor of Gyges' ring. The detour in the walk is analysed by Rousseau himself in the written *Promenade*. However, he does not analyse the detour

walk/
daydream

in the daydream which brings it to an abrupt end; in fact his usually clear and precise language breaks down, and the reader is left with a textual gap or enigma. The initial assertion at the beginning of the *Promenade* which is offered like a gift to the reader, a valuable jewel of wisdom, suggests that this apparently indifferent, even amusing, digression within the daydream cannot be unmotivated. This functions like a generous invitation to the reader to articulate what is unsaid, to fill the gap and to unfold the enigma.

Rousseau does not tell his reader anything about 'l'anneau de Gygès'; he assumes that it would be familiar to his contemporaries through their reading of Plato and Cicero. It is a device which makes the wearer invisible when he chooses; however, for anyone who has the privilege of reading the wearer's actions, that cloak of invisibility strips the subject of his social mask. In this way the ring retains its usual connotation of an invitation to penetration, while Gyges' ring also has the peculiar connotation of an instrument of penetration, the piercing of appearances, veils or walls.

The first well-known reference to the myth of Gyges' ring occurs in Plato's *Republic*, Book II. Rousseau's relationship with Plato, and particularly with the *Republic*, is a particularly interesting and not always comfortable one. It is worth pausing to consider some of the intricacies of Rousseau's attitude to that precursor in the light of this reference to Gyges' ring.[7]

In the *Republic*, Glaucon (Plato's brother)[8] tells the tale of Gyges to illustrate what he claims is man's natural tendency to be unjust when shielded from the consequences of discovery. The version of the myth of Gyges' ring which Glaucon tells is well suited to the pessimistic view of human morality which he propounds. The shepherd Gyges goes down into a crack in the earth caused by an earthquake and sees many marvels, including a hollow bronze horse in which lies a dead giant wearing the ring. The supernatural forces at play in this story are at best amoral, if not immoral. No retribution is exacted from Gyges for the criminal use which he makes of the ring; on the contrary he prospers greatly. Once the fortunate Gyges has realised that when he turns the ring so that the bezel faces inwards he is invisible, he contrives to be sent to court where he seduces the queen and, with her help, murders the king and seizes the throne of Lydia. His wealth becomes proverbial; indeed, he is associated in Greek thinking with the invention of coinage.[9] The exotic detail of the story of Gyges corresponds to the familiar tradition of Greek gods and heroes, who do not conform to the dictates of either Platonic or Stoic or, later, Christian morality. That is why Plato rejects Homer and the poets as guides to moral conduct, and will ban them from his republic – a project with which Rousseau sympathises. Glaucon claims that, in Gyges' place, no one, whether seemingly just or unjust, would have the strength of mind:

to stand fast in doing right or keep his hands off other men's goods, when he could go to the market-place and fearlessly help himself to anything he wanted, enter houses and sleep with any woman he chose, set prisoners free and kill men at his pleasure, and in a word go about among men with the powers of a god.[10]

Socrates responds to Glaucon's challenge with an alternative image of man and of society (the *Republic*) arguing that justice leads to happiness and true freedom, whereas injustice means the enslavement of reason, the most human faculty, to the base appetites and the worst passions. Plato and Rousseau are agreed that most human societies disguise the beauty of the Platonic soul or Rousseauian human nature, just as layers of weeds disfigured the sea-god Glaucus.[11] There are, however, certain important differences in the conclusions about relatively just societies reached by Rousseau and by Plato. One which has received less attention than it merits is the question of communal possession of spouses and children which is advocated for the Guardians in the *Republic*, and is denounced by Rousseau on two occasions in the most vehement tones. Yet the projected life at Clarens bears a certain resemblance to Socrates' scheme.

As the *Republic* is evoked in the *6^e Promenade*, it is tempting to turn to some 'rêveries d'un promeneur solitaire' in the *Republic*. Socrates' fancy, which he indulges 'like one who entertains himself with idle daydreams on a solitary walk' (p. 153), is the notion that the family may be replaced by a social structure in which spouses and children are held in common. He first suggests that women should be given equal opportunity with men; those women whose merits mark them as ranking as Guardians should receive the same education as the male Guardians, and eventually perform the same tasks. To that end, and also to prevent the formation of private families (and private loyalties), children should be reared in communal nurseries. 'Marriages' would be skilfully organised on eugenic principles. Amorous passion and pudicity would be replaced by a rational vision of the human body and a rationalisation of sexual conduct.

Rousseau finds this 'idle dream' totally aberrant:

Platon dans sa République donne aux femmes les mêmes exercices qu'aux hommes; je le crois bien! Ayant ôté de son gouvernement les familles particulières et ne sachant plus que faire des femmes, il se vit forcé de les faire hommes. Ce beau génie avait tout combiné, tout prévu: il allait au-devant d'une objection que personne peut-être n'eût songé à lui faire, mais il a mal résolu celle qu'on lui fait... je parle de cette promiscuité civile qui confond partout les deux sexes dans les mêmes emplois, dans les mêmes travaux, et ne peut manquer d'engendrer les plus intolérables abus; je parle de cette subversion des plus doux sentiments de la nature, immolés à un sentiment artificiel qui ne peut subsister que par eux; comme s'il ne fallait pas une prise naturelle pour former des liens de convention. (*Emile*, v, pp. 699–700)

Rousseau objects to the blurring of differences between men and women, in this case to the masculinisation of women, and to the destruction of the family and hence of familial affection, which is replaced by love of the state; this is a substitution, he says, of an artificial derivative for the natural source, which is impossible.[12] In the *Confessions*, Rousseau relates the unfortunate influence of Socrates' suggestion to his own abandoning of his children which he comes to regret: 'je crus faire un acte de citoyen et de père, et je me regardai comme un membre de la République de Platon' (*Confessions*, p. 357). Yet the dissolution of blood ties in favour of those of duty and affection is a feature of Rousseau's Clarens; in *La Nouvelle Héloïse* the nuclear family gives way to a community of like-minded individuals who love each other for their virtue. After Julie's death, Claire, Wolmar, Saint-Preux and Edouard are four adults who are not bound by

NB blood ties → duty, affn

any ties of blood; the closest legal bond is that Claire is Wolmar's cousin by marriage. Julie and Claire, the inseparables, appear to be interchangeable as mothers (and, it is hinted, as wives in that Julie offers Claire in her place to Saint-Preux).[13] The one opposition which remains clearly marked is that between men and women.

While Saint-Preux, 'le philosophe', is an advocate of Plato in general, and of the *Republic* in particular, Julie disagrees with him over the issue of sexual difference. She recollects: 'Te souvient-il qu'en lisant ta République de Platon nous avons autrefois disputé sur ce point de la différence morale des sexes? Je persiste dans l'avis dont j'étais alors, et ne saurais imaginer un modèle commun de perfection pour deux êtres si différents' (*La Nouvelle Héloïse*, p. 128). Julie, as befits a model of pudicity, bestows on this specifically feminine virtue the advantage of a grounding in nature, although it is not a defining characteristic of women according to Rousseau's state of nature. Pudicity, as described in the last chapter, is necessary as a shield against amorous passion. One effect of Plato's just city and of his rationalisation of male–female and parent–child relations among the Guardians is a taming of the passions, which makes virtue more easily achievable, relieving the need for a code of pudicity. Socrates opens conversation in the *Republic* by asking Cephalus about old age; Cephalus says that it is a blessing to be free of love, which is like bondage to a raving madman. This freedom seems to bless the just city.

The question of how to achieve virtue is traditionally dominated by two opposite attitudes – some sort of compromise must usually be reached. One attitude is to desire to devise an environment (and sometimes a nature, by eugenics) which is as conducive to virtue as possible. The other defines virtue as struggle against temptation. Rousseau explores (or would have explored) the first in his *morale sensitive*. The principle which conflicts to some extent with this is the belief that: 'Ce mot de vertu signifie *force*. Il n'y a point de vertu sans combat, il n'y en a point sans victoire. La vertu ne consiste pas seulement à être juste, mais à l'être en triomphant de ses passions, en régnant sur son propre cœur' (*Lettre à M. de Franquières*, p. 1143). This belief suggests that there would be no *virtue* in doing good if the environment made that the easiest option. Glaucon rejects Socrates' first 'healthy city', calling it the 'city of pigs'. In the 'city of pigs' man can be innocent and good, live off a simple vegetarian diet, experience perfect harmony between his natural gifts and natural preferences, between what is good for the individual and what is best for the state. Neither amorous passion nor death are mentioned in connection with this prelapsarian state. Glaucon emancipates desire for things beyond the necessary, which means the decay of the healthy city, but allows the emergence of the 'purified city'. In the purified city (in which the Guardians live communally) the struggle against the appetites seems already to have been fought and won. As Glaucon is dissatisfied with the city where virtue is unnecessary, so Rousseau is unhappy with the city where virtue is already achieved, which he finds implausible. His first example of virtuous struggle in the passage from the *Lettre à M. de Franquières* cited above is the following: 'Titus rendant heureux le peuple romain, versant partout les grâces et les bienfaits, pouvait ne pas perdre un seul jour et n'être pas vertueux: il le fut certainement en renvoyant Bérénice.' It is inconceivable to Rousseau that there should be no struggle against the temptation of women.

Rousseau is by no means the first to take up the idea of Gyges' ring as a test from Plato's *Republic*. Whereas Glaucon initially presents the ring as a test which all men will fail, the lawyer Cicero retells the myth and offers it as a trial for his readers in *de Officiis*. He is faithful to Glaucon's detail (earthquake, bronze horse, seduction of the queen and so on), abridging it very slightly. Cicero, adding Socrates' reassuring comments of Book x to Glaucon's story, suggests that Gyges' ring would be temptation only for the criminal. He holds that only some men are hypocrites who need to be stripped of their social masks. He states: 'The significance of the ring story is this: if you could do anything to satisfy your desire for riches, supreme rule, or sex, without anyone's knowledge or even suspicion, and if you were assured that neither gods nor men would ever know about it, would you do it?' (*de Officiis*, III, 9). Cicero asks the subjects of his moral test whether they would have to confess criminal intentions or whether they would 'agree that every wrong action is to be avoided simply because it is wrong'. He claims that 'if we have made any progress in philosophy at all, we ought to be convinced that even if all heaven and earth were ignorant of our actions, we should still do nothing which exemplified greed, injustice, lust or lack of self-control'. Rousseau adapts Cicero's test, using it to reveal the truth concerning the man who appears unjust (or, at least, ungenerous) rather than on the sanctimonious hypocrite. Rousseau claims that it is a rigorous test, and that the conclusions are not self-evident, since 'c'est bien là que la tentation d'abuser doit être près du pouvoir' (*Rêveries*, p. 1058). The test is applied to Rousseau himself, but by implication, it is a test of human nature to see how man might react when endowed with power and freedom such as this. Rousseau does not use the test as Cicero does, to see 'if we have made any progress in philosophy at all', but rather, to see how the natural man, the non-philosopher, the non-rhetorician will react. Indeed Rousseau does not claim to be an especially wise or virtuous man because he would behave justly and generously under these circumstances, which for him (as his daydream enables him to discover) make beneficence easier than in the unjust real world in which he lives. He says 'si j'eusse été invisible et tout-puissant comme Dieu, j'aurais été bien-faisant et bon comme lui' (*Rêveries*, p. 1057).

INVISIBLE OMNIPOTENCE

The setting is not supernatural in the exotic, amoral fashion of Glaucon's tale. Rousseau compares himself wearing the magic ring to the invisible beneficent God, like the Judaeo-Christian God;[14] or like the gods invoked by Socrates in the *Republic* (v, 452), 'simple Gods' who cannot lie, beings very different from the wise philosophers who rule the city and who know that the cause of *justice* may sometimes be served by convenient fictions ('noble lies'). The Socratic gods are not associated with justice as human virtue, they are simply and purely good. Rousseau proposes that strength and freedom make good men and good gods, whereas weakness (interdependence) makes men liable to do wrong and thereby gives them access to virtue. In *Emile* (p. 288), he states: 'Toute méchanceté vient de faiblesse; l'enfant n'est méchant que parce qu'il est faible; rendez-le fort, il sera bon: celui qui pourrait tout ne ferait jamais de mal. De tous les attributs de la divinité tout-puissante la bonté est celui sans lequel on la peut moins concevoir.'[15] This posits a kind of underlying identity of all action, whether *doing* good or *doing* bad – in circumstances which absolutely dictate the latter, the man who *is* good, can only *not do* – negative virtue.

It is man's weakness which is the origin of, and explanation for, human society. In *Emile*, IV (p. 503), Rousseau asserts: 'C'est la faiblesse de l'homme qui le rend sociable: ce sont nos misères communes qui portent nos cœurs à l'humanité, nous ne lui devrions rien si nous n'étions pas hommes. Tout attachement est un signe d'insuffisance: si chacun de nous n'avait nul besoin des autres il ne songerait guère à s'unir à eux.' Emile can only begin to understand this when he experiences it for himself at puberty, which is, according to Rousseau, man's second birth, his birth to his humanity. Suffering and weakness are an essential part of our humanity: they are what enable us to feel human pity, the emotional source of beneficent passion and action. If a man attempts to bypass this part of life through wealth or pleasure he becomes inhuman, and achieves at most a false, apparent happiness, in contrast to the beneficent man who has access to a deep contentment, knowing the truth of his own nature and of the human condition. In the sweet passions of pity and beneficence, in attachments, lies the 'frêle bonheur' accessible to social man – it is true 'bonheur' yet it is 'frêle' – that is the social condition. The only other true happiness is, according to Rousseau's theory, not accessible to us: 'Un être vraiment heureux est un être solitaire: Dieu seul jouit d'un bonheur absolu; mais qui de nous en a l'idée?' (*Emile*, p. 503). Complete independence (in the sense of freedom from attachments) is inconceivable for Rousseau; he writes in *Emile* (p. 503): 'Je ne conçois pas que celui qui n'a besoin de rien puisse aimer quelque chose: je ne conçois pas que celui qui n'aime rien puisse être heureux.' The Gyges' ring daydream is an attempt to imagine this impossible situation of freedom, independence, power and happiness in distributing benefits impartially, in dispensing invisible justice. Rousseau is testing (a) man who is outside the boundaries of humanity, man who is not weak, not part of society, man who does not need 'suppléments'. As well as a rejection of Glaucon's view of human and divine nature, this is clearly a subversion of Cicero's test: Cicero who is, to borrow Rousseau's phrase, 'l'homme de l'homme', social man and manipulator of language *par excellence*. Rousseau's imagined identification with God, or with a divine agent who is superior to the popular images of God ('Ministre de la providence et dispensateur de ses lois selon mon pouvoir j'aurais fait des miracles plus sages et plus utiles que ceux de la légende dorée et du tombeau de St. Médard', *Rêveries*, p. 1058), places him in a position of superiority even with respect to Plato, who he says himself overshadows Cicero as a moral authority. 'Les préceptes de Platon sont souvent très sublimes, mais combien n'erre-t-il pas quelquefois, et jusqu'où ne vont pas ses erreurs? Quant à Cicéron, peut-on croire que sans Platon ce rhéteur eût trouvé ses Offices? L'Evangile seul es, quant à la morale, toujours sûr, toujours vrai, toujours unique, et toujours semblable à lui-même' (*Lettres écrites de la montagne*, p. 728).

Yet the daydream of a fusion of strength and freedom enabling perfect happiness and triumph is burst like a bubble with a comic pin-prick.

Il n'y a qu'un seul point sur lequel la faculté de pénétrer partout invisible m'eût pu faire chercher des tentations auxquelles j'aurais mal résisté, et une fois entré dans ces voies d'égarement où n'eussé-je point été conduit par elles? Ce serait bien mal connaître la nature et moi-même que de me flatter que ces facilités ne m'auraient point séduit, ou que la raison m'aurait arrêté dans cette fatale pente. Sûr de moi sur tout autre article, j'étais perdu par celui-là seul. (*Rêveries*, p. 1058)

Rousseau tells his reader, who is the one privileged witness to Rousseau's love for mankind, that he knows that there would be one temptation which he could not withstand were he in possession of the ring; therefore, rather than be a malefactor, he would discard the ring at the very beginning. Thus it emerges

temp^ ? warren invisibille

Justice and difference in Rousseau

that the test of Gyges' ring is indeed a rigorous and revelatory one, even though at the outset Rousseau's theory of man's natural goodness would seem to suggest that success is inevitable. What is this temptation which can so powerfully negate all the good which has preceded it? Rousseau does not put it into words.

The Pléiade commentators, and other Rousseau scholars, have (rightly) assumed that the unspeakable (or, at least, unwritable) temptation is woman.[16] It is woman who destroys the god-like status of man. If we turn to the passage in the *Lettre à M. de Franquières* immediately preceding the reference to Glaucon, ('l'ami de Socrate dont j'ai oublié le nom'),[17] there is an imaginary acting-out, which may be what is 'forgotten' (or, at any rate, omitted) in the text of the *6ᵉ Promenade*:

Supposons votre cœur honnête en proie aux passions les plus terribles, dont vous n'êtes pas à l'abri, puisque enfin vous êtes homme... Supposons seulement qu'un cœur trop sensible brûle d'un amour involontaire pour la fille ou la femme de son ami, qu'il soit maître de jouir d'elle entre le ciel qui n'en voit rien, et lui qui n'en veut rien dire à personne; que sa figure charmante l'attire ornée de tous les attraits de la beauté et de la volupté; au moment où ses sens enivrés sont prêts à se livrer à leurs délices cette image abstraite de la vertu viendra-t-elle disputer son cœur à l'objet réel qui le frappe? (*Œuvres complètes*, IV, p. 1143)

It would be understandable for Rousseau simply to have drawn the daydream to a close as its function of reassurance is fulfilled, for it is clearly removed from the realities of social existence. Yet a certain logic or economy seems to require that *amorous passion* negates the dream of freedom and power exercised without injustice, as puberty brings to an end the (relative) strength and freedom of the child – a movement also echoed in Rousseau's theoretical account of the history of humanity: the *Discours sur l'inégalité*. While Socrates' dream is of a just city which successfully banishes the disruptive force of love, Rousseau's dream is set off course by that force.

The strange juxtaposition of beneficence, as perfect distributive justice, with amorous passion (achieved through the device of a 'penetrating' invisibility) leaves the reader with the sense of a gap or an enigma, precisely at the point where the reader is apparently privileged since she can *see* Rousseau (penetrate his motives) whereas the rest of humanity, Rousseau's imaginary beneficiaries, cannot. Spurred on by the sense that there is something to uncover, the reader desires to bridge the gap in the text. Just as the apparently idle detour in Rousseau's walk proved crucial, and the 'point de départ' for Rousseau's analysis of the relationship between benefactor and beneficiary, so will the 'égarement' in the daydream be the starting point for an unexpected development in the thinking about that relationship.

THE TRANSGRESSION OF PUDICITY

The magical invisibility of the benefactor, while freeing him from the possibility of being exploited or otherwise persecuted, could lead to an infringement of the privacy of the beneficiary. The device of invisibility is commonly associated with the invasion of privacy: the ability to go into places and to see and hear things which would otherwise be impossible.[18] There is little doubt that to be invisible at will is to have an advantage over those who enjoy merely human means of withdrawal or concealment. While Rousseau might seem to evade these connotations by his references to God, his selection of Gyges' ring rather than any other superhuman means of becoming invisible generates a number of transgressive associations in the minds of readers with a knowledge of the classics, as contemporary readers, for example, would have had.

The best known tale of Gyges, apart from that in the *Republic*, is in Herodotus' *Histories* ('Clio'). Rousseau recommends reading Herodotus in *Emile*, not because of the accuracy of his historical facts but because 'les anciens historiens sont remplis de vues dont on pourrait faire usage, quand même les faits qui les présentent seraient faux'. He asserts that 'les hommes sensés doivent regarder l'histoire comme un tissu de fables dont la morale est très appropriée au cœur humain' (*Emile*, p. 415).[19] The story about Gyges, which Herodotus recounts, should indeed be considered, as Rousseau suggests, for what it reveals about ideas and associations rather than as (possibly incorrect) historical fact.[20] It appears to be the second half of a myth of which Glaucon provides the first half in detail.[21] Herodotus elaborates Gyges' adventures at court; he omits the magical element of the ring, while still associating Gyges with willed invisibility and thus transgression of privacy, specifically of a woman's pudicity. The story is as follows: King Candaules is passionately in love with his wife, and believing her to be the most beautiful of all women, praises her beauty extravagantly. However, he suspects that merely hearing about her beauty will not convince anyone, and so, despite Gyges' (his favourite's) protestations, arranges that the latter should secretly look upon her naked.[22] When Candaules first proposes to Gyges that he should hide in the royal bed-chamber, Gyges replies: 'Oubliez-vous qu'une femme dépose sa pudeur avec ses vêtements? Les maximes de l'honnêteté sont connues depuis longtemps; elles doivent nous servir de règles: or, une des plus importantes est que chacun ne doit regarder que ce qui lui appartient.'[23] Candaules tells Gyges not to fear lest this should be a test, and that his wife will not harm him. However, the queen notices Gyges as he hides by the door, and, although she says nothing at the time, she summons him the next day. She offers Gyges the choice between killing the king, his friend, and dying himself. Despite misgivings Gyges does agree to murder Candaules; he again hides in the royal bed-chamber: he kills the sleeping king, and then succeeds him as king and as husband. He is confirmed as king by the Delphic oracle, in return for which he sends rich thank-offerings.[24]

In Herodotus' account, possessiveness is linked with pudicity. Gyges says that a man should look upon his own; he implies that the queen belongs to the king and that he should not share her, not even the sight of her. This is bound up with pudicity: Herodotus explains the queen's reaction by stating that like all 'barbarians' she felt that it was a great shame on her that she had been seen naked. The assumption is that only the man occupying the legal position of husband would have this privilege, and therefore Gyges must either die or become her husband. In Herodotus' story it is Candaules' momentary abandoning of possessiveness (in order to enhance the value of his property) and consequent transgression of the royal privacy and of his wife's pudicity which leads to violent death. It can also be assumed that the violent death arises in part because of Gyges' passion for the queen since he has seen her naked.[25] The threat that he will die if he does not act is, again in part, a taunt to his masculinity. Socrates' just city, which may usefully be juxtaposed with this, presents an alternative outcome. There the rational breaking down of possessiveness (all possessions held in common) and of pudicity (for example, the suggestion that women should exercise naked with men) is a stable and peaceful *modus vivendi*. Socrates characterises this as civilised: he contrasts Greek attitudes to male nudity with 'barbarian' pudicity, and advocates that women, too, should be unashamed of their nakedness.

HIERARCHY

A number of issues are raised in the *6ᵉ Promenade* which need to be explored further in Rousseau's writing. These issues are raised because Rousseau begins, unusually, with a story of an exploited benefactor, and proceeds to attempt to resolve the problem of the beneficiary's exploitation of the benefactor on the level of a daydream. This daydream is of a kind which has become of crucial importance in the study of Rousseau since Starobinski's seminal work, *La Transparence et l'obstacle*; it is a dream of perfect transparency: 'A la limite, la transparence est l'invisibilité parfaite.' While the example of Julie suggests that 'il faut mourir pour *être* définitivement du côté de la transparence', in the case of Gyges' ring: 'Devenir invisible: c'est le point où l'extrême nullité de l'être se convertirait en un pouvoir sans limite.' Starobinski suggests that Rousseau's departure from inaction armed with Gyges' ring will take the dual form also mentioned in the modern versions of the story of Gyges which are discussed in the appendix: 'il ferait le bien, il posséderait des femmes' (*La Transparence et l'obstacle*, p. 302).

The codes of beneficence and pudicity are both concerned with moral and emotional issues: Rousseau suggests that it is morally right to be a benefactor and also morally right for a woman to be pudic; the moral goodness of beneficence is associated with its natural emotional source (pity), whereas pudicity is intended both to arouse and to harness a social emotion (amorous passion) for the sake of virtue. Both codes are also concerned with property: beneficence is concerned with the circulation of goods (giving); pudicity is concerned with the retention of goods, that is to say, with making sure that your property remains yours alone (keeping). If generosity with goods should be extended to living goods, wives, then it contravenes pudicity.

The nature of this transparency as invisibility is intensely hierarchical. The possessor of Gyges' ring is a potent subject or self who is not only a just benefactor but also a literally invisible spectator: the recipients of his generosity are a spectacle, the highly visible objects of his gaze, which they cannot return. The tyrannical, transgressive and finally violent implications of this gaze are only apparent (and indeed meaningful)[26] when the object of the gaze is feminine.[27] For Rousseau, beneficence is the best possible relationship between non-equals, but women who are on view, like slaves, cannot be beneficiaries. Rousseau, in the *6ᵉ Promenade*, suggests (without naming 'women') that amorous passion puts an end to his god-like status and to his daydream of generosity outside social codes and contracts, because such a daydream will inevitably involve a transgression of pudicity. In later versions of the myth André Gide and Friedrich Hebbel, following a hint from Herodotus, will suggest that the impulse of generosity, of sharing possessions, will transgress pudicity because of that culmination of generosity which is sharing wives.[28] Rousseau only imagines being able to offer women to himself; the Candaules of Gide and Hebbel will choose to offer his woman to his friend.

The tyranny exercised over women by the invisible man is, according to Rousseau's account of the power struggle between the sexes, liable to be reversed. The shield of pudicity which woman holds before her is primarily supposed to protect men and to maintain the status quo in society. The Gygean figure is delivered up to woman's passive violence: 'sa violence à elle est dans ses charmes' (*Emile*, p. 694). Rousseau hints at terrible consequences; in the Herodotean tradition the king, the last of his dynasty, is overthrown (indeed brutally murdered), and a new order begins.

If Gygean invisibility is a form of tyranny, then the invisible Rousseau is an unjust source of justice like Deioces (the parallel figure to Gyges in Herodotus' *Histories*), the just man who becomes a tyrant hidden from his people by ring-walls.[29] Rousseau's own insight into his power is implicit in the sentence: 'Si j'eusse été possesseur de l'anneau de Gygès, il m'eût tiré de la dépendance des hommes et les eût mis dans la mienne' (*Rêveries*, p. 1057).[30] Rousseau does not conclude the *Promenade* on such an uncharacteristic note of actual mastery as distinct from moral superiority. Instead he turns to project the bad associations of Gygean invisibility onto the outside.[31] He says of his fellow men: 'C'est à eux de se cacher devant moi, de me dérober leurs manœuvres, de fuir la lumière du jour, de s'enfoncer en terre comme des taupes' (*Rêveries*, p. 1059). Yet while they take on the qualities of self-effacement, their tyranny is unsuccessful and they have no insight to accompany their blind penetration: 'Pour moi, qu'ils me voient s'ils peuvent, tant mieux, mais cela leur est impossible; ils ne verront jamais que le J.-J. qu'ils se sont fait et qu'ils ont fait selon leur cœur, pour haïr à leur aise.'

One recurring pattern which may be traced in this *Promenade* is that of man's or a man's development. The first stage is man as god, man untouched by amorous passion or death, innocent and good man. This is like Emile's brief summer, when the boy is awakened to pity and love for his fellows but is as yet untouched by amorous passion, a crucial but inevitably curtailed stage; the second moment is the eruption of sexuality, man's humanity, his weakness, his mortality. Herodotus, Hebbel and Gide do not go beyond this point – for them, Gyges succumbs. Despite the devastating nature of this negation of the daydream, it is far from being an entirely unwelcome development for Rousseau. Man is no longer good and 'celui que sa puissance met au-dessus de l'homme doit être au-dessus des faiblesses de l'humanité, sans quoi cet excès de force ne servira qu'à le mettre en effet au-dessous des autres et de ce qu'il eût été lui-même s'il fut resté leur égal' (*Rêveries*, p. 1058). But this discovery gives access to the third stage, virtue and realistic moral philosophy, which takes into account man's weakness, and aims at a synthesis of the best possible environment inhabited by ordinary men. In *Du contrat social*, Rousseau imagines 'les hommes tels qu'ils sont et les lois telles qu'elles peuvent être' (p. 351).[32]

Rousseau's imagined just state is, therefore, quite different from Plato's. He insists on segregation of men and women for much of the time; his model of the family is important because it reflects his model of the state, and he believes that familial affection will translate into affection for the state-mother. The two are mutually supportive. The notion of the contract is essential for relations between the sexes (marriage), a political system (the social contract) and for beneficence: Rousseau states in the *6e Promenade*:

Je sais qu'il y a une espèce de contrat et même le plus saint de tous entre le bienfaiteur et l'obligé. C'est une sorte de société qu'ils forment l'un avec l'autre, plus étroite que celle qui unit les hommes en général, et si l'obligé s'engage tacitement à la reconnaissance, le bienfaiteur s'engage de même à conserver à l'autre, tant qu'il ne s'en rendra pas indigne, la même bonne volonté qu'il vient de lui témoigner, et à lui en renouveler les actes toutes les fois qu'il le pourra et qu'il en sera requis. Ce ne sont pas là les conditions expresses mais ce sont des effets naturels de la relation qui vient de s'établir entre eux.

Gyges' ring, in enabling a man to be an anonymous benefactor, circumvents this structure, this relationship and its natural consequences. It is a dream solution to the problem of beneficence in a society in which men find it hard to be spontaneously grateful, and equally hard to be disinterestedly beneficent. This difficulty arises from their weakness, their enslavement, their concern for appearances rather than reality, their determination to succeed in a complex power-play with their fellows – the reign of *amour-propre*. In a world of appearances rather than reality, effects are more important than causes; the anonymous benefactor is therefore most welcome. This society is very close to that described by Glaucon in which justice is in danger of becoming nothing more than a social convention.

In a society in conformity with nature, the society of *Du contrat social*, Rousseau's Gyges' ring daydream would be an escape from moral responsibility. Real anonymous beneficence would already be an escape; a dream of such a thing would be like indulging in pity at the theatre. Indeed Rousseau writes of his fellow men, in the *6ᵉ Promenade*, 'ils peuvent encore m'intéresser et m'émouvoir comme les personnages d'un drame que je verrais représenter' (*Rêveries*, p. 1057). Pity experienced at the theatre is easy because the emotions aroused are 'pures et sans mélange d'inquiétude pour nous-même', because 'nous avons satisfait à tous les droits de l'humanité, sans avoir plus rien à mettre du nôtre' (*Lettre à d'Alembert*, p. 33). This relationship with a mere representation is a kind of deathly passivity. It may be compared with what Rousseau calls the dangerous supplement (masturbation) whose imaginary seductions and barren spilling of seed are, in Rousseau's eyes, an escape from the responsibilities of the marital contract and from the obligation to populate the state. It was noted earlier that Rousseau linked his unwillingness to conform to the contract of beneficence with an inability to perform marital duties on command. In the just state the social contract would protect contracts between individuals, and the observance of these interpersonal moral contracts would help to preserve the all-embracing social contract.

It is through borrowing the vocabulary and concepts of a legal contractual relationship, with rights and duties clearly defined, that the code of beneficence prevents itself from slipping into a relationship of pure emotional reciprocity.[33] A contract is, by definition, between two (or more) different parties (even though in the social contract one of the parties is created by that contract); thus, as husband and wife are maintained in their difference in Rousseau's just society, so are benefactor and beneficiary.

After the experience of degenerating social relations in the episode with the crippled boy, and all the remembered disappointments of the past, the Gyges' ring daydream is a reassuring image of transparency between Rousseau and his reader, who can observe Rousseau's impartial justice and beneficence; the obstacle of the false social image of Rousseau has been removed. All barriers (such as privacy, possessiveness and pudicity) are broken down between the self and the other. Initially, this imaginary fusion of strength and freedom, this abolishing of pernicious barriers and differences, is immensely pleasurable. However, the imagination is the faculty which permits inflation of desire, leading to a transgression of natural bounds (the natural equilibrium of desire and power); an imagined superhuman increase in strength and freedom will inevitably cause an expansion of desire. While this is not inconsistent with a surge of pity, it is incompatible with the strictures of pudicity, which is modelled on a natural reserve. Outside the rationality of the social codes (beneficence and pudicity) there is undeniable tension and even conflicts on the conceptual level which underpins these codes.

Nevertheless, in the *Rêveries*, which consistently move from disquiet to calm and reassurance, the final conclusion is an assertion of negative virtue: 'j'ai très peu fait de bien, je l'avoue, mais pour du mal, il n'en est entré dans ma volonté de ma vie, et je doute qu'il y ait aucun homme au monde qui en ait réellement moins fait que moi' (p. 1059). Rousseau finds a solution in abstention from action, which means that he escapes the possibility of being forced, perhaps unwittingly, to be an oppressor. In an unjust society, this is a remarkable achievement.

CHAPTER 6

Pudicity in some of Rousseau's minor writings: its relationship to beneficence

This chapter analyses in detail four in some ways uncharacteristic writings: *La Mort de Lucrèce, Les Amours de Milord Edouard, Le Lévite d'Ephraïm*, and *Emile et Sophie ou Les Solitaires*.[1] These are writings to which, in general, neither Rousseau nor his commentators have accorded the status allowed to his major works; this chapter seeks to show that they are nevertheless important both in their own right and for the light they shed on the major works. In each of these short fictions Rousseau presents a transgression of *pudeur*, and, to some extent, explores the consequences of this transgression. It might be expected that the transgression of pudicity would be linked to the antithesis of beneficence. That intuitive expectation is supported to the extent that, for example, rape, a dominant theme in these minor writings, and theft (the rich stealing from the poor) are both manifestations of the law of the strongest. Furthermore, rape, the most extreme assault on pudicity, shares certain particular associations with that theft which is the logical opposite to beneficence: there is a semantic (metaphorical) and formal linguistic overlap between the two domains. However, the instance of Gyges' ring has already suggested that the relationship between the codes of beneficence and pudicity is not so simple as one of perfect complementarity.

These four marginal works provide a series of further refinements to our understanding of that relationship, because they represent and analyse extreme social situations, which Rousseau prefers to exclude from his major fictional and philosophical writings. In *La Nouvelle Héloïse* or *Emile* there are no instances of rape, murder or suicide; they are first and foremost reflections on the conditions not of despair but of human happiness, albeit in an unjust society. Social injustice intervenes in as much as Saint-Preux may not marry Julie, for example, but brute force does not play any significant role. Rousseau's autobiographical writings do, of course, depict and analyse a more catholic range of situations, those which occurred during Rousseau's eventful and chequered career. But these are not so extreme as the situations to which his imagination turns in the short fictions under discussion. Indeed, he found it therapeutic on an occasion when his circumstances were distressing, during his flight into exile after the condemnation of *Emile*, to compose the *Lévite d'Ephraïm*, an exploration of the consequences of multiple rape, a reworking of violence into calm and order.

The fictions examined in this chapter are in two cases (*La Mort de Lucrèce* and *Les Solitaires*) unfinished, tailing off into fragments, and in two cases (*Les Amours d'Edouard* and *Les Solitaires*) supplementary to a major work. Equally, the *Lévite d'Ephraïm* might be viewed as a supplement to the *Confessions*, for, according to Rousseau, it is a testimony of his mildness towards his enemies. Each of the four writings, which might with justification be regarded as overspills from the main corpus of Rousseau's work, sheds new light on the figure of the benefactor and on his position as the superior in the best possible relation between non-equals. That light is cast by an analysis of the interplay between the hierarchical relationship which is beneficence and the hierarchy of masculine over feminine which is institutionalised in the code of pudicity.

In these four texts women are victims, they are abased. In three of the four they also achieve heroic status, although in quite different ways. Lucretia is the victim of male tyranny, specifically of rape by Sextus Tarquin, but she is exceptional in her subsequent espousal of a masculine heroic mode, her transfiguration into a public benefactor. Laure, the heroine of *Les Amours*, is sold into prostitution at a tender age, but later becomes a model of virtue and renunciation.[2] The Levite's beloved suffers multiple rape which causes her death; in the same story, Axa makes a heroic public sacrifice to bring to an end the carnage which follows the beloved's death. The exact nature of Sophie's abasement, in *Les Solitaires*, is a mystery; presumably more would have been revealed in later letters had Rousseau lived to write them. The reader learns that Sophie is pregnant by an adulterous liaison, but that there are significant mitigating circumstances: she may have been duped, drugged or otherwise forced. At any rate she lives to expiate her 'fault'.[3]

First, it is important to examine closely Rousseau's representation of these women and the extent to which they are defined with reference to the code of pudicity; second, I shall analyse the transgression of that code; and third, I shall look at the wider social import of that transgression and the role played by the code of beneficence. Finally, I shall turn to the question of the status of these writings and of their significance for the whole body of Rousseau's thinking. In each of the sections, the texts are considered in chronological order unless otherwise indicated.

THE PORTRAYAL OF WOMEN IN *LA MORT DE LUCRÈCE*, *LES AMOURS D'EDOUARD*, *LE LÉVITE D'EPHRAÏM* AND *LES SOLITAIRES*

Lucretia, in Rousseau's unfinished play *La Mort de Lucrèce*, is a perfect example of adherence to the social code of pudicity. She deliberately confines her existence to her home, to such an extent that her companion Pauline calls her life 'imprisonment', asking: 'Quel nom pourrais-je donner à cette réserve excessive, à cette humeur austère qui vous emprisonne dans votre maison, qui pour écarter de vous les sociétés dangereuses vous prive de celle des honnêtes gens et qui ôte en un mot au peuple Romain l'exemple de vos vertus et à vos attraits l'hommage de tous les cœurs?' (I, I). Lucretia answers with a rhetorical question: 'Appelez-vous une prison la douceur de vivre paisiblement dans le sein de sa famille?' She declares: 'Pour moi je n'aurai jamais besoin d'autre société pour mon bonheur ni d'autre estime pour ma gloire que celle de mon époux, de mon père et de mes enfants' (I, I). Like Candaules' wife in the myth of Gyges, Lucretia does not wish to be visible to men other than her husband, whoever he may be – whether or not he was her choice, whether or not he is worthy of her. She happily accepts a strict separation between the private feminine domain and the public masculine sphere of activity. She lives in relation to her husband, her father and her children; she has no independent concerns. Thus far she is a fiercer exponent of pudicity than, for instance, Julie, as befits a heroine from an earlier, starker age. She is deserving of the title 'Mater', yet would wish that such a title be unspoken outside the confines of her family home. She attempts to seal up her existence to the extent that not even her fame is spread abroad. Lucretia is convinced that her name will only become known outside her family circle at the cost of her happiness or of her innocence, referring to fame as 'ce funeste éclat' (I, I). She maintains: 'J'ai toujours cru que la femme la plus digne d'estime est celle dont on parle le moins même pour la louer.' In the light of later events her pious prayer has a note of dramatic irony. The bursting out of her name from the barriers which she has erected around it will indeed merit the adjective 'funeste' for it occurs only as a result of her suicide.

Lucretia restricts her actions, other people's access to her, even access to knowledge of her; and she also restricts her own knowledge and her critical faculties. She virtuously blinds herself to her husband's inadequacy, attributing to Collatin 'l'humanité et les passions douces et modérées qui d'un courtisan vulgaire en auraient fait à la place de Tarquin le meilleur de tous les princes' (I, I). Brutus, on the other hand, asserts that Collatin is 'ambitieux, faible, et peu adroit' (II, 4). On a personal level Lucretia claims that 'il est certain que l'amour constant et paisible de Collatin me rend heureuse' (I, I), although she seems far from happy at the opening of the play. Lucretia's account of the situation is incorrect on both the political and the personal side according to other evidence in the play, both that presented by the other characters and that of her own instinctive reactions or verbal slips; for example, in a moment of crisis she calls on her father before she calls on her husband (Fragment I). Although it seems that Lucretia's natural predilection would be for absolute honesty, instead, in accordance with the social code of pudicity, she settles for that which is suitable and appropriate encapsulated in her words:

'Puisqu'il est mon époux, il fut le plus digne de l'être.' The man who *is* her husband *must be* worthy to be her husband, and, in a reversal of cause and effect, *must (always) have been* worthy to be her husband.[4] This metaleptic structure is a characteristic of pudicity which constructs a causal fiction (that women are naturally timid, weak and passive, while men are the natural aggressors) as justification for the preservation of what Rousseau suggests is a socially necessary status quo. Whereas for man in general Rousseau seeks out what is in some way prior to social existence in order to prescribe right moral conduct in society, the code of feminine sexual modesty is a social exigence which necessitates an inscription of sexual difference in the heart of natural equality.

Not only must Lucretia deny her critical acumen with regard to Collatin, but also, according to Brutus, the very strength of her virtue is founded on the suppression of another kind of knowledge, that of her love for Sextus. Brutus explains to Lucretia's father:

Oui le fils de Tarquin est adoré de ta fille, mais sais-tu que ce sentiment caché pénétré par moi seul n'est pas moins ignoré de celle qui l'éprouve que du tyran qui en est l'objet; sais-tu que la découverte de ce funeste secret coûterait la vie à cette chaste et respectable femme; sais-tu quels prodiges de force et de vertu cet amour involontaire subjugué sans le connaître peut produire dans sa grande âme? (*La Mort de Lucrèce*, I, 5)

Brutus' affirmation may usefully be juxtaposed with Rousseau's later remarks on virtuous struggle in the *Lettre à M. de Franquières* (see Chapter 5) where he cites Brutus' own virtue and also that of Titus in sending away Bérénice. Commentators may feel that Lucretia's love for Sextus somehow makes her less admirable,[5] yet, for Rousseau, Lucretia would be less virtuous in rejecting Sextus and in inspiring his downfall if she had no affection for him, since her virtuous actions would be more easily achieved. Lucretia's existence is shaped by a pudic enclosure which is, in one sense, concrete (the physical boundaries of her home); in another sense it is moral, a stifling of thought and expression, a blocking up of any orifices, any chinks whereby dishonour might enter. This is not a state of peaceful stability but one of continuous struggle to maintain pudic reserve unbreached, which is impossible if only because the social situation, the network of social relations in which her household is engaged, is the unjust and unstable one of tyranny. Pudicity is not only necessary, according to Rousseau, for the conservation and growth of a stable society, but also itself necessitates a just society to shelter and protect it.

Lucretia suffers from a 'sombre terreur' which leaves her a prey to sleepless nights or nightmares. While on the one hand her failing health is a dramatic foreshadowing of her forthcoming death, on the other hand both are effects of the reserve constituting her virtue, according to the dictates of the social code, yet untenable under that society which is a tyranny. Pauline attributes the ebbing away of her health and vitality to her cloistered way of life; the link is not, however, simply on a physiological plane. It is Lucretia's sublime virtue which is a major factor in her fatal desirability; Sextus rapes her, in part, on account of her pudicity which he adores.[6] More importantly, after the rape, in order to maintain her virtue (although radically altered in character) even when her body has been violated, she needs a public voice which cannot be reconciled with her existence as a pudic woman; her pudicity thus necessitates her self-destruction.

Lucretia's pudicity confirms, in Rousseau's terms, her potential association with a republican political force. Although the code of pudicity holds women apart from any role in the political sphere, the very adherence of women to this code is itself contrary to aristocratic pretensions. The code of pudicity sets up the difference, and indeed the hierarchy (unavowed by Rousseau), between the sexes at the expense of other sociopolitical differences. The aristocracy are, according to Rousseau, so concerned to mark their rank that they will happily sacrifice such signs of their sex as feminine pudicity or male virility. Pudicity is upheld by the virtuous populace, and according to Saint-Preux's letter from Paris which deals with women's fashions: 'les idées de pudeur et de modestie sont profondément gravées dans l'esprit du peuple' (*La Nouvelle*

Héloïse, p. 267). Saint-Preux makes a harsh judgement on court ladies:

> Cette pudeur charmante qui distingue, honore et embellit ton sexe leur a paru vile et roturière; elles ont animé leur geste et leur propos d'une noble impudence, et il n'y a point d'honnête homme à qui leur regard assuré ne fasse baisser les yeux. C'est ainsi que cessant d'être femmes, de peur d'être confondues avec les autres femmes, elles préfèrent leur rang à leur sexe, et imitent les filles de joie, afin de n'être pas imitées. (*La Nouvelle Héloïse*, p. 267)

The male–female hierarchy of pudicity is not stated explicitly by Rousseau; he suggests that, on the contrary, pudicity is a solution to the entrapping of male–female relations in the recurring pattern of his master–slave dialectic. Yet he shows the hierarchy at work in the relationship between dominant fathers and their pudic obedient daughters. These fathers typically have no surviving biological sons, and so select their successors in their daughters' husbands. While the husbands are sometimes less dominant as characters than their fathers-in-law, they are heirs to the authority of the head of the household. Lucretia's father chooses Collatin as her husband although he is neither loved by Lucretia at that time, nor a suitable husband. Wolmar is, of course, forced upon Julie by her father although she is in love with Saint-Preux (as is Lucretia with Sextus). The Baron d'Etanges chooses Wolmar because Wolmar saved his life, and not because he would make a good husband, although in this case (a novel of moral elevation) he does become a good husband. In the *Lévite d'Ephraïm*, Axa is persuaded by her father to renounce her fiancé (her father's first choice); for reasons of acute political expediency she must succumb to a brutal Benjamite. Saint-Preux takes on the role of father for the fatherless Laure in the story of *Les Amours d'Edouard*. He encourages her to give up the man she loves, Edouard, and become a bride of Christ. This last example is a significant modification of the theme in that it is a move away from the biological family.

Les Amours d'Edouard present a reversal of the pattern to be found in the lives of Rousseau's other female characters. Lucretia, Sophie and the women in the *Lévite d'Ephraïm* are all encouraged by their education or their environment to live lives of absolute modesty and virtue. Their pudicity is subsequently breached by an exterior force, which may be aided and abetted by internal factors. At the beginning of *Les Amours*, on the other hand, the two female characters are respectively the adulterous Marquise and the prostitute whom she hires as her surrogate. The Marquise dies unrepentant, but Laure, the former court-esan, embraces the extreme of pudicity; she takes a vow of chastity in becoming a nun. Her new-found modesty comes to her by the agency of an exterior force, the Englishman Edouard, but clearly touches an inner chord: she has an intrinsic capacity for self-sacrifice. Julie comments to Claire: 'Quel prodige ne doit pas être cette étonnante fille que son éducation perdit, que son cœur a sauvée, et pour qui l'amour fut la route de la vertu? Qui doit plus l'admirer que moi qui fis tout le contraire, et que mon penchant seul égara, quand tout concourait à me bien conduire?' (*La Nouvelle Héloïse*, p. 627). Julie is intrigued by this reversal of the common train of events, again asking: 'Comment l'amour qui perd tant d'honnêtes femmes a-t-il pu venir à bout d'en faire une?' What Julie does not recognise is that Laure's love for Edouard is saturated with feelings of gratitude to a benefactor, and that he regarded her first and foremost as a beneficiary. The love between Julie and Saint-Preux is saved from being criminal by its links to beneficence (as Wolmar points out),[7] but these links are contingent rather than essential to their passion. Laure's achieving of pudicity will be discussed in a later section of this chapter, which investigates the relationship between the codes of pudicity and beneficence.

Les Amours d'Edouard also contains a portrait of the most violent and impudic woman within the corpus of Rousseau's writing; in general, Rousseau prefers to write about the morally admirable rather than the execrable. The Marquise is not only an adulteress but also a deceiver and would-be murderer: she represents the violence of extreme amorous passion, that which pudicity exists to prevent. She is the indirect agent of her husband's death, she makes numerous attempts on the lives of Edouard, her former lover, and Laure, the courtesan she offered him. Her passion also brings about her own destruction; it is

a'evany ereses sell diffeu 137

'une passion violente qui la dévora le reste de sa vie, et finit par
la mettre au tombeau' (*Les Amours d'Edouard*, p. 749). The price
of pudicity appears small set against the devastation caused by
unbridled desire within society, as Rousseau represents it.

The Marquise is the embodiment of a mythic Italy ('un
climat où les sens ont tant d'empire', p. 750), a country of high
and illicit passions, of courtesans, vendettas, of the legendary
Medicis and the Borgia popes and indeed of Lucrezia Borgia,
the modern antithesis of the ancient Roman Lucretia. The
Marquise is at the opposite pole to Lucretia historically; her
story is enacted in degenerate modern Rome as opposed to that
of Lucretia who represents the virtue of the ancient Romans.
Geographically she is at the opposite pole to the Swiss women,
the women of the Valais, Julie and Claire. Socially she is set
against Laure, a child of the people who retains the possibility
of redemption; the Marquise is a maleficent aristocrat who is
known by her title, unlike Rousseau's heroines whom we know
familiarly by their first names: Julie, Claire, Lucrèce, Laure,
Axa, Sophie. Her impudic behaviour favours an erosion of
sexual difference which is, according to Rousseau, characteristic
of aristocratic pretensions. In eighteenth-century terms she acts
like a man: making sexual advances, manipulating, exchanging
women (she procures Laure for Edouard). Her attempted
forcing of Edouard is the first vestigial rape in the story. From
the outset she obtains his sexual favours by deceiving him: he
believed that 'ils lièrent ensemble un commerce intime et libre',
but in reality this free and mutual seeming exchange is founded
on deception. Their relationship is only permissible, in
Edouard's eyes, because she is a widow; in fact she has
anticipated her husband's death.

This sham widowhood on the part of a predatory aristocrat is
reminiscent of the sham weddings which occur in eighteenth-
century novels; these were part of the stock-in-trade of rapacious
noblemen intent upon snatching the virtue of innocent young
girls. Mr B. and Lovelace, in *Pamela* and *Clarissa* respectively,
both plan sham marriages in order to succeed in their designs on
the virtuous girls they desire, and both are also prepared to
stoop to rape, in which Lovelace succeeds when Clarissa has

been drugged. He does not achieve his purpose while her will is active for she can always oppose him, using as her final weapon the threat of suicide. The famous penknife scene in *Clarissa* is echoed in *Les Amours d'Edouard*, with the roles reversed in that it is a man, Edouard, who is the victim and a woman, the Marquise, the aggressor. This scene occurs after Edouard has discovered how he has been tricked and made 'coupable sans le savoir, d'un crime qu'il avait en horreur' (p. 749). He breaks off the liaison, but continues to see the Marquise and thus be a prey to a series of ruses and wiles. In this he is, like Saint-Preux in the brothel, unwisely self-confident: Rousseau's maxim is that you should (if at all possible) avoid situations where your duty conflicts with your self-interest. Rousseau describes Edouard's threat of suicide as follows:

Une fois la séduction devint trop pressante; le moyen qu'il allait prendre pour s'en délivrer retint la Marquise et rendit vains tous ses pièges. Ce n'est point parce que nous sommes faibles, mais parce que nous sommes lâches que nos sens nous subjuguent toujours. Quiconque craint moins la mort que le crime, n'est jamais forcé d'être criminel. (*Les Amours d'Edouard*, p. 750)

Laure, like Edouard, has the courage to prefer death to what she recognises as crime. Although sold into prostitution at an early age, and therefore obliged to suffer many indignities, once she has come to know love (through witnessing Edouard's love for the Marquise) she refuses Edouard's advances so that he might not be defiled by contact with one so unworthy as herself. When he attempts to force her she insists that she would prefer death: 'Tuez-moi si vous voulez; jamais vous ne me toucherez vivante' (p. 752). The tableau of love of which she was a spectator teaches her that she has a will, a choice, whereas up to that moment, like the Levite's beloved, she is completely passive in the face of her destiny.

One unexpected consequence of the Marquise's sham widowhood is that when she is indeed a widow Edouard refuses to marry her. 'Il lui trouva tant d'empressement à mettre à profit sa liberté recouvrée, qu'il frémit de s'en prévaloir' (p. 759). Her haste is not only a feature of her widowhood but also of the time before her husband was even in danger of death; indeed, her adulterous relationship is the indirect cause of that death, for her husband is wounded in a duel with Edouard. Edouard, who cultivates a stoical love of order, cannot tolerate this reversal of nature's purpose: 'La raison seule ne nous dit-elle pas que les plaisirs attachés à la reproduction des hommes ne doivent point être le prix de leur sang; sans quoi les moyens destinés à nous donner la vie seraient des sources de mort, et le genre humain périrait par les soins qui doivent le conserver!' (*Les Amours d'Edouard*, p. 759). The preservation of the species can only be achieved, it seems, by pudic sexual union, by a union of opposites. Impudicity and women who behave like men (at their worst) not only prevent the multiplication of the species, but may even diminish its numbers. An interesting result, however, of the scruples of Edouard and of other characters in *La Nouvelle Héloïse* is that the majority of them actually remain childless: life is not given to another generation. The individuals in *Les Amours* all choose sterility, in the case of the Marquise out of vice, but in the other cases out of virtue. Rousseau's didactic assertion (that pudicity is necessary for generation) is undermined by his representation of pudicity allied with childlessness.

There are two female characters in the *Lévite d'Ephraïm*: the first, the Levite's concubine (to give her her biblical appellation) or wife (as she is also called), is a key figure in the Old Testament story on which Rousseau's 'prose poem' is based; the second, Axa, is Rousseau's invention. Rousseau apostrophises the female sex at one point in the narration: 'Sexe toujours esclave ou tyran, que l'homme opprime ou qu'il adore, et qu'il ne peut pourtant rendre heureux ni l'être, qu'en le laissant égal à lui' (*Le Lévite d'Ephraïm*, p. 1221). Women are, he says, caught up in a masculine master–slave opposition, they are constituted as either tyrants or slaves by men, and are equally unfree in either role. The Levite's concubine or wife is a perfect example of this; she is like a blank sheet or a nameless space, to be inscribed, named or filled by others. In the first Canto Rousseau states that she and the Levite enjoy free and reciprocal love. Yet she was the passive object of the Levite's choice; he sees her, likes her and addresses her: her only response is a silent smile. He takes her to the mountains to worship her: 'sur un sistre d'or fait pour chanter les louanges du Très-Haut, il chantait souvent les charmes de sa jeune épouse' (*Le Lévite d'Ephraïm*, p. 1209). He brings her offerings of honey and doves as if she were an idol. These are erotic symbols which also foreshadow her own fate as a sacrifice.

When the Levite first addresses her he calls her 'Fille de Juda', later 'Fille de Bethléem' (p. 1209) and 'Fille d'Israël' (p. 1210). Rousseau refers to her as 'une jeune fille' or as 'sa jeune épouse' although she is not the Levite's wife and the Levite has told her that they cannot be married. The girl has no fixed name, no individual identity: she is the daughter of a succession of patriarchal groups, Bethlehem, Judah, Israel; she is the wife or concubine of the Levite. Even her status in relation to someone else is ill-determined: she is not consistently the daughter of any one entity, and her position with regard to the Levite is uncertain.[8] The Levite by way of contrast has a clearly defined priestly function. Axa, who is named, is not only a victim, but also a heroine.

When the Levite places his concubine above him to be worshipped the young girl is depicted as unhappy; he asks her 'pourquoi pleures-tu toujours ta famille et ton pays?' (*Le Lévite d'Ephraïm*, p. 1209). Rousseau adds 'la jeune fille s'ennuya du Lévite, peut-être parce qu'il ne lui laissait rien à désirer' (p. 1210). This statement need not necessarily be understood as criticism by Rousseau of the girl; it is, on the contrary, an accurate perception: that it is intolerable to be refused existence as a desiring subject. The one independent action taken by the Levite's wife is her flight from him, but this only returns her to her father's house, and so to an impossible regression into childhood. She therefore welcomes the Levite's pursuit of her and greets his arrival with caresses. Her only means of communication or expression appear to be the smile, the caress and the tear: when the Levite reproaches her she hides her face and weeps silently, she does not speak. Her language is the most basic one of the body in what seems to be an almost involuntary revelation of her emotions. On the one hand their very simplicity may to a certain extent invoke complexity, the complexity of mystery; in other words, the reader might wonder what her real feelings for the Levite are. The unanswerability of the enigma means that whoever attempts to read her feelings may inscribe upon her whatever he desires. The alternative is to understand her language as the most basic code: she can signify happiness, affection and sorrow but little else. By way of contrast a dialogue is instituted between the Levite and the girl's father; for example, the Levite points out to the father that the girl is devalued as a marriageable commodity for she is no longer a virgin; if she is not with the Levite she will be alone and abandoned. Words are thus shown to be the prerogative of the father and the husband.

In the second Canto the roles of master and servant are completely reversed: the Levite delivers up his beloved to a band of rapists as if she were a thing that belonged to him, to sacrifice when necessary. Her lack of identity and diminished value make her the fit substitute as a victim. The rapists' desire is, in the first place, for the Levite, who as a priest and as a man could not be given up to them. Secondly, their host offers his virgin daughter but, as the host's daughter and as a virgin, she is also too precious to be sacrificed. The Benjamites, whose original desire (for a man) is already, within the terms of reference of the story, a substitution of an unnatural passion for a natural one, accept the series of substitutions without complaint.

Throughout the story substitutability is associated with the role of victim, and feminine identity or lack of it. Another chain of substitutions occurs in the fourth Canto, where the virgin daughters of Israel become the victims/wives/concubines of the Benjamites. The sacrifice of the concubine is thus ritually repeated on a massive scale for the sake of social order, to prevent further destruction, just as the concubine is sacrificed for the sake of the safety of the Levite and of the host and his family. The virgin daughters are not brutally raped as she was, but they are taken captive during a religious festival. While they are dancing joyfully they are surrounded by the Benjamites: 'la terreur succède à leur innocente gaité' (*Le Lévite d'Ephraïm*, p. 1222); their dancing turns to running, but the author tells them 'en fuyant l'oppresseur qui vous poursuit vous tombez dans des bras qui vous enchaînent'. As the concubine discovered, there is no escape. In despair the parents of the victims ask: 'Des filles d'Israël seront-elles asservies et traitées en esclaves sous les yeux du Seigneur?' (*Le Lévite d'Ephraïm*, p. 1222).

Once the decision to allow the Benjamites to be 'ravisseurs autorisés' is revoked, and the Israelites decide that the daughters may choose whether or not to accept these new suitors, the girls move from a position of servitude to one of courtly tyranny: 'Les ravisseurs forcés de céder à ce jugement les relâchent à regret, et tâchent de substituer à la force des moyens plus puissants sur leurs jeunes cœurs.' The girls remain the 'sexe toujours esclave ou tyran', even though their slavish 'tyrannical' role is clearly preferable to their slavish 'enslaved' role. Rousseau modifies this unhappy biblical situation by introducing a heroine, Axa. Axa is another Julie. Where force fails, her father employs emotional pressure and an appeal to virtue to bend her (and with her all the other daughters) to his will, in his new choice of husband. He asks her to save him from the shame of going back on his word, evoking 'l'honneur de ton père' at the same time as 'le salut de ton peuple' (*Le Lévite d'Ephraïm*, p. 1223). Like the concubine she is 'demi-morte' as she falls into the arms of a Benjamite. She is, however, in a position which is significantly displaced from that of the passive and anonymous concubine. She embraces what she believes to be, and what society presents to her as, virtuous action.

In *Les Solitaires*, it is Sophie fallen who is significant; whereas in *Emile*, Book v, before the first letter of *Les Solitaires*, Sophie is woman, a model of pudic femininity.[9] It is suggested that she regains her former status in a time which follows the events recounted in the two letters of *Les Solitaires*. In the time preceding the letters Sophie achieved the virtue of a mother of a family. The tutor says to Emile on his wedding day: 'J'abdique aujourd'hui l'autorité que vous m'avez confiée, et voici désormais votre gouverneur' (*Emile*, p. 867). The reign of the tutor is over and that of Sophie begins. Her pudicity is to guarantee the authenticity of Emile's affections towards her, his wife, and towards the children he knows are his own. This permits him to be not only a good head of the household, but also an exemplary member of the community and to that extent a citizen. Rousseau appeals to the mother at the beginning of *Emile*:

C'est à toi que je m'adresse, tendre et prévoyante mère, qui sus t'écarter de la grande route, et garantir l'arbrisseau naissant du choc des opinions humaines!... Forme de bonne heure une enceinte autour de l'âme de ton enfant: un autre en peut marquer le circuit; mais toi seule y dois poser la barrière. (*Emile*, pp. 245–6)

The circle is complete when at the end of *Emile*, the tutor learns that Sophie is pregnant; she is now ready to be the mother addressed at the beginning of the book, to provide that benign enclosure, and Emile is absolutely determined to take over as tutor for his son. Plato suggests in the *Republic* that loyalty to the family may detract from loyalty to the state. Rousseau claims in *Emile* that, on the contrary, family affection enables and promotes affection for the state. The wife's reserved-ness is the condition of possibility of social equilibrium and morality, although her domain is strictly that of her home and not outside it. Sophie endeavours to the best of her ability to maintain the role for which she was educated; Emile later asks himself reproachfully: 'Quels sujets de plainte t'a-t-elle donnés dans la retraite où tu l'as trouvée et où tu devais toujours la laisser?' (*Les Solitaires*, p. 896). It was his decision to take her away from her home, and furthermore, away from the country-side to the city in an attempt to distract her from a protracted period of mourning. However, neither city life nor the distractions and pleasures of the town can, according to Rousseau, be reconciled with the simple and virtuous life which had hitherto been sufficient for Emile and Sophie. They cannot go back to what they once were, and will only be able to retrieve their former happiness in another place.

[handwritten margin notes: "breakdown of pudity does not bring there", "// indy species", "/"]

THE BREAKDOWN OF PUDICITY

These four writings are not of course chiefly of interest on account of their portrayal of virtuous femininity. To learn more about Rousseau's analysis of the code of pudicity it might be more fruitful to turn to *Emile*, Book v, *La Nouvelle Héloïse* or the *Lettre à d'Alembert*. It is the depiction of the breakdown of pudicity which makes these four writings exceptional. It is as if Rousseau had felt that life for the fictional characters in his major texts had been too uneventful, that, for example, Emile's education had not really been tested since his adult life had been unusually free of problems. It is as if the series of natural disasters which wrench humanity out of the state of nature, according to Rousseau's hypothesis in the *Discours sur l'inégalité*, must also fall upon the individual, Emile, and so cause his historical degeneration. Emile and Sophie are therefore struck by natural disaster in the form of bereavement, and then by human aggression in the shape of an assault on feminine virtue.

In three of these four works the initial situation is that of a woman who abides by the code of feminine virtue instituted by the society in which she lives; the degree of relativity inherent in the code is suggested by the ambiguous marital status of the Levite's wife, which would be morally censured at Clarens but not in ancient Israel. The fourth work, *Les Amours d'Edouard*, will be considered last because it is a reversal of the pattern to which the others to some extent conform. The reader's expectation, governed by the ethical framework of Rousseau's writing, is that Lucretia, the Levite's wife, and Sophie would each live happily and peacefully. All three adhere to the social code, more or less explicitly expressed, which should, according to Rousseau, bring them the inner contentment of well-doing and the affection and respect of their families. Yet all three, for different reasons, are unhappy even before the violations which they are to endure. Julie d'Etanges, it should be remembered, is also less than perfectly happy despite her numerous reasons, in her own terms, to be so.

At the opening of *La Mort de Lucrèce*, Lucretia, as a virtuous matron, accepts the limitations on her existence which her moral code dictates to her. However, her father has, we learn, forced her to marry a man who is unworthy of her; she is attempting, by clinging to the regulations of the code of pudicity, to maintain this unstable situation. According to Rousseau, Lucretia is unhappy because she lives in a city governed by a tyrant, and her husband has responded to this by becoming a slave: he does not wish for equality but for the chance to be a tyrant himself. The demeaning nature of Lucretia's marriage forces upon her a mutilation of her critical faculties. Her unease with the fictions which shape her life is, however, concealed (or revealed) in her refusal to admit any limit to virtue. 'Les vertus n'ont jamais d'excès, et quiconque les aurait toutes ne serait jamais accusé d'en avoir trop' (*La Mort de Lucrèce*, I, I). It is in this verbal slip that Lucretia is shown to be potentially beyond the code of pudicity, and beyond its refusal of the woman as a public benefactor or even as a public speaker. Lucretia claims that virtues have no excess, yet excess is a necessary implication of the notion of a limit or a boundary, just as transgression is implied (and required by) interdiction. Thus Lucretia's moral pleasure in the bounds around her life breaks down at the point of the sublimity of her virtue, of her moral strength.

The logic of the code of pudicity is thus already stretched almost to breaking point in the first scene of *La Mort de Lucrèce*. As pudicity is a code primarily concerned with appearances, it can still function in spite of internal inconsistencies. It can incorporate the metalepsis of Lucretia's statement, 'since he is my husband he was the most worthy to be my husband', or the paradox of rejecting a limit to a virtue which consists in limitation. In that first scene the code of pudicity involves Lucretia's implicit belief in things which she knows not to be true. However, her awareness of being trapped in an unlivable state of hypocrisy is expressed only in nightmares until Sextus' tyranny extends to the point of raping his former beloved, Lucretia.

Collatin, far from safeguarding his wife's pudicity in fulfilment of his part of their marriage contract, actually makes the first break in it. He fails to uphold the secondary barrier of

Collatin exposes Lucr. to other men

privacy which should shield an outsider from the potential functioning of a woman's pudicity to excite desire. In Livy's account of the rape, to which Rousseau refers, it is Collatin who awakens Sextus' desire for Lucretia by boasting of her virtue while away from home in the army.[10] In order to prove his claim he brings a group of men, including Sextus, to his home late at night where they find Lucretia, a picture of modest devotion, working on her wool. Collatin subsequently invites Sextus to enjoy their hospitality; he instructs Lucretia to welcome him and, in Rousseau's version, to bear in mind that his fortune depends on Sextus. Collatin is blamed for permitting this threat to his wife at several points in the text for it is assumed that a tyrant will not hesitate to destroy liberty nor to enforce his desires without question on a personal level, just as he does on a political level. Collatin first brings trouble upon his household by his desire to see for himself, and to let others see, his wife when he is absent in the army.

This desire to *see* is contrary to the aims of pudicity, which is a veiling, a covering, a structure of appearances which should not be penetrated by men bursting into the female domain. Collatin has the same weakness as Candaules in the story by Herodotus, without the emotional generosity of Gide's Candaule: Collatin's offer of hospitality is entirely self-seeking. He abandons his duty as master of the household because he has implicitly agreed to be a slave to the Tarquins in the hope of eventual mastery over the Romans. Sextus' servant, Sulpitius, expounds the invidious collaboration of the enslaved with their masters; his words apply to Collatin as well as to himself:

dans notre condition les vices de nos maîtres nous servent de degrés pour monter à la fortune...c'est en excitant leurs passions que nous parvenons à contenter les nôtres. Nous serions perdus s'ils étaient assez sages pour savoir se passer des secrets services par lesquels nous les enchaînons. C'est ainsi qu'à son tour on se rend nécessaire à ceux de qui l'on dépend, et le plus grand malheur qui pût arriver à un courtisan ambitieux serait de servir un prince raisonnable et juste qui n'aimerait que son devoir. (*La Mort de Lucrèce*, I, 3)

Collatin is less perceptive than Sulpitius but equally ambitious; he admits to Brutus: 'Ta grandeur est toute au fond de ton âme

master/slave

et j'ai besoin de chercher la mienne dans la fortune' (*La Mort de Lucrèce*, II, 4). The route to fortune, according to the astute Sulpitius, is through the vices and weaknesses of Sextus. Collatin's willingness to bring Lucretia into danger, with the words 'Il me suffit de connaître Lucrèce; que m'importent les sentiments de Sextus', appears at least foolhardy if not sinister. His father-in-law tells him what his duty as a husband should be:

Le respect même que vous devez à votre épouse vous oblige à venger ou prévenir tout sentiment qui l'outrage. Apprenez qu'une femme chaste ne doit entendre que les discours qu'elle peut approuver et qu'auprès d'elle une entreprise formée est nécessairement un affront reçu. (*La Mort de Lucrèce*, I, 4)

Collatin will defend neither his wife's pudicity nor his country's freedom; indeed he sets in motion the chain of transgression of social and moral codes.

Sextus' attack on Lucretia is first of all an attack on her will rather than on her body. In several speeches in the play he makes it clear that his fascination with Lucretia is a fascination with her virtue and innocence as well as with her beauty: 'Idolâtre de Lucrèce, j'en voulais à son âme toute entière' (II, 1). He realises that in possessing her in the manner in which he intends he will lose most of what he desires. Sulpitius, his servant, believes that words have no objective meaning and that each individual merely employs them as counters in a power-play, in an attempt to dupe those who believe in morality. He is the only character in the play who does not find Lucretia's virtue sublime; he encourages Sextus to believe that she can be caught in a (linguistic) double bind. Sulpitius asks his accomplice Pauline,

Serez-vous toujours la dupe de ces grands mots, et ne comprendrez-vous jamais que devoir et vertu sont des termes vides de sens auxquels personne ne croit mais auxquels chacun voudrait que tout le reste du monde crût? (*La Mort de Lucrèce*, I, 3)

Sulpitius' account of human relations resembles the hypothesis put forward by Glaucon in Book II of Plato's *Republic*: that justice and virtue are only practised for the sake of reward or a good reputation and to prevent others from wronging you with impunity, that if a man possessed Gyges' ring he would steal, seduce women and murder. No one cultivates virtue for its own sake, only for lack of power to do wrong without fear of retaliation. Sulpitius attempts to teach Sextus to use words (and silence) as tools without any meaning other than their power to achieve what he wants of them.

This account of language is appropriate to political tyranny. Rousseau writes in the *Essai sur l'origine des langues*: 'Les langues se forment naturellement sur les besoins des hommes; elles changent et s'altèrent selon les changements de ces mêmes besoins' (chapter 20). It means that after the rape Lucretia's pudic silence would become mere concealment, something which Sextus should promise to maintain for the sake of her reputation. Equally her verbal account of the rape could be estimated no more than rhetoric, debased persuasiveness for political and interested ends. According to Livy (and from the remaining fragments of Rousseau's play, we can deduce that he intended to reproduce this tradition in some form) Sextus offers Lucretia an explicit choice between two equally impossible alternatives. She may preserve her innocence in reality but die and appear guilty of the most shameful adultery or, on the other hand, she can live, guilty, but preserving an appearance of virtue. In this way Sextus separates the appearance from the reality of pudicity to an extent which makes the code no more than a hollow sham; there is a complete loss of even that illusion of meaning which the code retained for Lucretià in the first scene of the play.

Rousseau entitles his rewriting of the story the *death* rather than (as Shakespeare had) the *rape* of Lucretia. The focus of the play is her death; the rape is relegated to the position of occasion, to the fleshing-out of a tyranny over her will. The role of Sextus Tarquin is thus diminished to that of catalyst. Brutus is also presented in relation to Lucretia's death; it is her independent action which is named, not the ignominious outrage of which she was the victim, nor the revolution which succeeds it.[11] The rape itself is missing from the fragments of Rousseau's play. According to Livy, Lucretia is unmoved when threatened by Sextus' sword; this would accord with Edouard's threat of suicide when tempted beyond endurance by the Marquise, and with Laure's response to Edouard's attempt to take her by force: death is preferable to dishonour. Lucretia appears to yield only to Sextus' threat that when he has killed her he will also kill his slave and lay him naked by her side that she might be said to have been put to death in adultery. It is fitting that it should be a slave whose death would replace the tyrant's pleasure; it is a reminder that Sextus' tyranny implies the servitude of those around him. It is this attack on her pudic appearance which decides Lucretia to act in the full force of her will to truth. She will suffer the physical humiliation, but refuse the choice of life in guilty silence or death with dishonour.[12]

The events of the *Lévite d'Ephraïm* follow a quite different path. Unlike Lucretia, the Levite's wife is unable to exercise her will; she never achieves a role as a speaking subject. Whereas Lucretia has intrinsic (and very high) value, this nameless woman has only the value which the Levite chooses to put upon her. Because she has no brothers the Levite cannot marry her, for it would be wrong for her father's inheritance to pass outside his tribe. She has, therefore, lost the possibility of being a bringer of wealth; that role will presumably be left to her sisters. The Levite invests her with the value he chooses, first that of goddess or concubine; then that of a beloved child (he was 'comme une mère qui ramène son enfant de chez la nourrice et craint pour lui les injures de l'air', *Le Lévite d'Ephraïm*, p. 1212); finally that of a substitutable victim. The rape is the focus of the story, but she who silently suffers it is barely present even at that moment: 'elle est déjà morte' (*Le Lévite d'Ephraïm*, p. 1215). The rapist is not one desiring subject as in the case of the pitiful tyrant Sextus, but an anonymous band of brutes whose assault is described in terms of animality:

tels dans leur brutale furie qu'au pied des Alpes glacées un troupeau de loups affamés surprend une faible génisse, se jette sur elle et la déchire, au retour de l'abreuvoir. (*Le Lévite d'Ephraïm*, p. 1214)

The event is marked by *silence*. The Levite pushes his beloved companion outside 'sans lui dire un seul mot' and without even communicating with a look, 'sans lever les yeux sur elle' (p. 1214). He does not ask her to volunteer to sacrifice herself, he does not discuss the matter or give her even the briefest explanation or reassurance. This stands in bleak contrast to the experience of the other women victims whose self-sacrifice is permitted to be an achievement of virtue rather than a resignation enforced by physical weakness. During the outrage the woman loses even the limited ability to communicate by gestures which she previously enjoyed 'elle n'a plus de voix pour gémir, ses mains n'ont plus de force pour repousser vos outrages' (p. 1215). The Benjamites lack that defining human emotion of pity. Rousseau addresses them thus:

Barbares, indignes du nom des hommes; vos hurlements ressemblent aux cris de l'horrible hyène, et comme elle vous dévorez des cadavres. (*Le Lévite d'Ephraïm*, p. 1215)

The reader has the unpleasant sensation that he is becoming a voyeur of this scene:

Voyez ses yeux déjà fermés à la lumière, ses traits effacés, son visage éteint; la pâleur de la mort a couvert ses joues, les violettes livides en ont chassé les roses. (*Le Lévite d'Ephraïm*, p. 1215)

There is a hint of Sadeian (or rather pre-Sadeian) necrophiliac pleasure in the sight of the perfectly helpless victim. In Rousseau's translation of the second canto of Tasso's *Jerusalem Delivered*, he also introduces roses: 'Les roses éteintes sur son visage y laissent la candeur de l'innocence plutôt que la pâleur de la mort.'[13] The erotic and the deathly are conjoined in the spectacle upon which we are invited to turn our gaze. The reader, placed in the role of invisible spectator, thus experiences himself how a spectacle which should arouse pity (and hence inspire beneficence) may instead arouse impudic amorous passion (and hence inspire maleficence, in this case of the most extreme kind). At the same time there is a moral imperative not to avert our eyes from suffering or from criminal action out of a false modesty which would leave the criminals free to commit further atrocities:

O vous, hommes débonnaires, ennemis de toute inhumanité ; vous qui, de peur d'envisager les crimes de vos frères, aimez mieux les laisser impunis, quel tableau viens-je offrir à vos yeux ? Le corps d'une femme coupé par pièces. (*Le Lévite d'Ephraïm*, p. 1208)

It is a formal re-enactment of the assault, the dismembering of the woman's body, which makes the crime, committed in the depths of night, visible to the whole people of Israel, forcing them to see, to understand and to act. But it is the Levite who is the agent of this powerful silent rhetoric; his wife is no more than the physical material which composes the message. The tale is, after all, entitled *Le Lévite d'Ephraïm*: it is the man who is the lover of the rape victim, who makes vengeance possible (who was also the one who aroused the rapists' desire), who occupies the primary and authoritative position rightly accorded to Lucretia in *La Mort de Lucrèce*.

The Levite blames himself for having been the unwitting cause of his beloved's death: 'Je suis cause de ta perte... c'est donc pour cela que je t'ai tiré de la maison de ton père? Voilà donc le sort que te préparait mon amour?' (*Le Lévite d'Ephraïm*, p. 1215). He traces the cause of the event back to his having taken her from her father's house, and 'forgets' that he was also the one who thrust her out of the house in Gibeah on that fateful night. While Rousseau places a heavy burden on the shoulders of the pudic woman, he never fails to depict the guilt of the husband in creating the circumstances in which his wife is brought into peril.

Emile, too, is culpable – for having brought Sophie away from her home and the peace of the countryside to the corruption of the city, where he himself becomes a different man and neglects his wife. He says to himself in his despair: 'C'est toi qui du sein de la paix et de la vertu l'entraînas dans l'abîme de vices et de misères où tu t'es toi-même précipité' (*Les Solitaires*, p. 896). He takes her to a place where there is total inversion of what is proper, where women blush to be chaste. In the state of nature, we may presume, there are no blushes. In virtuous social existence women learn to blush at what seems to be immodest, indeed at any suggestion of the sexual. The society in which women blush to be chaste is degenerate indeed. Emile's instincts

[handwritten margin note: E's overconfidence — takes S to city / power of envt]

warn him that he is unwise to take the lovely Sophie to such a place, but foolishly he ignores his feeling. He is over-confident like Collatin or like Saint-Preux in the Parisian brothel: 'Sûr d'elle et de moi, je méprisais cet avis de la prudence.' Emile forgets the lesson of the 'morale sensitive' and underestimates the effect of the environment on virtue. In the city he himself becomes frivolous and cold; neither his nature nor his education leave him proof against the force of example and the desire to imitate. He comes to believe that he no longer desires Sophie because he already possesses her; later he will reproach himself with the words 'son inconstance est l'ouvrage de la tienne' (*Les Solitaires*, p. 896). It would seem that Emile's education should have left him impervious, yet he succumbs. This mystery relates to that concerning the 'fall' of natural man in the *Discours sur l'inégalité*: natural man appears to be complete and perfect as he is, and so, why does he change, why does he enter history? One answer is that of the external natural catastrophe, another that of man's inherent weakness; both play their part in *Les Solitaires*.

In the city Emile is no longer himself, he is detached from himself, split between reality and a mask. On another level he and Sophie are no longer one, no longer inseparable, but two separate individuals. Their honest acceptance of this state of affairs is a remnant of their self-respect and of their respect for each other. Whereas in a fashionable marriage of convenience the couple are apparently united because they are both self-interested and uninterested in each other, Emile and Sophie live apart because they are not yet indifferent to each other. 'En paraissant nous être mutuellement à charge, nous étions plus près de nous réunir qu'eux qui ne se quittaient point' (*Les Solitaires*, p. 888).

There are a series of enigmas in *Les Solitaires*. The first is the mysterious departure of Emile's tutor without a word of explanation; there are a host of potential explanations but the absence of one in the text confers upon the event the air of a divine act or a natural catastrophe. The second is Sophie's inability to conquer her grief after a certain period of mourning; she sinks into melancholy. This would seem to point to a flaw or inadequacy in her education as a pudic woman. The third enigma is Emile's sudden moral degeneration in the city. One further enigma concerns the circumstances of Sophie's fall from virtue. The reader is told that she 'n'avait plus ce goût décidé pour la vie privée et pour la retraite' (*Les Solitaires*, p. 887). To that extent she, like Emile (perhaps following his example), has departed from her code of virtue. In addition to this, a role is played by false friends who, to our surprise, have also come from the country. Despite this rustic origin they are the epitome of what Rousseau presents as aristocratic, modern and Parisian. As the Marquise procures Laure for Edouard, so Sophie's friend acts as procuress for her husband. But she is worse than the Marquise in that she does not seek out women who have already decided to sell themselves (or rather, in Laure's case, been forced to do so), she attempts to corrupt her friend, a woman of hitherto impeccable pudicity. The mystery is how she succeeds, a mystery to which, we presume, Rousseau would have revealed the answer at a later stage in the correspondence.

The fact that Emile does not know to what extent Sophie is to blame, and can presume, for example, that she loves another, enables Rousseau to elaborate arguments concerning a husband's reaction to his wife's infidelity as, in *La Nouvelle Héloïse*, he elaborates those concerning suicide or duelling. Whereas in *La Nouvelle Héloïse* the arguments for and against a certain position are put forward by different characters, in *Les Solitaires* Emile argues with himself. His desires argue against his reason and vice versa. His desire to be reunited with Sophie presents him with a series of arguments to the effect that in the city a wife's infidelity is taken lightly, and anyway cannot dishonour her husband who is responsible only for his own actions. In a second line of reasoning he claims that even if public opinion condemns Sophie, he ought to be above these prejudices and pity her. At the same time Sophie's case is quite different from those women who either conceal their crimes or flaunt them; she has confessed and is repentant, and will probably make a better (less proud) wife on account of her slip from virtue. Emile concludes after thinking through these apparently sensible arguments:

Quand les passions ne peuvent nous vaincre à visage découvert elles
prennent le masque de la sagesse pour nous surprendre, et c'est en
imitant le langage de la raison qu'elles nous y font renoncer. Tous ces
sophismes ne m'en imposaient que parce qu'ils flattaient mon
penchant. (*Les Solitaires*, p. 901)

This, however, creates a problem, at least for the reader if not
for Emile. If the strategy of the passions is to assume the guise of
wisdom, how do we know when it is wisdom itself which is
speaking to us? Emile says confidently: 'Je ne pus me dissimuler
que je raisonnais pour m'abuser, non pour m'éclaircir' (*Les
Solitaires*, p. 901). But how can we trust this new enlightenment?
Rousseau's final testing of Emile will be another version of the
Gyges' ring test. Emile will be placed outside society, in a
daydream-like and exotic other place where the actions of men
cannot touch him. There his judgement and capacity for
virtuous action (beneficence) will be vindicated – but as if in a
daydream of virtue.

Emile proceeds to argue against any further contact with
Sophie. He dismisses the views of the city and decides that
Sophie's infidelity does dishonour him because he is largely to
blame for it: 'Si Emile eût toujours été sage Sophie n'eût jamais
failli.' Thus far Emile's new thoughts are in accordance with his
beliefs before he entered the city, and appear to conform to his
earlier moral framework. He then argues that Sophie's character in fact makes his case more, not less, desperate: 'Oui, Sophie
est coupable parce qu'elle a voulu l'être' (*Les Solitaires*, p. 901).
Emile now assumes that Sophie has retained all her pride, and
would not deign to return to him once she has deceived him.
This line of reasoning has the air of being once again disguised
passion (anger) even though Emile does not recognise it as such.
Sophie goes to great pains to discover Emile's whereabouts;
after the death of her son, when she is free to travel, she seeks
him out and finds him although he is far away.[14] Her love for
him, we are told, never diminishes.

Emile's dilemma is of considerable importance for Rousseau's
theory of pudicity, and of the consequences of the transgression
of the code, which is, in this case, presumed to be voluntary.
One of Rousseau's chief pragmatic arguments for the necessity

of a wife's absolute fidelity, is that without that safeguard there is the disastrous possibility that a man might not know whether or not he is the father of his wife's children. In this instance Emile actually knows that Sophie is pregnant with another man's child; it is this fact which arouses his anger and jealousy as the mere knowledge of her love for another could not. It is well known that Rousseau holds that true love is not in general characterised by jealousy, hence the relatively peaceful triangles which haunt his life and novel (the triangles centred on Mme de Warens, Mme d'Houdetot, or Julie, for example). But the idea that the mother of his son is also the mother of another man's son is unbearable for Emile:

> Cette idée, plus horrible qu'aucune qui m'eût passé dans l'esprit m'embrasait d'une rage nouvelle; toutes les furies revenaient déchirer mon cœur en songeant à cet affreux partage. Oui, j'aurais mieux aimé voir mon fils mort que d'en voir à Sophie un d'un autre père. (*Les Solitaires*, p. 904)

Emile decides that Sophie should be separated from their son, which would act as a punishment for her. He is saved from committing this unjust act by Sophie's secret visit to look upon him unseen while he is at work. When he learns of this pathetic scene, it works like a benign charm preserving him from his own anger and bitterness. The harsh edict of separation is, however, carried out, unbeknown to Emile, by his family. They take on the punitive paternal role, which would be inappropriate for Rousseau's hero, and as a result Emile's son dies as if in fulfilment of the hostility expressed in Emile's darkest moment and enacted by his family.

Sophie watching Emile at work is presented to the reader as Emile's vision of Sophie watching him at work. In this way it becomes a spectacle which arouses pity, pity for a mother who fears that her child might be torn away from her, like the model spectacle from Mandeville which Rousseau evokes in the *Discours sur l'inégalité*. It has an added poignancy because it reminds Emile an earlier happier occasion when Sophie had watched him at work, prompted by love rather than fear. A picture of Sophie which would arouse amorous passion (of which there are many examples in *Emile*, Book v) cannot now please Emile, but an image which arouses nothing but pity has a benign effect in directing Emile towards charitable thoughts. The reassurance which Sophie finds in the sight of her husband calmly going about an honest humble task, which represents a rejection of the city with its idle aristocratic frivolity based on the values of *amour-propre*, gives Emile strength. It strengthens him in his rejection of *amour-propre*, and affirms him in those emotions rooted in pity. Images of Sophie which arouse pity had been a constant source of comfort to Emile from the beginning:

Malgré l'horreur de mon sort je sentais une sorte de joie à me représenter Sophie estimable et malheureuse; j'aimais à fonder ainsi l'intérêt que je ne pouvais cesser de prendre à elle. Au lieu de la sèche douleur qui me consumait auparavant, j'avais la douceur de m'attendrir jusqu'aux larmes. (*Les Solitaires*, p. 898)

Emile eventually takes flight, deciding that he cannot be far enough away from Sophie's physical presence; but he can take with him a mental image of her as worthy of pity.[15] In distance he thus achieves a kind of proximity.

Les Amours d'Edouard differs from the other works discussed in that it sets out from a situation of impudicity. The Marquise is, as has already been detailed, the antithesis of a pudic woman. So, initially, is Laure by virtue of the social role which she has been forced to play, that of courtesan. Prostitution is obviously quite a different transgression of pudicity from those so far considered, rape and infidelity. It is generally something which continues over some time and involves no mitigating passionate motivation. This is the point which Claire, speaking with the voice of the pudic woman, makes to Julie with regard to the differences between Laure's fault and Julie's own now that both have repented:

Je ne méprise point Laure; à Dieu ne plaise: au contraire, je l'admire et la respecte d'autant plus qu'un pareil retour est héroïque et rare. En est-ce assez pour autoriser les comparaisons avec lesquelles tu t'oses profaner toi-même; comme si dans les plus grandes faiblesses le véritable amour ne gardait la personne, et ne rendait pas l'honneur plus jaloux? (*La Nouvelle Héloïse*, p. 639)

In the terms dictated by society, Laure's loss of honour appears irrevocable. When she attempts to stop being a courtesan she is forced to take refuge in a convent, for nowhere else is safe: 'Elle éprouva que celle qui renonce au droit sur sa personne ne le recouvre pas comme il lui plaît, et que l'honneur est une sauvegarde civile qui laisse bien faibles ceux qui l'ont perdu' (*Les Amours d'Edouard*, p. 756). Such a loss of the right of self-determination cannot take place *de iure*, but it may take place *de facto*. Up to the moment when she falls in love with Edouard, Laure has indeed relinquished her right to determine her own fate; she succumbs to force rather than using her will-power, which always leaves open the option of suicide rather than dishonour. Laure's passivity in the face of her fate is understandable in terms of the *morale sensitive* which explains, although in social terms it does not excuse, her inability to fight against her situation until the moment when she has come to know something different.

In general Rousseau has little sympathy for prostitutes: 'J'ai toujours eu du dégoût pour les filles publiques' (*Confessions*, p. 316); but he made particular exceptions to this general rule. In the *Confessions* he relates experiences with Venetian courtesans which must have contributed to the thinking and emotion which fuelled his characterisation of Laure. In Zulietta he encountered a courtesan for whom he felt admiration as well as desire, despite his knowledge of what he considers to be the degrading nature of her profession. He describes himself in an emotional turmoil, 'inquiet encore malgré que j'en eusse de concilier les perfections de cette adorable fille avec l'indignité de son état' (*Confessions*, p. 322). In Laure, a fictional creation, he is able to reconcile this contradiction which he finds so disturbing by reforming her through love. At the end of the story her way of life matches her beauty and generosity rather than standing, in Rousseau's terms, in flagrant contradiction to them. She therefore gains ground on the Marquise, who previously had at least her passionate nature as mitigation for her crimes:

La Marquise perdait toujours du terrain par ses vices; Laure en gagnait par ses vertus. Au surplus, la constance était égale des deux côtés; mais le mérite n'était pas le même et la Marquise avilie, dégradée par tant de crimes finit par donner à son amour sans espoir les suppléments que n'avait pu supporter celui de Laure. (*Les Amours d'Edouard*, p. 759)

THE RELATIONSHIP BETWEEN PUDICITY AND BENEFICENCE

The third section of this chapter concerns the relationship between the code of pudicity and other social codes, in particular at the point at which pudicity can no longer function. The relationship between pudicity and beneficence, a code which should encourage social cohesion, is ambivalent; pudicity tends to exclude women from many of the actions or emotions which beneficence promotes. Not only is it impudic for women to be benefactors in a public sense, but it might be impudic for them to be beneficiaries. Equally, pudicity can co-exist with a social system in which women are the chattels of their fathers or husbands, but it cannot permit men to be generous with possessions which are women as they may be with other possessions. Pudicity confers value on women but its system of value functions according to different criteria from those governing value within the code of beneficence (where, for example, a gift's value may lie in the emotion which prompted the giver). Nevertheless, conceptual contradictions between the two codes must often be overcome in practice for, according to Rousseau, both are necessary for the best possible social existence.

Clearly, under conditions other than those of the best possible social system, the strains between the codes, as well as strains internal to any given code, are intensified. Lucretia's intimate confrontation with the reality of tyranny means that, for her, pudicity can no longer be more than a sham : she must speak out with a public voice. According to the code of pudicity, women should speak with a gentle voice, should be an imperceptible influence like the chief minister whispering in the king's ear.

Luc. becomes public bf by renouncing pud

Otherwise women should only speak amongst women as in the Genevan *cercles*. In order to deny a public voice to women, Rousseau sometimes suggests that if women persist in speaking or writing for an audience beyond their home or their circle, their words are empty and worthless:

Mais ce feu céleste qui échauffe et embrase l'âme, ce génie qui consume et dévore, cette brûlante éloquence, ces transports sublimes qui portent leurs ravissements jusqu'au fond des cœurs, manqueront toujours aux écrits des femmes : ils sont tous froids et jolis comme elles. (*Lettre à d'Alembert*, p. 139)

Lucretia, however, does not compose cold and pretty books like the traditional 'précieuse', she accedes to a rhetoric of inspiration by the disfigurement and destruction of her body. It is a body language which stands in sharp contrast to the silent communication of the body allowed to women in Rousseau's theory of pudic eroticism.[16] In choosing Lucretia as a heroine, Rousseau chooses a woman who rouses a people to bring vengeance upon a powerful tyrant. Her success is that of a public benefactor of the highest kind; her example brings freedom to the people of Rome.

Lucretia's words, in telling of the rape, cannot enter into the restricted economy of exchange because they are uttered at the same time as her self-inflicted death. She gives without asking for material reward, and she inspires a mimetic response, in the first instance from Brutus, and then from the people of Rome. Brutus takes the very dagger with which she has stabbed herself, and swears an oath on it to avenge her; in Rousseau's Fragment 11 Lucretia says: 'Tiens, Brutus, j'ai fait mon devoir, fais celui de Rome et le tien.' Rousseau's Lucretia has a far less passive role than the Lucretia imagined by other writers who is merely a useful symbol of the suffering of Rome which may be exploited by the politician, Brutus. Lucretia herself, within Rousseau's frame of reference, goes beyond private (feminine) concerns to enter the political (masculine) arena. While Brutus' determination to overthrow tyranny is not dependent on the rape of Lucretia, her sublime virtue triumphant over passion and over tyranny furnishes a model for him. He says: 'Et pour tout dire en un mot soyons dignes s'il est possible d'être les vengeurs de Lucrèce' (Fragment 12). Up to the moment of Lucretia's suicide Brutus is a dissembler, feigning stupidity or even madness; Sextus refers to him as an 'insensé' (II, 1) and is quite unaware of his true ability. When Brutus hears Sextus approaching he says: 'Il faut me contraindre. O lâche et vile feinte, de tous les sacrifices qu'exige la patrie tu es le seul qui coûte à mon âme' (Fragment 2). Rousseau's Brutus is not happy to have to deceive rather than fighting openly, but it is only through Lucretia's courage that he is able to break out of his ignominious role.[17]

Brutus calls Lucretia 'more than a man'; this means that his imitation of her is not the 'becoming-woman' of a man, but a 'becoming-more-than-a-man' of a man. Nevertheless, the clear boundaries of sexual identity which make Lucretia the epitome of pudic femininity and Brutus her virile counterpart (who sternly asks Collatin 'Sais-tu être homme et saurais-tu mourir?') become somewhat blurred: it is Lucretia, not her husband, who knows how to die and when that action is appropriate.

After ridding Rome of the Tarquins, Brutus becomes famed for the austerity of his virtue; he is one of Rousseau's most revered heroes from classical antiquity.[18] In the *Lettre à M. de Franquières*, Rousseau cites Brutus as a model of that virtue which conquers passion. He describes Brutus' action, watching the execution of his sons which he has ordered, as self-mutilation, as if he were stabbing himself as Lucretia did:

Brutus faisant mourir ses enfants pouvait n'être que juste. Mais Brutus était un tendre père; pour faire son devoir il déchira ses entrailles, et Brutus fut vertueux. (*Lettre à M. de Franquières*, p. 1143)

As it is necessary for Rousseau that Brutus should have loved his unworthy and ambitious sons in order for his act to have been a virtuous one rather than simply a just one, so Lucretia's presumed love for Sextus makes her act a virtuous one.

In the *Essai sur l'origine des langues*, Rousseau claims: 'Ce que les anciens disaient le plus vivement, ils ne l'exprimaient pas par des mots, mais par des signes; ils ne le disaient pas, ils le montraient' (chapter 1, p. 89). Lucretia speaks before she dies, and speaks in public, but her message is above all conveyed in her body, in the message of her wound. One of the examples which Rousseau gives to support his statement in the *Essai* is that of the Levite of Ephraim who, in a demand for retribution, dismembers the body of his wife who has died as a result of being raped. He explains his message in simple terms to the assembled Israelites, but it is his mute sign which rouses them to action; likewise, it is Lucretia's suicide and the sight of her body with the fatal stab wound which rouses the Romans to action. Yet, in terms of feminine identity, the two cases are quite different. When the assault is re-enacted on the body of the Levite's wife, she is once again a passive victim, for she is already dead. Lucretia herself re-enacts the violent entering of her body, this time with a dagger, for her own purpose. The result of Lucretia's action is the liberation of Rome, whereas in the biblical story, avenging the woman becomes proliferating carnage which threatens to wipe out an entire tribe. Only the voluntary sacrifice of Axa and the other daughters of Israel can bring this to an end.

In choosing Lucretia as a heroine, Rousseau is focussing on a female benefactor. He also mentions her in *Sur les femmes*, where he claims, 'nous verrons dans l'autre sexe des modèles aussi parfaits dans tous les genres de vertus civiles et morales' (*Œuvres complètes*, II, p. 1255). These are both relatively early works. Once it is decided that in the family 'il faut que le gouvernement soit un, et que dans les partages d'avis il y ait une voix prépondérante qui décide' (*L'Economie politique*, p. 242), then, having settled that it is man who has the preponderant voice ('car quand la balance est parfaitement égale, une paille suffit pour la pencher'), for the sake of harmony woman must follow a code of feminine virtue which muffles her voice, excluding her from other kinds of 'vertus civiles et morales'.

In *La Mort de Lucrèce*, Lucretia's rejection of a strict pudicity which has lost all semblance of meaning makes her into a public benefactor in death. *Les Amours d'Edouard*, however, unlike the unfinished play, has its denouement in one of Rousseau's major works, *Le Nouvelle Héloïse*. Whereas the *Amours* sets out with a

depiction of aristocratic manipulation of social codes, false
beneficence, the ending within the novel is the triumphant
reunion of beneficence and pudicity – at the cost of banishing
sexual relations altogether.

The Marquise uses the language of the code of beneficence to
mask her impudic self-interest. Rousseau employs a kind of
style indirect libre to represent the Marquise's emotions in the
light in which she wishes them to be interpreted:

> Elle commença d'aimer avec générosité; avec un tempérament ardent
> et dans un climat où les sens ont tant d'empire, elle oublia ses plaisirs
> pour songer à ceux de son amant, et ne pouvant les partager, elle
> voulut au moins qu'il les tînt d'elle. (*Les Amours d'Edouard*, p. 750)

The Marquise offers Edouard a gift, something she has sought
at great cost and effort because she thinks it will please him:
Laure, the prostitute. She hopes that in using what she has given
him, he will remember his benefactress with gratitude: 'C'est
assez pour moi si quelquefois auprès d'elle vous songez à la main
dont vous la tenez.' Edouard is about to refuse her offer when
the Marquise asks: 'Pourquoi mon bienfait vous est-il à charge?
Avez-vous peur d'être un ingrat?' This apparent generosity is
clearly false beneficence; the Marquise is not motivated by pity
or justice; she wants to arouse Edouard's desire for her by
mingling sensuality with gratitude as the senses alone have
failed. She is using Edouard's goodness against him, attempting
to make an ally of her enemy. She almost succeeds: 'Sa
reconnaissance lui donna plus de peine à se contenir que son
amour, et ce fut le piège le plus dangereux que la Marquise lui
ait tendu de sa vie' (*Les Amours d'Edouard*, p. 751). However, as
events turn out, she is defeated by her own stratagem: 'On peut
juger du désespoir de cette femme emportée quand elle crut
s'être donnée une rivale, et quelle rivale! par son imprudente
générosité' (*Les Amours d'Edouard*, p. 758).

The vocabulary of beneficence is commonly employed both
displaced to serve amorous passion, and inverted to serve as a
disguise for self-interest. Here the Marquise uses it to both ends.
Her 'gift' not only abuses Edouard in arousing his gratitude
under false pretences, but also misuses Laure. The Marquise

treats a fellow woman as a slave, a thing who may be exchanged, sold, or given by the person who has bought her, without consulting her in any degree. Unexpectedly it is Laure who profits from the seductive and touching scene arranged by the Marquise; she is awakened by the sight of passion striving to be virtuous to the possibility of making choices herself, and of, to some extent, determining the course of events.

Edouard is accustomed to plain dealing; he is an Englishman, and therefore, according to eighteenth-century theories of environmental determinism, quite different from the subtle Italians. He is easily deceived in matters of the heart, and misunderstands the finer points of the code of beneficence, despite being a model benefactor in the most important sense. He does not realise that the Marquise will be angered by the fact that he goes to visit Laure without using her for the purpose intended by the Marquise. He thinks that to hide his visits 'eût été de sa part une ingratitude' (*Les Amours d'Edouard*, p. 755). He neither sees through to the Marquise's true purpose which has been thwarted, nor understands that, on the level of the appearance of beneficence, he has left untouched the Marquise's gift (of Laure as prostitute). He is enjoying and cultivating that part of Laure (her moral being) which the Marquise did not give to him, indeed whose existence the aristocratic Marquise did not wish to acknowledge. The Marquise has sent Laure to him as a *res* not as a *persona*.

Edouard ('n'oubliant pas la magnificence anglaise') sends Laure a lacquered cabinet and some jewels. She returns them with a note saying:

J'ai perdu le droit de refuser des présents. J'ose pourtant vous renvoyer le vôtre; car peut-être n'aviez-vous pas dessein d'en faire un signe de mépris. Si vous le renvoyez encore, il faudra que je l'accepte: mais vous avez une bien cruelle générosité. (*Les Amours d'Edouard*, p. 754)

A courtesan's possessions both are and yet are not her own. Because she cannot refuse gifts, her acceptance of them has no meaning other than confirmation of her humiliating lack of status a courtesan. It is a similar situation with the gifts she gives: as she cannot refuse to give certain things, her giving of them is only a sign of her situation. Laure hopes to escape from her place outside the social code of beneficence, and outside normal human transactions, by not giving her body to Edouard and by not accepting his magnificent presents. As she moves towards the assumption of a pudic veil, she simultaneously adopts other codes in the social network, but paradoxically by a refusal, by a not-doing. It is because she must regain her place as a pudic woman in order to have a place at all, that ultimately her entry into social acceptance will be a withdrawal from society.

Edouard, unlike Laure, does not fully understand the delicate intricacies of the significance of gifts which he treats as material objects. He sends the Marquise the presents which Laure has refused, as if the significance of the objects were unchanged by this episode. At first, ignorant of their history, the Marquise accepts the gifts, which underlines the difference between her position as a recipient and that of Laure: 'Elle l'accepta; non par avarice, mais parce qu'ils étaient sur le pied de s'en faire l'un à l'autre.' However, once she learns that Laure has already refused the same offering 'à l'instant tout fut brisé et jeté par les fenêtres' (*Les Amours d'Edouard*, p. 755). This act of destruction is partly a demonstration of the violence of her anger, but it also has a symbolic character. She can no longer send the gift back, for Laure has forestalled her in that gesture of disinterestedness. She must show that she cares even less for possessions than the courtesan, as if they were engaged in a potlatch competition of magnanimity.

Edouard excels as the highest kind of benefactor, as moral example and teacher. He is a benefactor to Laure as he is to Saint-Preux. He teaches Laure how to be virtuous and how to attain self-respect: 'Par ces soins bienfaisants, il la fit enfin mieux penser d'elle.' Laure is the perfect beneficiary, responding not only with gratitude, but with the evidence of her improvement. In Edouard's absence she learns English and memorises every book which he recommends to her. 'Elle s'instruisait dans toutes les connaissances qu'il paraissait aimer: elle cherchait à mouler son âme sur la sienne' (*Les Amours d'Edouard*, p. 759). She has the advantage over Saint-Preux, who frequently back-slides, that her benefactor and her love object coincide. Also her harsh experience as a courtesan, socially unacceptable, leaves her eager to embrace all the aspects of a respected social existence epitomised by the very letter of the moral codes.

Laure is, at this stage, beautiful not only without but also within. Edouard discovers that 'il avait rendu Laure trop estimable pour ne faire que l'estimer'. While her love for him pre-exists his generosity towards her, he loves her as his creation, as what he has made her: 'Où est l'homme bienfaisant dont l'utile amour-propre n'aime pas à jouir du fruit de ses soins?' (*Les Amours d'Edouard*, p. 758). This is the positive side of the phenomenon analysed by Aristotle (see Chapter 2). The origin of Edouard's love for Laure (his success as a benefactor) helps to explain why he is consoled for her loss by the proof of Saint-Preux's devotion to him. He says: 'J'oubliai la Marquise et Laure. Que peut-on regretter au monde quand on y conserve un ami?' (*Les Amours d'Edouard*, p. 653). He has devoted more time and effort to retrieving Saint-Preux than to saving Laure, and is correspondingly more pleased with the success of his benefi-cence.[19] Saint-Preux has the possibility of becoming Edouard's equal, of entering into a relationship of reciprocity. The code of pudicity dictates that Laure cannot be a benefactor in the same way Edouard or Saint-Preux can be; she has only one possibility, that of sacrificing herself for Edouard. Saint-Preux demonstrates that he has reached social maturity by acting as a benefactor to Edouard and like a father to Laure – dictating her role as sacrifice. Laure becomes a nun in order to save Edouard from wedding a former prostitute. This mirrors her first rejection of him, but is a far greater act, befitting her increase in moral stature. She writes: 'Le sacrifice de tout mon bonheur à un devoir si cruel me fait oublier la honte de ma jeunesse' (*Les Amours d'Edouard*, p. 653).

La Nouvelle Héloïse represents the triumph of social compro-mise at a certain price. Despite the egalitarian moral philosophy which is held by many of the characters, the realities of a hierarchical social system cannot simply be abolished. The Wolmar family continue to employ servants and therefore treat them differently from their social equals, although their treatment may be the kindest and wisest under the circumstances. Furthermore, Julie accepts that she cannot marry Saint-Preux because of her father's prejudices, and Laure accepts that she cannot marry Edouard. Throughout the novel there is flirtation with the possibility of an earthly paradise, but the eighteenth century prevails, albeit in a form modified in accordance with Rousseau's dreams. It is to be expected that within this compromise the codes of beneficence and pudicity should unite, but the price for Laure is voluntary immolation. And Julie, on the other hand, aware of the dangers to her purity, if Wolmar's generous plan to invite her former lover to live with them comes to fruition, dies as a result of saving her son from drowning. It could be said that she gladly embraces death and thus prevents the transgression of her pudicity which might result from her husband's hospitality. Laure embraces what amounts to a living death; after all, she does not claim a religious vocation. Edouard and Saint-Preux both vow not to marry since they cannot marry the women they have chosen. Claire and Wolmar will not remarry. Thus the triumph of social existence is, up to a point, sterile.

The *Lévite d'Ephraïm* is a story which takes place much earlier, in the distant age of the Patriarchs, a time before any recognised civil authority: 'Dans les jours de liberté où nul ne régnait sur le peuple du seigneur, il fut un temps de licence où chacun sans reconnaître ni magistrat ni juge, était seul son propre maître et faisait tout ce qui lui semblait bon' (*Le Lévite d'Ephraïm*, pp. 1208–9). The one stable element in this society, an element on which Rousseau lays great store, is the code of hospitality. In the opening paragraph of the prose poem he urges: 'Mortels, respectez la beauté, les mœurs, l'hospitalité' (*Le Lévite d'Ephraïm*, p. 1208). Hospitality is one of the oldest manifestations of a code of beneficence, and one which could come into conflict with the code of pudicity in so far as pudicity lays down that the home is the private sanctum of women, who should be preserved·as much as possible from contact with outsiders. Hospitality attempts to render the outsider harmless by bringing him within the confines of the home and of the social code which governs

hosp 9

the transaction. The contract of hospitality is a promise for the host to watch over the safety of the guest and also for the guest to protect the host. In *La Mort de Lucrèce*, a guest transgresses the code and reverts to being an enemy by attacking his host's wife, as, in an even older tale, Paris does, starting the Trojan Wars.

The Levite and his wife have to make the journey from Bethlehem to Ephraim; they decide to seek hospitality in Gibeah, an Israelite town but of the tribe of Benjamin, whereas Bethlehem is in Judah. Contrary to their expectations no one offers them shelter; the strangeness of this failure is brought into relief by Rousseau's celebration of those times when 'l'hospitalité n'était pas à vendre...le voyageur dépourvu de tout ne manquait de rien' (*Le Lévite d'Ephraïm*, p. 1212). Finally an old man takes them into his home, saying 'si quelquechose vous manque, que le crime en soit sur moi' (*Le Lévite d'Ephraïm*, p. 1213). The old man is not one of the tribe of Benjamin himself, he too is a stranger in the town and is originally from Ephraim like the Levite. Thus to some extent both are guests in the town, and the long-term guest has taken it upon himself to offer hospitality to another stranger for the night. When the Benjamites surround the house, making it explicit that the household is enclosed by the town and the tribe, they cry:

Livre-nous ce jeune étranger que sans congé tu reçois dans nos murs, que sa beauté nous paye le prix de cet asyle, et qu'il expie ta témerité. (*Le Lévite d'Ephraïm*, p. 1213).

The Benjamites claim that the old man has no right, as a foreigner himself, to invite other strangers into his household, which is already, in a vestigial sense, receiving the hospitality of the town. As a consequence, they argue, they are permitted to enter his home with violence despite his plea: 'Ah! ne faites pas ce mal devant le seigneur; n'outragez pas ainsi la nature, ne violez pas la sainte hospitalité' (*Le Lévite d'Ephraïm*, p. 1214). Their argument appears contrived because it is known that they had designs on the Levite before he met the old man. Yet not one of them individually had dared to offer the Levite hospitality and then rape him. Although they are 'sans joug, sans frein, sans retenue' (p. 1213) they have 'un reste de respect pour le plus sacré de tous les droits' (p. 1214). Hospitality is the only social or moral code which appears to have any hold over them; they are even, as Rousseau points out, emancipated from the taboos concerning corpses, yet 'ils n'avaient pas voulu le loger dans leurs maisons pour lui faire violence' (p. 1214).

The Benjamites' sense that it would be wrong to invite the Levite into their homes in order to rape him shows the moral codes working together as they should, in order to protect individuals and social order. However, the strategies involved in the codes of hospitality and pudicity are quite different; they are different on a conceptual level. Pudicity, as has already been observed, functions by the rigid demarcation of difference, by separation maintained by barriers or shields. Hospitality, on the other hand, welcomes the stranger in to accommodate him, to make him closer to the host. The two terms 'guest' and 'host' inhabit each other in a certain sense, and the term 'enemy' is occulted.[20] Host and guest share food (salt) and the roof over their heads; this engages them in a series of duties towards each other which temporarily supersede duties towards families. When the Benjamites threaten to break into the old man's house to seize the Levite, the old man's sense of his duty as a host is such that he offers his own daughter as a substitute for his guest 'pour racheter son hôte aux dépens de son propre sang' (p. 1214). The Levite, however, must defend his host and his host's family; he sends out his wife unprotected to be raped by the Benjamites. The Levite, aware of the perils of travel, attempted to shield his wife from the heat and the dust during the journey; it is when they are indoors, within someone else's house that she is in fact most at risk.

The code of pudicity indicates that women should stay at home, in their own homes, and not travel out and so not be guests in other people's houses. Mobility is for men.[21] Sophie's displacement to the city proves to be her undoing; the Marquise, a Neapolitan in Rome, is impudic in her masculine independence. Emile ignores his forebodings as he enters the city; likewise, the Levite ignores the forebodings which delay his departure from his wife's father's house.

Much of Rousseau's writing appears to be structured by an

Solving independence vs rel's of dependence

opposition between the independence of the solitary and the network of relations which inevitably create some degree of dependence for social man. The *Lévite d'Ephraïm* takes place during a transitional stage between the solitary state and fully developed society. In *Les Solitaires* (p. 905), Emile writes: 'Il y avait longtemps que je n'étais plus un être isolé sur la terre: mon cœur tenait, comme vous me l'aviez prédit, aux attachements qu'il s'était donnés.' It is the transgression of pudicity which will force Emile to leave his community and become a solitary; this reinforces Rousseau's claim that pudicity is essential for a just society. While *Emile* has the name of one individual as its title, the sub-title, *De l'éducation*, implies that the eponymous hero will eventually be engaged in some kind of social relations or else that education would be superfluous. The sequel is entitled *Emile et Sophie* which, after Emile, suggests a couple, the unity of married life, the founding of a dynasty and social existence. In fact for most of the two letters (which are all that Rousseau was able to write) the reader encounters Emile without Sophie rather than Emile and Sophie; the copulative *et* in fact represents a disjunction. The sub-title, *Les Solitaires*, suggests that the sequel will relate a withdrawal from social life. Even once the couple are reunited they will no longer form that basic social unit which the family may be considered, and which Rousseau opposes to Plato's dream of communal living in the *Republic*.

At the end of *Emile*, Emile is a member of a small, close-knit, rural community; this stands in sharp contrast to the busy life of the city where many individuals live in close proximity but where each is emotionally isolated from the other. The eighteenth-century city represents the society which Plato's Glaucon evokes, the society in which the Marquise or Sulpitius are at home, skilled at manipulating social codes (language and behaviour) in order to gain power over others. Emile's tutor advises him that he will be both more happy and more effective in the country than he would be in the city for 'un homme bienfaisant satisfait mal son penchant au milieu des villes' (*Emile*, p. 859). Emile's happy fate is contrasted with something like Rousseau's exile:

Mais toi, bon Emile, à qui rien n'impose ces douloureux sacrifices, toi
qui n'as pas pris le triste emploi de dire la vérité aux hommes, va vivre
au milieu d'eux, cultive leur amitié dans un doux commerce, sois leur
bienfaiteur, leur modèle, ton exemple leur servira plus que tous nos
livres, et le bien qu'ils te verront faire les touchera plus que tous nos
vains discours. (*Emile*, p. 859)

Emile's social relations, his attachments, are based on beneficence; this is the result of his education, for which he expresses
his gratitude in *Les Solitaires* (p. 883):

Ne pouvant donc me garantir de toutes les affections qui nous lient
aux choses, vous m'apprîtes du moins à les choisir, à n'ouvrir mon âme
qu'aux plus nobles, à ne l'attacher qu'aux plus dignes objets qui sont
mes semblables, à étendre, pour ainsi dire, le moi humain sur toute
l'humanité, et à me préserver ainsi des viles passions qui le concentrent.

There is a difference between the specific relations with his
fellows which the tutor recommends to Emile and the more
general kind of beneficence to which Emile refers in the second
quotation. When Sophie's adultery has caused the disintegration of Emile's family life, and hence his abandoning of his
responsibilities as a citizen, he substitutes general duties towards
humanity for those particular relations with a wife, parent,
children, friends, servants and so on. He writes 'j'en devenais
d'autant plus homme en cessant d'être citoyen' (*Les Solitaires*,
p. 912). This does not mean a return to the state of nature, for
Emile is a moral being and so cannot choose to be otherwise. In
other words, his relations with his fellow men are governed by
morality, even though his commitments are not durable as they
would have been in his home community. This intermediate
position, somewhere between natural goodness and republican
virtue, bears some resemblance to that of Rousseau in his
daydream of possessing Gyges' ring. In that daydream the
spectacle of women without the veil of pudicity (which
necessarily arouses amorous passion) is threatening as it would
be, Rousseau suggests, in society. Rousseau's proposed conclusion to *Les Solitaires* included an imaginary multiplying and
actual doubling of Emile's wife. Perhaps Emile can feast on the
spectacle of women with impunity because there is no other man
on his desert island.

THE FUNCTION OF THE MARGINAL WORKS AS TESTS OF
THOSE HIERARCHIES WHICH ROUSSEAU
ACKNOWLEDGES

Rousseau's work appears consistent in its protest against power, against inequality and injustice. But as I have already indicated, he suggests that certain hierarchies are necessary; or, at least, that the maintenance of a distinction between the two parties or groups is necessary. These hierarchies are those between the benefactor and the beneficiary, between men and women, and between the writer and his reader. A clear distinction between the two parties is essential for an exchange or a contract to take place between them. If, for example, the differences between men and women are eroded, then, Rousseau implies, sexual relations (understood as a meeting of opposites) become difficult, if not impossible. These binary oppositions have a tendency to be hierarchical; to some extent Rousseau is prepared to legitimate or, at any rate, to exculpate the existence of these hierarchies, particularly with regard to the masculine–feminine opposition, less so with that between benefactor and beneficiary.[22] To reinforce the sense of the necessity of these hierarchies, he convincingly represents the potential tyranny of the weaker party: the crippled boy in the *6ᵉ Promenade*, women in, for example, the *Lettre à d'Alembert*, and the reader (who refuses to read) in the *Dialogues* (p. 659) ('très sûr d'avance que cette grâce [being read] ne me sera pas accordée').[23]

A combination of 'superior' qualities (beneficence, masculinity, authorhood) is to be expected; indeed, on a conceptual level, benefactors are men, and writers should be male benefactors. The most dangerous of the weaker parties, women, may not on a conceptual level even be beneficiaries or readers (let alone benefactors or writers).[24] The repressive aspects of this system make it, within Rousseau's generally egalitarian thinking, a precarious one. The minor writings discussed in this chapter function like a safety valve ensuring the serenity of the major works. They reveal as breakdowns what are only fissures or cracks in much of Rousseau's writing. They demonstrate the cost, the sacrifice of women and children, of what is elsewhere simply accounted a moral necessity.

The status of these four texts is that of tests or experiments; they are tests which *must* be passed, but, in a sense, they cannot be passed in a completely satisfying way. *La Mort de Lucrèce* is an early attempt to test the model woman, to see if she can approximate to masculine virtue, an attempt which is abandoned in favour of Julie, the feminine heroine. *Les Amours d'Edouard* are the test of Saint-Preux, the beneficiary, as benefactor. *Le Lévite d'Ephraïm* is a test of Rousseau, the writer, and by implication of his reader (as judge of the writing); is the writer fit as a benefactor? *Les Solitaires* would be a trial of the educations in *Emile*, or, in other words, of the possibility of human happiness in Rousseau's here and now.

Rousseau describes his choice of Lucretia thus:

Je méditais... un plan de tragédie en prose, dont le sujet qui n'était pas moins que Lucrèce ne m'ôtait pas l'espoir d'atterrer les rieurs, quoique j'osasse laisser paraître encore cette infortunée, quand elle ne le peut plus sur aucun théâtre français. (*Confessions*, p. 394)

His subject is 'no less than' Lucretia, a woman who passes from feminine silence and reservedness to acting and speaking out to influence public and political events. She is not only his subject-matter but someone whose cause he champions; he hopes to 'atterrer les rieurs', those who would turn tragedy into comedies at the Théâtre de la Foire.[25] Rousseau hopes that at this historical moment characterised by French (Parisian) mockery of virtue (like Sulpitius' mockery within the play) he can nevertheless make Lucretia a worthy spectacle again. Lucretia is an 'infortunée' both because her positive influence on events in Rome arises out of the extreme of male tyranny, and because those who support a monarchical political system (the French) will no longer suffer her appearance in public.[26] Yet the play which would tell of Lucretia is unfinished; her written existence is fragmented: she does not appear once more in public.

A later attempt at creating a female heroine who will stun Rousseau's public into acquiescence is Julie. The novel, which is complete, is successful on every count: it is an acknowledged masterpiece. Julie, like Lucretia, is a model of pudicity, even though somewhat tempered. She, too, has a husband, chosen by her father, who urges her to be more welcoming to guests. Wolmar warns: 'La modestie extrême a ses dangers ainsi que l'orgueil' (*La Nouvelle Héloïse*, p. 494), words which could have been addressed to Lucretia. He, too, is eager to invite his wife's former lover or suitor into his house. Although Wolmar's motives are on a higher level than those of Collatin, Julie's response to him in one curt note could have been Lucretia's answer to her husband:

Wolmar, il est vrai, je crois mériter votre estime; mais votre conduite n'en est pas plus convenable, et vous jouissez durement de la vertu de votre femme. (*La Nouvelle Héloïse*, p. 514)

Claire's role is like that of a superior Pauline, her advice not motivated by base concerns. She urges Julie to trust herself: 'Tout ton mal vient de toi ô Israël' (*La Nouvelle Héloïse*, p. 499). Julie's death, which is altogether less violent, less shocking, and with a purely private significance, is a more suitable (in terms of the code of pudicity) form of feminine self-sacrifice than that of Lucretia. Her relief at death may be due to her fear of the consequences of sharing her house with Saint-Preux, but the cause of her death is her action in saving her son's life, not rape by a tyrant. Julie is a private 'household' benefactor. Her moral influence is greater perhaps than that of any other character in the novel, but it is a passive rather than an active influence. Julie inspires those around her to love goodness by her very being, by her moral beauty; she is almost like the 'true spectacle of nature' which exists within men's hearts. Rousseau celebrates this 'quiet voice' to the full, and presents it as uniquely satisfying. Yet the existence of the incomplete play, *La Mort de Lucrèce*, which sketches another mode of heroism, a model of civic virtue which equals if not surpasses those Greek and Roman heroes of Rousseau's boyhood, arouses the modern reader's desire for a female public benefactor to succeed, although the unfinished state of the text means that on one level she cannot.

The function of *Les Amours d'Edouard* is to elucidate the testing of Edouard's beneficiary Saint-Preux. Edouard fears that Saint-Preux's motives for wanting to live at Clarens may not be entirely dictated by virtue, and uses the possibility of his marrying the Marquise or Laure as a means of testing this. He believes that such a marriage could not be encouraged by a true friend, but pretends that only if he marries will he settle at Clarens. As Saint-Preux has vowed to spend the rest of his life with his benefactor, it would be in his interest to agree that Edouard should marry Laure.[27] The test develops from an artifice into a real crisis: Edouard loses control of events and falls in love with Laure whom he is then genuinely determined to marry. This means that Saint-Preux does not simply have the chance of passing the test with flying colours, but can repay his benefactor in some measure, and be a benefactor himself in his turn.

Edouard, like Wolmar, is a model benefactor; he thus contributes to the moral atmosphere of *La Nouvelle Héloïse*. He is not governed entirely by reason and love of order, as Wolmar is, despite his belief that he judges only according to stoical principles. Julie, Saint-Preux and Claire feel that he is swayed by his good heart and spontaneous passions; he is closer to the natural source of beneficence (pity) than he is prepared to acknowledge. When Saint-Preux describes their first encounter it is in passionate terms:

nous sentîmes que nous nous convenions; il y a un certain unisson d'âmes qui s'aperçoit au premier instant, et nous fûmes familiers au bout de huit jours...pour toute la vie. (*La Nouvelle Héloïse*, p. 125)[28]

Edouard's expansive nature, as might be expected, means that he is not only prone to beneficence, but also to amorous passion. 'Cet homme, âpre et peu galant, mais ardent et sensible, extrême et grand en tout, ne pouvait guère inspirer ni sentir d'attachement médiocre' (*Les Amours d'Edouard*, p. 749). This statement refers to his relationship with the Marquise, but could equally well refer to that with Saint-Preux.[29]

Benefactors are always given the name of father in *La Nouvelle Héloïse*; Saint-Preux names Edouard successively 'friend', 'benefactor' and 'father', each title redefining and reinforcing the others. The role of blood-fathers in *La Nouvelle Héloïse* (as to some extent in *Le Lévite d'Ephraïm* and *La Mort de Lucrèce*, and in a vestigial sense in *Emile*[30]) is to decree the sacrifice of their daughters to some other interest, such as honour or political necessity. As Saint-Preux rises to the status of benefactor to Edouard, he also takes on the characteristic of the blood-father to Laure. Previously (see Chapter 3) it has seemed that the juxtaposition of the terms 'benefactor' and 'father' involves primarily a redefinition of 'father'; in the case of Saint-Preux it appears that the connotations of 'father' have shaped his role as a benefactor.[31]

Saint-Preux presents Laure's self-sacrifice as *his* work: 'Voyez ce que j'ai fait', he says to Edouard, 'je sondai le cœur de Laure, et y trouvant toute la générosité qui est inséparable du véritable amour, je m'en prévalus pour la porter au sacrifice qu'elle vient de faire' (*La Nouvelle Héloïse*, pp. 652, 653). The hierarchical role of the father as head of the household is a social convention, according to Rousseau, but a just one as long as the head does not become a tyrant. It is just because the father will have been, in a certain sense, a benefactor to his children and thus they owe him gratitude. This may be illustrated by the example of Julie; she holds that she cannot take up Edouard's generous offer to give her and Saint-Preux a refuge in Yorkshire, because her ingratitude towards her parents would make her unfit to gain a new father-benefactor:

Plus riche, plus honorée de vos bienfaits que de mon patrimoine, je puis tout recouvrer près de vous, et vous daignerez me tenir lieu de père. Ah Milord! serai-je digne d'en trouver un, après avoir abandonné celui que m'a donné la nature?... Depuis quand un cœur sensible marque-t-il avec tant de soin les bornes de la reconnaissance? N'est-ce pas être déjà coupable que de vouloir aller jusqu'au point où l'on commence à le devenir, et cherche-t-on si scrupuleusement le terme de ses devoirs, quand on n'est pas tenté de le passer? (*La Nouvelle Héloïse*, p. 208)

Edouard's proximity to the natural source of beneficence (pity) makes him vulnerable to its social perversion, amorous passion. The same was true of Saint-Preux, who demonstrates that he is cured of his adulterous desires by taking up the colder,

more conventional side of the role of benefactor; he speaks
'froidement' (*La Nouvelle Héloïse*, p. 652). As the blood-father
rejects love on behalf of his child in favour of what he names
duty, so Saint-Preux rejects love on behalf of Edouard and
Laure in favour of duty. The crucial difference lies in the extent
to which the father *names* duty arbitrarily (in which case his will
is a tyrannical one).

Amorous passion is thus banished in favour of friendship
between moral equals. But pudicity is praised by Rousseau
because of its maintenance of sexual difference, which permits
sexual union, and hence the preservation of the human race by
sexed reproduction. It also permits a father to be sure that his
children are his own and entitled to inherit his property. In this
instance the benefactor has enforced a pudic veil so thick that
for Laure sexual difference becomes sexual isolation; she enters
a convent, something of which Rousseau does not, in general,
approve, because monastic vows are contrary to nature and so
are unlikely to be kept. Saint-Preux passes his test; he is
pronounced fit to raise Julie's and Wolmar's children and to live
at Clarens. It is assumed that amorous passion between him and
Julie has been banished. However, beneficence has only
succeeded in reimposing pudicity and controlling desire between Edouard and Laure by an extreme social artifice (the
convent); sexual segregation at Clarens is not so strict.
Paradoxically it is in the novel that the benefactor/host will be
shown to have initiated a breach in his wife's pudic reserve.

In the prefaces to the *Lévite d'Ephraïm* Rousseau lays claim to
the text as a demonstration of his good character. In proving his
good character, Rousseau wishes to assert the beneficent quality
of his writing; he is defending himself primarily against the
attack on the author of *Emile*. At the same time the work
contains an allegory of writing which undermines the possibility
that it could serve as a test of the author as benefactor.

At the end of his first preface Rousseau writes:

Si jamais quelque homme équitable daigne prendre ma défense en
compensation de tant d'outrages et de libelles, je ne veux que ces mots
pour éloge: Dans les plus cruels moments de sa vie, il fit *Le Lévite
d'Ephraïm*.

Pour moi je me console. Le seul éloge que je désire et que je m'accorde sans honte parce qu'il m'est dû. Dans les plus cruels moments de sa vie il fit *Le Lévite d'Ephraïm*. (*Le Lévite d'Ephraïm*, p. 1206)

At the end of the second preface Rousseau says of the work:

Elle a un côté par lequel les honnêtes gens l'applaudiront j'en suis sûr et ils sentiront qu'un homme qui s'occupe ainsi quand on le tourmente n'est pas un ennemi bien dangereux. (*Le Lévite d'Ephraïm*, p. 1207)

In so far as the fact of having written such a work under such circumstances is a test, it is a test which Rousseau has already passed; the reader's judgement, if he is 'honnête' or 'équitable', will be a eulogy.

Rousseau's satisfaction with the work rests on a kind of textual mastery, that of reshaping existing material into a happier form, rather like the creative work which the benefactor performs on his beneficiary. In the *Lévite d'Ephraïm* Rousseau is at once substituting a literary reality for his present unhappy circumstances, as he so often substitutes daydreams for the misery of the present, and rewriting a sombre biblical tale as pastoral prose poem. After the condemnation of *Emile* he is haunted by the thought of men's injustice and ingratitude:

J'imaginai de donner le change à ma rêverie en m'occupant de quelque sujet; celui-ci me vint dans l'esprit; je le trouvai assez convenable à mes vues. Il m'offrait une espèce d'intermédiaire entre l'état où j'étais et celui où je voulais passer, je pouvais de temps en temps m'y livrer à mon humeur sombre puis y substituer de plus doux objets et sitôt que mon sujet le permettait j'imitais mais...les délicieuses images de M. Gessner. (*Le Lévite d'Ephraïm*, p. 1206)

However, within the work there is a violent representation of the activity of writing.[32] This is the dismemberment of a woman's body, which Rousseau cites in the *Essai sur l'origine des langues* as an example of 'éloquence muette', the most powerful and effective form of language.[33] Yet it is hardly the reshaping of existing matter into a happier form; it is lethal writing, its matter a corpse, a woman's body divided up by her lover's knife in a horrible parody of the strokes of the pen dividing up the page. The effectiveness of this silent rhetoric brings about a

disinemberment

retribution which finally far exceeds the measure of the crime, however horrible, causing extraordinary death and devastation. Despite his power over the living woman, the Levite has no authority over his message: he is the instrument by which the message is written. Rousseau describes him as if already dead, but his body briefly surviving him in order to accomplish the rhetorical purpose. The message is dispersed by synecdoche (each twelfth representing the whole). The Levite cannot follow his dismembered wife to re-establish mastery over her as he could when she was a living body; the corpse has scattered in twelve different directions. When the woman is reassembled for burial he, too, is dead: they are reunited in the grave. In all, this episode makes the writer subordinate to the writing; his authorship does not vest him with any authority nor is his message in any way expressive of himself.

The metaphor of a dismembered body for writing is one which suggests a mental suffering and anguish; in *Les Solitaires* Rousseau represents extreme anguish by the sensation of being torn into pieces and sent in different directions losing any sense of a unified identity, yet each part seeming whole in its experience of pain. This is a synecdochal experience like that of the fragment-message; Rousseau calls it 'se multiplier pour souffrir' (*Les Solitaires*, p. 892). However, a dismembered corpse still permits the memory of unity and wholeness like something once had and now lost.[34] There is a still more radical image of writing in the *Lévite d'Ephraïm*, which is that of the machine of war. In the last chapter of the *Essai sur l'origine des langues*, Rousseau represents the end of the speaking subject in language by the arbitrary command *tel est mon plaisir* backed up by cannon and soldiers.[35] In the *Lévite d'Ephraïm* the revenge wreaked on the Benjamites for the rape also becomes mechanical and infinitely proliferating violence at the service of an impersonal and absolute command (that of the invisible God). Rousseau compares the Israelite army to cannon balls hurled by blazing machines which destroy everything which lies in their random path.[36] The violence of the army, generated from a univocal source, appears to have its own momentum of performance; it produces reasons (revenge, then lack of women) *allegorical reading*

to explain the performance just as much as it performs in order
to keep up with the reasons for performance. In this case both
cause and effect (terms which become infinitely substitutable)
equal *death*, death which (unlike that of Lucretia) is not invested
with any meaning.

The four Cantos of the *Lévite d'Ephraïm* may be interpreted as
a textual allegory, which is not surprising since this pastoral
prose poem is related on every level to Rousseau's passionate
concern with, and equal fear of, the experience of writing. In the
first Canto there is an illusion of meaning in the reciprocity or
love between the Levite and the woman, where in fact there is
a hidden power structure behind the illusory reciprocity; where
the woman is treated as a goddess, she is soon to be a slave. In
the second Canto there is the memory of the illusion of meaning:
the dismembered body may be re-membered, if only in a coffin.
In the third Canto there is the loss of illusion of meaning; this is
made explicit in the fourth Canto when the army turn against
Jabesh-Gilead for its 'unjust pity', or because the remaining
Benjamites require wives, or perhaps simply because once
started the army cannot stop in its execution of devastation.
However, Rousseau finally invests the tale with a more positive
significance; he invents Axa's sacrifice, another illusion of
meaning, but significantly displaced from the first. The meaning
accorded to the sacrifice is the return to virtue in Israel; the
reality is another woman delivered up to the ravishing
Benjamites. Yet the violence is no longer represented as animal
and silent. The illusion of truth and meaning is on the level of
language; Axa chooses to attain what she knows as feminine
virtue.

The *Lévite d'Ephraïm* suggests, by its textual allegory, that the
imposition of meaning on arbitrary and violent events (linguistic or otherwise) is above all an *imposition*. Rousseau cannot fail
to pass his test, but finally that proves above all his skill and
sensitivity as a writer. Writing is not the transparent medium
which could permit more.

Whereas Emile's education is only putatively tested under the
best possible circumstances within *Emile*, in *Les Solitaires* it is
tested under extremely difficult circumstances.[37] The education

outlined in *Emile* is at the same time an analysis of the conditions for human happiness within social existence; these conditions are markedly different from those of Rousseau's own beginning described in his *Confessions*. In *Les Solitaires*, on the other hand, Emile's situation bears a strong resemblance to that of Rousseau in the *Rêveries d'un promeneur solitaire*. The difference lies only in their histories and how they have been marked by them.

Emile is tested in *Les Solitaires* by the corruption of city life, by the loss of what was dearest to him, by what he believes to be betrayal, and finally by being taken captive by Turks who make him a slave. The corruption of city life proves the most difficult (because the most insidious) trial to withstand. As already remarked, he does succumb to a certain extent and thus initiates his own betrayal by Sophie. However, his decline is only superficial, and he is able paradoxically to rediscover freedom as a slave.

There is a delicate pattern of interdependence of freedom and enslavement which runs through *Les Solitaires*. The first sentence of the work runs: 'J'étais libre, j'étais heureux, ô mon maître!' (p. 881). Emile expresses his happiness in *freedom* under the *mastery* of his tutor, a structure which is familiar to the reader of *Emile*.[38] Emile's tutor is also his creator, he says, 'Vous m'aviez fait un cœur...', and benefactor, 'vous m'aviez donné Sophie'. Emile remembers his education (*Les Solitaires*, p. 882); he received from his tutor the invaluable gift of a happy childhood, the acquisition of reason and judgement in adolescence which brought him wisdom and contentment and the acceptance of the laws of necessity. In other words, he learnt, thanks to his tutor/master, that he is truly free when he is happy within the bounds of his freedom.

Emile also experiences enslavement to love:

aux pieds d'une épouse adorée, j'étais le plus heureux des êtres; c'était l'amour qui m'asservissait à ses lois, qui me tenait dans sa dépendance; son tyrannique pouvoir était l'ouvrage de ma tendresse, et je jouissais même de ses rigueurs. (*Les Solitaires*, p. 895)

Because Emile has chosen (has been given) a beloved who is worthy of his adoration, and who exercises her erotic power in accordance with the dictates of the code of feminine virtue, his happy subjugation to love is again a kind of freedom. He is free as Edouard could not be while he was being deceived by the Marquise and believed that her husband was dead. He is free in that he has knowingly chosen bonds which he has no desire to break, and which he may virtuously enjoy. To be freed of (the freedom of) the tyranny of love is a burden to be shouldered rather than any kind of liberation. Emile writes: 'Je suis libre; au moins je dois l'être: que mon cœur ne l'est-il autant que ma foi!' (*Les Solitaires*, p. 903).

Emile paradoxically retrieves a freedom within bounds (as opposed to that false freedom of loss) as a slave. In this case he has not chosen the bonds, nor are they just ones, but he regards them as an extension of the law of necessity. He writes regarding his enslavement 'que m'ôtera cet événement? Le pouvoir de faire une sottise. Je suis plus libre qu'auparavant' (*Les Solitaires*, p. 916). Emile considers that his masters will not be harsher on him than nature, the master of all, could be: 'Qu'un maître m'assomme ou qu'un rocher m'écrase, c'est le même événement à mes yeux' (*Les Solitaires*, p. 917). A human being cannot be more unyielding than a stone must be according to the laws of nature. Emile's philosophical resignation to his exterior change in circumstances, which is the result of his education, contrasts sharply with the attitude of the knights who share his plight. They are at once less physically fit to bear their work load, and less mentally prepared to endure their subordination. While Emile feels emancipated from his desires, they cannot accept that freedom does not consist in doing as you will, but in willing what you do. Emile retains his sense of his duties towards humanity; to prevent death through exhaustion for himself and his fellows he organises a strike. His cool determination and practical statement of the case improve the situation for everyone. This is the final test of Emile's education and shows, like a philosophical example, the beneficial results which it has had. As Emile expounds his sense of freedom to his tutor ('le temps de ma servitude fut celui de mon règne', *Les Solitaires*, p. 907), he addresses him as 'father' which serves as a reminder that he owes his contentment to his first and major benefactor.

Emile's language in *Les Solitaires* bears a striking resemblance to that of Rousseau in his autobiographical works, in particular *Les Rêveries*. Emile is alone ('mon sort est de vieillir et mourir seul', *Les Solitaires*, p. 881) as Rousseau is: 'Me voici donc seul sur la terre' (*Rêveries*, p. 995). Neither has chosen to be alone; solitude is forced upon them by their ill-treatment at the hands of their fellows. Solitude extends to the lack of a destined reader for their writing. Emile addresses his tutor, who, he believes, may well be dead. If he is not dead it makes little difference for, Emile writes, the letters will never reach him. The form of the letter is a constant reminder of distance and separation; during Emile's happy youth there would have been little need to write to his tutor who was always present. That the letters will not be read denies the need for communication. Emile writes for himself, as Rousseau does in the *Rêveries*, 'je n'écris mes rêveries que pour moi' (*Les Solitaires*, p. 1001). Emile states that:

Ce ne'est pas ici l'histoire des événements de ma vie; ils valent peu la peine d'être écrits; c'est l'histoire de mes passions, de mes sentiments, de mes idées. (*Les Solitaires*, p. 890)

Rousseau, too, wishes to reflect on his 'dispositions intérieures' and his 'contemplations charmantes' (p. 999); he says: 'Je dirai ce que j'ai pensé tout comme il m'est venu' (p. 1000). This solitary contemplation of the inner self takes place within a kind of eternal present:

Je me disais qu'en effet nous ne faisions jamais que commencer, et qu'il n'y a point d'autre liaison dans notre existence qu'une succession de moments présents, dont le premier est toujours celui qui est en acte. Nous mourons et nous naissons chaque instant de notre vie, et quel intérêt la mort peut-elle nous laisser? S'il n'y a rien pour nous que ce qui sera, nous ne pouvons être heureux ou malheureux que par l'avenir, et se tourmenter du passé c'est tirer du néant les sujets de notre misère. (*Les Solitaires*, pp. 905–6)

These thoughts of Emile could find a place in the *Rêveries*; Rousseau speaks in the 5ᵉ *Promenade* of 'un état où l'âme trouve une assiette assez solide pour s'y reposer tout entière et rassembler là tout son être, sans avoir besoin de rappeler le passé ni d'enjamber sur l'avenir' (*Rêveries*, p. 1046).

The testing of Emile's education is thus, by extension, the testing of Rousseau, had he enjoyed Emile's education and Emile's status as a private person rather than a writer (a public figure). In other words, it bears a certain resemblance to the daydream of possessing Gyges' ring in its function of testing Rousseau by placing him outside and above social existence. Testing Rousseau, it must be remembered, is also a way of testing the capacities of man in general. Rousseau attempts to find the resignation to fate which Emile enjoys, and which is freedom, but his task is sadly far more difficult. Emile's enslavement is a physical representation of what Rousseau feels his own fate to be, yet his enslavement is less restricting on his thoughts and actions than Rousseau's intangible servitude is felt to be. Nevertheless, Emile's practical general beneficence is replaced, in Rousseau's case, by the general beneficence which is writing.

THE LESSONS OF THE MARGINAL WORKS

Social existence is impossible without pudicity. This is stated in other works by Rousseau, but nowhere is it illustrated graphically as in *Les Solitaires*, in which a man who has received the best possible education for social life (and for beneficence) abandons all ties (including those of a citizen) when his wife's pudicity is transgressed. He does not flee her because he no longer loves her, but because he knows that his love for her would lead him to attempt to affect a reconciliation, and believes that this would now be morally wrong. This turns on the question of the legitimacy of children, which is an integral part of the argument for pudicity. The structure of the family requires, according to Rousseau, that the husband believe that he is the father of his wife's children. *Les Solitaires* shows how beneficence is dependent on a man's relationship to society (which is in turn dependent on his wife's pudicity); Emile does not abandon beneficence altogether, but he moves from particular beneficence extended to selected individuals (which we imagine to be like that of Julie and Wolmar at Clarens), to general beneficence directed towards humanity represented in any human individuals whom he may encounter. At the same time, his inner self becomes more accessible to the reader in writing.

While beneficence and pudicity are mutually supportive as two social codes which, according to Rousseau, promote the right functioning of social existence, and while the breakdown of pudicity usually involves some kind of tyranny which is the antithesis of beneficence, the expansive and public force of beneficence is opposite in nature to the reservedness of pudicity. The public beneficence of Lucretia would be impossible while she adheres to the code of pudicity. Just as a pudic woman cannot be a (public) benefactor, so she cannot be a beneficiary in so far as this involves contact with others, outside the family home. Crudely, beneficence brings people together, pudicity keeps people apart. Women are vulnerable as guests (*Le Lévite d'Ephraïm*) or hosts (*La Mort de Lucrèce*). And where social codes combine, as in the case of Saint-Preux's role in the resolution of *Les Amours d'Edouard*, a certain price has to be paid. This price may be the very prize (legitimate fecundity) which should have rewarded the strict maintenance of the social codes. There remains, it should be said, the satisfaction of virtue.

 The minor works present extreme situations which intensify latent hierarchies and suppressed strains or tensions. The example of these writings allows a rereading of the major works in which a precarious status quo is maintained. The conceptual underpinning of *La Nouvelle Héloïse* thus becomes clearer. Rousseau attempts to unite beneficence and the maintenance of pudicity by the agency of Wolmar. This is feasible so long as beneficence is restricted to the practical 'household' level (directed at those who are clearly inferiors), but as beneficence becomes superabundant generosity (Wolmar invites his wife's former lover into his house), so pudicity becomes correspondingly extreme culminating in Julie's death, a final retreat behind a veil.[39] The woman is sacrificed, or sacrifices herself, to preserve a (just) social order. This is a theme which recurs in these works: Emile, for example, leaves Sophie behind rather than endanger social order by appearing to condone impudicity.

It is particularly the role of the father to sacrifice his daughter.

The hierarchy of masculine and feminine is deemed to lie first and foremost in that relationship of father to daughter, but this is transposed on to husband and wife, if only in a vestigial sense. The hierarchy of beneficence also borrows the image of parent to child, chiefly in order to suffuse the term 'father' with the connotations of 'benefactor', something which reinforces the stability of the family. However, the father-tyrant (against whom Rousseau writes *Du contrat social*) lurks behind the structure of masculine virtue, as daughter-slave is implicit in the code of pudicity.

Les Solitaires, the latest of the four works discussed, would, it is suggested, have involved a daydream-like other place, a distant exotic island where social existence would take a form prior to the establishment of conventions, where, for example, a man might have two wives. However, the end of *Les Solitaires* is in its beginning: the solitary Emile writing. Social illegitimacy leaves the virtuous man the possibility of the negative virtue which closes the *6ᵉ Promenade*, a withdrawal into a kind of voluntary masculine pudicity, different from the feminine kind because supplemented by written daydreams.

Conclusion

This book begins with a consideration of what Rousseau presents as the best possible relationship between non-equals, something which is the epitome of social virtue, that is to say beneficence. Rousseau's treatment of the relationship between benefactor and beneficiary is characteristic of the main thrust of his work. He attempts to specify conditions which promote moral freedom. A paramount condition is potential equality, an equality which may be achieved through the moral growth of the weaker party. He takes from his predecessors those elements which support this, and so his treatment of beneficence has much in common with (and indeed goes beyond) Seneca's enlightened treatise, *de Beneficiis*. He opposes aristocratic, hierarchical formulations such as those to be found in Aristotle. He protests fiercely against both literal and analogical situations of servitude. A study of beneficence alone would confirm that Rousseau's position is one of protest against the constant exercise of power.

However, the analysis of the relation of benefactor to beneficiary in certain of Rousseau's writings stumbles unexpectedly upon the relation of men to women. This is represented as a relation between non-equals which is constant and static. Whereas the beneficiary must be able in some way to grow to resemble the benefactor in order for the relationship to have a tendency towards equality, the relation between men and women does not have this dynamic element. The code of

Women anomalous a/in code of b/pe [handwritten annotation]

pudicity holds women back, preventing them from being like, or close to, men.

Although in a literal sense the position of women advocated by Rousseau is not that of a slave, there is a resemblance between the two, in that the exercise of power by men over women is both constant and, to some extent, arbitrary. It is not supported by Rousseau's description of the state of nature in the *Discours sur l'inégalité*. Whereas, in the case of beneficence, Rousseau selects the most egalitarian and just elements of his classical precursors, in the case of the relation between men and women, he reproaches Plato for his attempt to make men and women resemble one another. His model is similar to that of Plutarch who, like Rousseau, warns against the enslavement of the wife by the husband yet prescribes an affectionate subordination, restriction and confinement of the wife which makes her situation in some respects slave-like.

Rousseau explains his anomalous treatment of women on the grounds of necessity; he insists that social existence is impossible without a code of pudicity. According to Rousseau, amorous passion should lead to the creation of new life, but unexpectedly, if it is unchecked it brings death. It leads to death for a society by enabling women to seize power, an act which will eventually lead to an erosion of sexual difference and leave men impotent. In other words, successful sexual relations, those which lead to the birth of a new generation, require a strict maintaining of sexual difference along the lines laid down by the code of pudicity. In the case of beneficence, Rousseau suggests that there is an alternative to the two extremes of identity or absolute irrevocable difference. But there is no such third alternative in his major statements on the relations between men and women.

The mark of successful living in society is, for Rousseau, being a parent. In *Du contrat social* (pp. 419–20), he suggests that the success of any society may be calculated by its population growth:

Quelle est la fin de l'association politique? C'est la conservation et la prospérité de ses membres. Et quel est le signe le plus sûr qu'ils se conservent et prospèrent? C'est leur nombre et leur population…

Calculateurs c'est maintenant votre affaire; comptez, mesurez, comparez.

Rousseau's footnote to this passage reinforces the point that the virtue and the morals of a people are signalled by their multiplying. This rule of thumb might not always be applicable to the individual, but the refusal to be a parent or the abandoning of children would suggest that something is wrong.

Rousseau's argument requires that social codes work together, that beneficence and pudicity function in harmony: the one to promote social cohesion, the other to preserve the life of the society. Certain major strands of his writing encourage this supposition. Rousseau's autobiographical works narrate, by his own judgement, a gradual decline. He ends, he tells us, *alone*, outcast from the society of men, lacking all freedom or occasion to be virtuous, possessing only his inner moral liberty and negative virtue. These are considerable achievements under the circumstances, but far from the happy, free and virtuous life within a community which he would wish for anyone. The final proof of his failure would be, applying the calculation of *Du contrat social*, his abdication as a father, the fault which torments him, yet which he could excuse in terms of his position (or lack of one) within society.

The *Confessions* calls upon a certain figure of a benefactor (or benefactors) who would have given the young Jean-Jacques moral guidance at his most impressionable age. Instead of that, he is formed by fictions (the books he reads) and by false benefactors. The right benefactor would have enabled Rousseau, the man, to be a benefactor (and a father) in his turn as Emile would be, rather than a benefactor-writer who fathers books. Rousseau's earlier works (*La Nouvelle Héloïse*, *Du contrat social* and *Emile*) attempt to outline model benefactors, who make their beneficiaries into men who are successful at virtuous living within society. These benefactors could, it is presumed, have altered the story told in Rousseau's autobiographical works.

It might then be thought that Rousseau presents as legitimate a happy co-existence of, on the one hand, justice and freedom in relations between men, and, on the other hand, an inflexible hierarchy of men and women. Yet this is not quite the case. The works of Rousseau studied in Chapters 5 and 6 suggest certain problems in the co-existence of the codes of beneficence and pudicity. To understand why this might be so, it is necessary to look closely at Rousseau's conceptual underpinning of the codes in his analysis of human nature in the *Discours sur l'inégalité* and *Emile*. Pudicity is based on reservedness, beneficence upon imaginative expansion. Pudicity involves retention, whereas beneficence involves giving. The latter requires a penetrating observation of its object, the former veils the object from the gaze.

In the writings examined in Chapters 5 and 6 it emerges that the conceptual opposition between beneficence and pudicity may lead them into conflict so that beneficence transgresses pudicity, or pudicity stifles beneficence. Alternatively, they may unite repressively, whereby the benefactor takes on the despotic characteristics of the father, and pudicity stifles sexual union and reproduction altogether. In that case the price to be paid is the prize that was to be won: beneficence no longer tends towards the equality and reciprocity which promote social cohesion, and pudicity no longer preserves the life of the society.

Rousseau's early work, *La Mort de Lucrèce*, points to a different path, a path which is only residually present in his later works because it is blocked by the imposition of pudicity. That alternative is the one of womanly beneficence. *La Mort de Lucrèce* is unfinished and tails off into fragments; it presents only the possibility of a female benefactor who would arise as a result of the extreme of male tyranny and out of transgression of pudicity.

The classical code presents a model of masculine virtue, which Rousseau follows in his male benefactors, Wolmar, the legislator and the tutor. Yet these men are so much like gods that they are effaced as men, as living presences. They become conditions of enabling or the answer to the beneficiary's needs. They bear the mark of the abstraction of the figure of the benefactor which occurs in the general prescriptions of a classical treatise. The extreme example of this divine abstraction or effacement occurs in the *6ᵉ Promenade*, where Rousseau suggests that in order to be a successful benefactor he must be an invisible god. This daydream of an impossible, magical kind is at the greatest possible distance from real presence. Inevitably, humanity re-emerges, and so characteristically Rousseau deviates from his path. In so doing he reveals a new repressive potential in beneficence, that of excessive generosity transgressing feminine pudicity, of looking at what should be hidden, or offering to another the sight or even the touching of what should, he claims, be hidden.

Traces of the potential for a female benefactor in Rousseau's work lie, for example, in his use of the maternal metaphor, although not in his recommendations for real mothers. Mother Nature – one way of referring to God – is a public benefactor; Rousseau often refers to 'la bienfaisante nature' (for example, in the *Discours sur l'inégalité*, p. 202), or speaks of life itself as 'un bienfait de la nature' (*Du contrat social*, p. 376). God the Father may be represented as an awesome, terrifying divinity who condemns to eternal damnation. He has to be recuperated by the connotations of the term 'beneficent'. Mother Nature, on the other hand, is characteristically benign.

The analysis of women in Rousseau's writing presents them as more human than men, more perfected (and, therefore, more degenerate) and thus with more scope to be virtuous. Where a man is so divinely good that he requires little effort to do good, he is not truly virtuous, for virtue implies struggle. Furthermore, where women are oppressed (and so resort to slavish wiles) Rousseau frequently identifies with them, as he tends to identify with the powerless in general. Yet the possibility of women becoming less weak is rarely characterised as a potential for equality; instead it is represented as a potential for domination.

The only completed model of feminine beneficence in Rousseau's writing is Julie. She is restricted in her scope by her adherence to the code of pudicity. Her sphere is domestic, and her death, which preserves her virtue, is a private one. That achievement may be compared to Rousseau's achievement of negative virtue. Under the circumstances imposed, it is outstanding. In the case of Rousseau, however, it is made explicit that the conditions of his life are pernicious, whilst he applauds Julie's narrowness of sphere.

Les Amours d'Edouard elucidate the repressive side of the union of beneficence and pudicity in *La Nouvelle Héloïse*. Saint-Preux's beneficence towards Edouard consists in inspiring Laure to retreat behind a pudic veil; it is thus the antithesis of the Gyges story. Doubts about this solution are expressed by Julie, whose pity always threatens to overcome her pudicity until the moment of her death, but her voice is not heeded. Of three men who finally come to live at Clarens, only one is a father; this failure to multiply condemns their little society according to the guideline of *Du contrat social*. It also suggests that absolute adherence to both moral codes under one roof is far from life-giving.

Both *Le Lévite d'Ephraïm* and *Les Solitaires* reaffirm descriptively the breakdown in social relations attendant upon a breakdown of pudicity. In *Le Lévite d'Ephraïm* the assault on virtue is the most extreme to be found in any of Rousseau's works, and the consequences are correspondingly atrocious. A solution which permits a return to social existence is, however, found in paternal authority and daughterly sacrifice, reviving the problem of women treated as objects to be given by men. *Les Solitaires* presents a less extreme case, but, nevertheless, Sophie's fall marks the end of Emile's beneficence other than towards society in general. The only solution to the crisis is a return to something which approaches in its solitude the state of nature.

Le Lévite d'Ephraïm also represents the violent side of writing; *Les Solitaires* suggests the role of writing as supplement to a solitary existence, and as substitute for particular and active beneficence. While it is Rousseau's writing-beneficence which survives to tell the tale, and to benefit future generations, that very writing will not permit the reader to view writing as an unmitigated benefit, nor as something which accords well with the dictates of pudicity.

The insoluble problem on which the issue turns is that of the vulnerability of justice in relations between non-equals. Society has been predicated upon differences as oppositions, which always involve a hierarchy. The hierarchy of benefactor and beneficiary must tend towards reciprocity. The masculine–feminine difference, which, Rousseau claims, safeguards the survival of a society, cannot, he says, involve a tendency towards identity of roles, nor an oscillation of roles on the part of men and women. Rousseau suggests a balance of power predicated upon difference, yet that fixed and absolute difference cannot escape a hierarchy. Pudicity, the code which enforces that difference, touches upon all aspects of social life. The importance of that ineffaceable inequality is paramount, and helps to explain the precariousness of all attempts to sustain justice within society.

The reader can feel grateful to Rousseau that the hierarchy of writer (benefactor) and reader (beneficiary) still allows the reader a chance for moral growth by not presenting a total solution to the problems of social existence.

TOWARDS A RECONSTRUCTIVE READING

In the *6ᵉ Promenade*, meaning can be unfolded from obscure places (reminding us of the cavern in which Gyges found his ring) in Rousseau's would-be transparent prose. Meanings available to the reader depend on her socio-historical context, which closes off some possible interpretations, renders others obsolete, and makes some of particular strategic interest. Looking beyond the golden guardrail of scholarly research, some earlier political readings of Rousseau adopted the strategy of discovering 'totalitarian', inegalitarian, mysogynistic, or simply inconsistent elements in his writing, in order to castigate or discredit this 'Great Man' and 'Founding Father' who preceded us. The difference between dynamic inequality (potential equality) between men, and the imposition of a static difference between men and women, which I have emphasised in this book, could be treated as simply more grist to this mill. Another reading of Rousseau associates his ideas with those guiding the revolutionary class of the eighteenth century. From there it can be argued that his views on women are coextensive with those which were eagerly adopted by the rising bourgeoisie, who celebrated motherhood and the home in a way which marked them out from the degenerate aristocracy. A reading with that emphasis alone has to explain away the essential anti-capital (indeed anti-market) strands in his philosophy. It is not only women who are to withdraw from the labour-market and from any mediated exchange, according to Rousseau. It seems to me, in any case, that that kind of historical reading, while locating a writer in his/her own time, is incomplete if it does not go on to consider the position of today's reader, and the utility which can be produced from the text here and now.

An alternative reading which I should like to propose is one which draws upon the full force of metaphor and fictionality in Rousseau's work, and which draws upon the lessons of the violent, excited 'marginal' works as well as the main corpus from which they overspill. The reading produced today can be one which continues to draw the gift of sustenance from the donor text. For example, Rousseau's *Emile* is a treatise on human happiness four books long. The fifth book 'Sophie', which is self-avowedly a fiction rather than a philosophical treatise, places a restriction on human happiness. It does this, I would suggest, with a figure: the suggestion that the first four books apply to only half of mankind, named 'men', and that another half, completing the first, named 'woman', is created both to suffer and to please.

There have been many (if not plenty of) referential readings of Rousseau's writing, which conclude at the attribution of real biological referents to Rousseau's 'Emile' and 'Sophie' – showing that he intended men to be like Emile and women to be like Sophie. There have been many recuperative readings which return to attributing humanity to Emile, and forget about the embarrassing (frivolous and constrained) Sophie – perceived as an unfortunate eighteenth-century aberration. I should like to suggest a third alternative, a figural reading which sees Rousseau's representation of women via pudicity and, in the marginal and autobiographical texts, transgressions of it, as adding humanity to the otherwise too divine model men (Emile/his tutor, Wolmar, the legislator). The Rousseauian benefactor, drawing from the classical treatises on beneficence, is strong in his virtue employing reasoned justice as well as pity.

Rousseau's women, particularly at the margins of his writing, constitute a device whereby the pole of suffering, darkness and death is not altogether abolished from the picture of transparency, immediacy and light. The pole of suffering, weakness, obscurity and death is one with which he clearly identifies at many points in his autobiographical writings – and sometimes this identification is explicitly figured as a feminine one. The classical (Roman, Spartan) thrust of his work is to repress weakness, but it always returns. The persistent return of weakness, albeit projected onto women, is, I would suggest, a strength in his work. A useful reader's task is to weld the two halves together; the political significance of Rousseau's gendered representation need not be lost, but the chance to adopt both crucial elements for one ungendered humanity should be gratefully accepted as a benefit.

APPENDIX

Generosity and pudicity in Gyges und sein Ring *and* Le Roi Candaule

The relationships and oppositions which are so important in Rousseau's treatment of generosity and pudicity can be further elaborated with the help of some much more recent accounts of the myth of Gyges. Both Friedrich Hebbel and André Gide expanded the story of Gyges into a play, and these plays provide a useful imaginative commentary on the implications and assumptions of the classical source texts.[1] Both plays, inspired by the myth, make a statement about generosity. Gide makes it explicit in a quotation from Nietzsche, in a footnote to his preface to *Le Roi Candaule*: '"Généreux jusqu'au vice," écrit Nietzsche; et ailleurs: " C'est une chose curieuse à constater que l'excessive générosité ne va pas sans la perte de la pudeur." La pudeur est une réserve.'[2] Gide also claims to have made a rare encounter with the spirit of emotional generosity which his Candaules displays in the works of Rousseau:

Je relève cette phrase des *Confessions*: 'Enfin, de quelque violente passion que j'aie brûlé pour elle, je trouvais aussi doux d'être le confident que l'objet de ses amours, et je n'ai jamais un moment regardé son amant comme mon rival, mais toujours comme mon ami. On dira que ce n'était pas encore là de l'amour: soit, mais c'était donc plus.' (Il s'agit ici de Mme d'Houdetot et de Saint-Lambert; il eût pu s'agir de Mme de Warens et de Claude Anet.) ... L'expression de ce sentiment (qui est aussi celui de mon *Candaule*) – que je n'ai recontré *que là* – est de la plus haute importance. (*Journal* 2/12/05)[3]

Both Hebbel and Gide insert the device of the ring into Herodotus' story. Both also portray Candaules as having the character of a benefactor, desirous of enriching Gyges first materially, and then by showing him the queen. Again, in both,

197

Candaules and Gyges share the ring of invisibility (an important development, as it seems that Rousseau's daydream must concern both men), as well as the queen. These texts will be considered in this appendix only in so far as they cast light on the implications of the classical sources from the point of view of Rousseau's writing, and not in their own right as works of literature.

In all versions of the story, the queen represents pudic woman; so far this representation has not suffered the literary fate of, for example, that of Lucretia, of whom it has come to be said that she desired the transgression which she suffered. It is a constant that the queen is veiled, that she is the forbidden object of the gaze. In the *6ᵉ Promenade* woman is not even named; there is a textual veiling even when Rousseau's daydream features an imaginary peek behind the veil. While the queen is still unseen she conforms to the position of the chief of her husband's possessions. Gautier suggests this in a way which is later echoed in Gide's preface to *Le Roi Candaule*. Gautier classifies Candaules as an aesthete and art-lover who 'avait en quelque sorte, honte d'accaparer un si riche trésor pour lui seul, de faire au monde le vol de cette merveille, et d'être le dragon écaillé et griffu qui gardait le type vivant de l'idéal des amoureux, des sculpteurs et des poètes' (p. 34).[4] Candaules feels guilty about keeping the queen from the world not because she herself (as subject) might make a different choice, but because he feels selfish with regard to other men who would enjoy the sight of her (as object). Gide explains in the preface to his play that part of his motive in writing *Le Roi Candaule* was to warn of the dangers of 'communism', provoked by a suggestion made by a contemporary that the rich and powerful should educate the populace by organising exhibitions of their beautiful possessions. Gide claims that the next question to ask is: if the people are allowed to *see*, may they *touch*? Supposing a man's most beautiful possession is his wife, should she be hidden as a miser hoards his gold, or put on public display for the benefit of the spectators? If the latter, then will they be content only to look?

GYGES UND SEIN RING (1854)

In Hebbel's play, Kandaules is, from the outset, a benefactor to Gyges, and the two are the closest of friends. Kandaules is a benefactor to Gyges in the highest sense, even allowing him to repay him as far as he can. In a lyrical exchange just before Kandaules' death, Gyges realises and recognises the nobility of the king's generosity:

GYGES   You could have saved yourself from that tiger which was ready to pounce on you. I, with my superfluous arrow, instead of saving you from death robbed you of the best shot of the day.

KANDAULES   That is true, I had indeed noticed him and was prepared, but when I saw how your eyes shone, your cheeks burned and your chest heaved, then I suppressed a quiet smile and thanked you.

GYGES   He was always so noble, even then when I had no idea!

GYGES   Du hattest dich des Tigers
Wohl selbst erwehrt, der auf dich lauerte,
Und ich, mit meinem überflüssgen Pfeil,
Beraubte, statt vom Tode dich zu retten,
Dich nur des Meisterschusses.

KANDAULES   Das ist wahr,
Ich hatt ihn wohl bemerkt und war bereit
Doch, als ich sah, wie dir die Augen blitzten,
Die Wangen glühten, und die Brust sich hob,
Da unterdrückte ich ein stilles Lächeln
Und dankte dir.

GYGES   So edel war er stets!
Auch da, wo ich nichts ahnte![5]

Kandaules allows Gyges to believe that he is his beneficiary, that he owes him his life. The apparent benefactor is in fact obliged to his beneficiary; this could be seen as an enactment of Rousseau's remark to Mme d'Houdetot, 'entre deux amis, celui qui donne est sans contredit fort obligé à celui qui reçoit'. Kandaules recognises that it is Gyges' intention which counts.

I also saw straightaway that in a situation of even greater danger, you would act again even more bravely; if the situation never arose, that was not your fault. (Act v)

> Ich sah es auf den ersten Blick ja auch.
> Dass du in einer grösseren Gefahr
> Die Tat noch kühner wiederholen würdest;
> Wenn die nicht kam, so war's nicht deine Schuld!

From the beginning, Gyges' ring signifies, or is a means of promoting, the emotional generosity between the two friends. Gyges offers it as a gift to Kandaules in Act I, scene i, with these delicate words expressing how, before he has recognised its great value, Kandaules will still accept it gratefully because of the spirit which prompted it.

Take it! It is a princely ring! You are looking at it and see nothing special about it. You are amazed that I dare to offer it to you. You will take it as a flower from a child just because you do not want to hurt the poor innocent spirit who plucked it for you, not because you like the thing itself.

> Nimm! Es ist ein Königsring!
> Du siehst ihn an, du findest nichts an ihm,
> Du staunst, dass ich ihn dir zu bieten wage,
> Du wirst ihn nehmen, wie vom Kind die Blume,
> Nur um die arme Einfalt nicht zu kränken,
> Die dir sie brach, nicht, weil sie dir gefällt.

The queen, Rhodope,[6] says to the king when he tells her that the ring is a gift from Gyges: 'Da wird er dir unschätzbar sein!' (Then it will be beyond price for you.)

The two men, although there is much to separate them (for example, Gyges is a Greek and Kandaules a 'barbarian') become almost as one through the strength of their affection for each other. The positions of benefactor and beneficiary become merged to some extent; it is not clear whose generosity is the force which permits Gyges to see the queen: Kandaules shares his marital rights, but Gyges acepts the honour in order to make Kandaules happy. When Gyges finally has to kill Kandaules in a fight, he feels as if it is he who has died.

> It is as if I myself had lost the blood which flowed from him!
> I am as cold as death. (Act v)
> Mir ist, als hätt ich selbst das Blut verloren,
> Das ihm entströmte! – Ich bin totenkalt.

Kandaules is represented as a man who wants to break down barriers, as a force for change, a man ahead of his time. He is eager to break with ancient customs and conventions; he wishes to be respected as king for himself, and not because of the traditional trappings of his office. Gyges' ring will, he thinks, help him to erode the barriers of privacy and pudicity on which his wife, Rhodope, insists.

Rhodope clings to conventional codified behaviour. In accordance with custom, she intends never to be seen unveiled by any man other than her husband. The husband is less a chosen individual than the occupant of a legal position, and so Rhodope repairs her modesty by going through a wedding ceremony with Gyges because he has seen her uncovered. She is immediately suspicious of the ring and of the uses to which it could be put; she rebukes the king for his unseemly behaviour with it even before his invitation to Gyges to look at her. She claims that it is terrifying for any good person, and that it should be thrown into the deepest river. The king refuses to give it to her unless she will show her face in public – which she will not do. Thus the ring is associated from Act I with opposition to privacy and pudicity. Before the breaching of Rhodope's pudicity her status is similar to that of a valuable object; Hebbel expressed in a number of letters relating to *Gyges und sein Ring* the view that Rhodope, like Helen of Troy, is treated like a piece of furniture or a precious jewel.[7] In a letter to Arnold Schloenbach he goes on to remark: Herodotus' story, which served as my material, shows that this object, even among the barbaric Lydians, was transformed into a person. 'Dass diese Sache siche aber doch selbst unter den barbarischen Lydiern zuweilen in eine Person verwandelte, zeigt die Fabel des Herodot, die mir als Stoff diente' (3 June 1856, *Werke*, II, pp. 698–9). Rhodope becomes a person, in fact a force for destruction, when her existence as a possession of one individual, as a slave of one master, is threatened. At that point she puts aside her veil, throws open the doors to her apartment and acts.

Once Gyges has seen Rhodope and therefore fallen in love with her, the relationship of beneficence between himself and Kandaules is disrupted on a material level although not on an emotional one. Gyges refuses Kandaules' gifts in Act II in these terms:

Forgive me for my disobedience! All your gifts have suddenly become an encumbrance, and if the beautiful slave-girl were added to the gold and jewels, then I would use her slim white neck to hang the treasure on. I no longer need anything apart from my sword, but if you want to show yourself gracious towards me, send me the heads of your enemies, I will collect those to the last man.

> Verzeih mir, wenn ich nicht gehorchen kann!
> Das alles ward auf einmal mir zur Last,
> Und da sich jetzt zu Gold und Edelstein
> Die schöne Sklavin noch hinzu gesellte,
> So nutzt ich ihren schlanken, weissen Nacken
> Und hing die Kostbarkeiten daran auf.
> Ich kann nichts weiter brauchen, als mein Schwert,
> Doch, wenn du dich mir gnädig zeigen willst,
> So schenke mir die Köpfe deiner Feinde,
> Ich sammle sie bis auf den letzten ein.

Gyges generously allows Kandaules to keep the ring of invisibility, and he returns Rhodope's diamond to him, which he had secretly taken from her; this means that Kandaules should be able to hide the night's activities from his suspicious wife. Gyges' own selfish desire would be to reveal himself to Rhodope; he also wants to sacrifice himself for Kandaules, but Kandaules refuses his sacrifice.

LE ROI CANDAULE (1900)

Gide makes it explicit that he is dealing with attitudes towards property in this play. The fact that the most valuable piece of property which a man owns is, in this case, his wife, makes the question more complex since a wife is animate and can act as an autonomous being even when her husband assumes that she is an object. Both Gygès and Candaule regard their wives as pieces of property, but their attitudes towards property are quite different.

Candaule is a man of great generosity. In the prologue
Gygès says of him nostalgically: 'C'était une donnante nature.'
In the first scene of Act I, the courtier Syphax says:

> Je commence à croire en effet
> Que, si le roi nous retient ici dans les fêtes
> Et nous comble de ses bienfaits
> Ce n'est par politique ni par sottise,
> Mais, comme tu me la disais,
> Par une sorte de générosité indécise.

Candaule's generosity is not codified beneficence; it is not
subordinate to justice. It is a 'générosité indécise' which is
lacking in direction until he meets Gygès whom he chooses as a
friend. Candaule's great desire is to have a friend with whom he
can share everything; this is not because he imagines that
friendship can be bought, for Phèdre states

> Malgré tous ses trésors, il sait encore le prix de l'amitié;
> Il sait qu'elle ne s'achète pas avec l'or.

Phèdre's testimony on this point is important, for Phèdre and
Simmias are perfect friends or Platonic lovers; they provide a
model which Candaule greatly admires. Candaule wishes to
hold everything in common with a friend so that there will be no
giving or taking, only sharing.

> Qu'importe que l'un donne et que l'autre reçoive,
> Où deux jouissent ensemble des mêmes biens.

It is suggested from the outset that Candaule regards his wife
as his best possession, and so might wish to share her in order to
seal his friendship. He says in public,

> ...je croirais voler à tous
> Le bien dont je reste seul à jouir

The queen, Nyssia, reminds him:

> Fi, Seigneur! Vous semblez oublier
> Que le bien dont on parle, c'est moi.

Her intervention reminds us that in fact she is not simply
another of his possessions but a human being with the potential
to rebel against tyranny.

Gygès, unlike the king, is a man who wants neither to give nor to receive. He tells the audience:

> Moi, Gygès le pauvre,
> Pour les mieux posséder je ne tiens que
> quatre choses sur la terre:
> Ma hutte, mon filet, ma femme et ma misère.

Gygès is fiercely independent and possessive, even refusing the king's hospitality for as long as possible. He believes:

> Il vaut mieux pour moi, n'avoir que peu
> Mais l'avoir seul.

His wife is characterised as 'plus facile' than he, a recipient and a giver of favours. She meets with a violent death at his hands, in front of the king and queen, when he discovers that he is not alone in possessing her. As he stabs her he utters the words: 'Elle est à moi. – Elle est à moi.'

When Gygès is persuaded to come and live at court, Candaule wants to shower gifts on him. At first Gygès is reluctant, he asks:

> Roi Candaule pourquoi tiens-tu tant
> A ce que je connaisse ta fortune?

Candaule does not want Gygès to know his wealth by reputation nor even by seeing it, but by participating in the enjoyment of it. The term 'connaître' slips towards the biblical sense; Candaule wants Gygès to know his wife to the point of possessing her sexually. The king convinces Gygès of his true affection through the magic ring which binds them together as friends. Gygès had, unbeknownst to him, sent the ring to Candaule in a fish. Candaule gives it back so that he can enter the royal bed-chamber unseen. Like their counterparts in Hebbel's drama they are friends to the last; although Nyssia persuades Gygès to kill Candaule, Gygès' last words to the king are 'Candaule! mon ami'.

Nyssia, although not as fierce in her pudicity as Hebbel's Rhodope, prefers to remain veiled and withdrawn from male society. She understands Gygès' murder of his wife and, unlike her husband, agrees with it:

> Il a bien fait de la tuer. –
> Appartenir à deux...oh! c'est horrible!

Nyssia throws off her status as property, to be hidden away or displayed at will, when she discovers that her husband does not want to enjoy sole ownership. She demands vengeance, using the love which she inspires in Gygès; she throws off the veil of pudicity which previously she wore with pride. However, her new husband, Gygès, is determined to reintroduce her code of pudicity by force if need be. The power struggle between men and women becomes overt violence at the end of the play.

Notes

INTRODUCTION

1 We are still concerned to know what kind of behaviour on the part of a benefactor (for instance someone who is doing a favour for a friend) is most likely to provoke resentment or disappointment in her or his beneficiary. The distinction between casual or general-ised beneficence and long-term specific beneficence remains an important and difficult one. Certainly the problem of state benefits, Third World aid, charity and so on could profit from study of the accumulated thinking on beneficence if only in order to emphasise the point that many so-called gifts or hand-outs would not match up to the standards of beneficence on account of the attitude of the donor or the strings attached.

2 This argument has been put forward by a number of neo-classical or new classical economists. One prominent example is Gary Becker's *The Economic Approach to Human Behaviour* (Chicago, 1976). He argues that all behaviour is maximisation, that markets (which tend towards equilibrium) allocate all scarce resources and that the preferences which dictate our objects are broadly universal. All scarce resources (including, for example, spouses) which appear not to have quotable market prices nevertheless have shadow prices and are allocated by (shadow) markets.

3 One example is the work of Pierre Bourdieu on pre-colonial feudal structures in Algeria; see, for instance *Algérie 60. Structures économiques et structures temporelles* (Paris, 1977). He argues against the ahistorical approach of many economists 'qui transfigure les exigences objectives d'*une* économie en préceptes universels de la morale, prévoyance, abstinence ou épargne hier, crédit, dépense et jouissance aujourd'hui' (p. 8). He claims that in pre-capitalist gift exchange, 'Le contre-don étant différé, chaque acte de don peut être saisi comme un commencement absolu et non point comme continuation imposée d'un échange déjà commencé' (p. 35).

4 Jean-François Lyotard, *Economie libidinale* (Paris, 1974). In this work Lyotard's analysis suggests that on the one hand apparently primitive societies as described by Marcel Mauss, for example, share the characteristics ascribed to capitalism, and on the other hand 'toute économie politique est libidinale' (p. 133), including capitalism.

1 THE PROBLEM: THE INTERSECTION OF BENEFICENCE AND PUDICITY

1 In recent years the most intensive analysis of binary oppositions has been carried out by Jacques Derrida. In 'Signature événement contexte' (in *Marges de la philosophie* (Paris, 1972), pp. 367–93), he writes: 'Très schématiquement: une opposition de concepts métaphysiques (par exemple, parole/écriture, présence/absence, etc.) n'est jamais le vis-à-vis de deux termes, mais une hiérarchie et l'ordre d'une subordination' (p. 392). In *On Deconstruction*, chapter 1, section II 'Reading as a Woman' Jonathan Culler elucidates how Derrida's work on oppositions is relevant to the opposition between the masculine and the feminine.

2 I should like to thank Felicity Baker for suggesting to me the importance of the code of beneficence in Rousseau's moral and political thinking, and also for directing me to relevant classical and other sources.

3 For example some Marxist theorists have identified Rousseau as a spokesperson for the rising (petty) bourgeoisie, others have perceived him as even more radical, in a recent work entitled *Rousseau, le luxe et l'idéologie nobiliaire* (Oxford, 1989), Renato Galliani enlists Rousseau in the conservative cause of the rural aristocracy Lester G. Crocker claims him as a fascist...

4 While it must not be assumed that there were no changes in the social and economic relations between the sexes in the long period between Socrates and Cicero, I shall not devote any time to the analysis of those changes since my focus is to be the Enlightenment reading of these texts rather than the conditions of production of the texts themselves. Rousseau's citation of classical history tends to be for rhetorical (didactic) purposes and to fall into two modes: either a period is presented as 'early' and virtuous compared to the present or as 'late' and decadent like the present. In the 'early' version relations between the sexes would be governed by the code of pudicity; in the 'late' version women would be condemned as impudic.

5 One of the earliest critiques is to be found in Mary Wollstonecraft's

A Vindication of the Rights of Woman (New York, 1975), pp. 72–92, which was first published in 1792. See, for a modern example, Eva Figes, *Patriarchal Attitudes*, London, 1970 or Susan M. Okin, *Women in Western Political Thought* (Princeton, 1979). Rousseau's attitude towards women is conservative compared to many of the *philosophes* as Jean Bloch has pointed out, for example in 'Women and the Reform of the Nation' in *Woman and Society in Eighteenth-Century France* (London, 1979).

6 Adam Smith, *The Wealth of Nations*, first published 1776 (Harmondsworth, 1970). In his introduction to this edition Andrew Skinner comments: 'the book sold well, not least because the general "philosophy" which it contained was so thoroughly in accord with the aspiration and circumstances of the age... Indeed, the arguments of *The Wealth of Nations* seemed to lend a certain sanctity to the self-interested pursuit of gain, by showing that such activity was productive of benefit to society at large' (p. 11). As Skinner points out, a closer reading of the text shows its argument to be less optimistic than this would suggest, but a long tradition has nevertheless associated the name of Adam Smith with such ideas.

7 See Derrida, *De la grammatologie* (Paris, 1967), for example:

> L'on peut suivre partout, dans l'œuvre de Rousseau, une théorie de *l'innéité* comme *virtualité* ou de la naturalité comme potentialité sommeillante. Théorie peu originale, certes, mais dont le rôle organisateur est ici indispensable. Elle commande de penser la nature non pas comme un donné, comme une présence actuelle, mais comme une *réserve*. (p. 263)

8 While that tradition has often been a misogynistic one, it has been reappropriated in various guises, for example, in Derrida's reading of Nietzsche (*Eperons* (Paris, 1978)) or in post-1968 French theorists associated with the group 'Psychanalyse et politique' or with accounts of *écriture féminine*, such as that given by Hélène Cixous in *La Jeune née* (Paris, 1975). Luce Irigaray writes of 'un "autre" commerce' between women:

> Où le plus de valeur serait, aussi bien, le moins de réserve. Où la nature se dépenserait, sans épuisement; s'échangerait, sans travail; se donnerait – à l'abri des transactions masculines – pour rien: plaisirs gratuits, bien-être sans peines, jouissances sans possessions. Ironie pour les calculs, les épargnes, les appropriations plus ou moins v(i)oleuses, les capitalisations laborieuses. (*Ce sexe qui n'en est pas un* (Paris, 1977), p. 193)

9 An interesting figure in this context is Saint-Preux. He is 'educated' to be a benefactor by Julie, Wolmar and Edouard. The end result appears to be a dangerous tension between passion and

(self-) mutilation. It is not surprising that he is the character who is seen as most closely resembling Rousseau. I shall return to Saint-Preux at greater length in the last chapter.

10 Raymond Trousson gives some examples from Rousseau's correspondence of love letters from readers in *Jean-Jacques Rousseau. Le deuil éclatant du bonheur* (Paris, 1989). Panckoucke writes to Rousseau after reading *La Nouvelle Héloïse*: 'Il fallait un dieu et un dieu puissant pour me tirer de ce précipice et vous êtes, Monsieur, le dieu qui venez d'opérer ce miracle. . . .J'adore votre personne et vos sublimes écrits' (cited by Trousson, p. 121). A more recent example which comes to mind is that of Annie Leclerc, *Origines*, Paris, 1988, who recounts at length (to Jean-Jacques, her ideal reader) how she fell in love with Rousseau. When she read *La Nouvelle Héloïse* 'je n'ai jamais tant aimé vivre qu'en ces instants-là. . . Instants où la jouissance tiendrait dans le tracé d'un livre' (p. 13). For an example of the hatred which Rousseau also inspires, one could cite Voltaire's *Sentiment des citoyens* in which the apostle of tolerance concludes: 'Il faut lui [Rousseau] apprendre que si on châtie légèrement un romancier impie, on punit capitalement un vil séditieux.' I shall cite just one twentieth-century case: Bertrand Russell in *The History of Western Philosophy* (London, second edition 1961), a work with an impeccably scholarly title, writes as follows about Rousseau: 'there is abundant external evidence that he was destitute of all the ordinary virtues' and 'At the present time, Hitler is an outcome of Rousseau; Roosevelt and Churchill of Locke' (p. 660). Both Voltaire and Russell attack not only the works, but the man ('un homme qui porte encore les marques funestes de ses débauches', writes Voltaire); likewise Rousseau's admirers regularly praise his qualities as a saintly individual as well as a writer.

11 Take the example of Seneca since it is particularly relevant to beneficence. In a footnote to *La Nouvelle Héloïse*, the editor (Rousseau) quotes these words of Seneca: 'si l'on me donnait la science à condition de ne la pas montrer je n'en voudrais point' (p. 57). Rousseau chides what he terms philosophical vanity; the Pléiade editors point out that Seneca makes this remark in the context of his praising the virtue of helping others through teaching: he is speaking in a generous and not a vainglorious spirit.

2 THE CODE OF BENEFICENCE

1 It could be compared to one of the codes which Roland Barthes identifies in *S/Z* (Paris, 1970), his *code gnostique* or his

code culturel (pp. 26–7). Elements of a moral code can be deduced from all kinds of different information in a text, directly from prescriptive statements or discourses, and indirectly from behaviour of characters which is clearly well or ill regarded, asides to the reader and so on. The term *code* is employed in this book to refer to a set of prescriptions which are not enforced by law but are upheld by social approval or disapproval and by the individuals' personal sense of satisfaction or dissatisfaction regarding their own conduct.

2 *Pour une critique de l'économie politique du signe* (Paris, 1972), p. 19.

3 All quotations from Aristotle will be from the *Ethics*, translated by J. A. K. Thomson (Harmondsworth, revised edition, 1976) unless otherwise stated. For information on Rousseau's reading, see Marguerite Richebourg, *Essai sur les lectures de Rousseau* (Geneva, 1934).

4 All quotations from Cicero will be from the edition translated by Walter Miller (London, 1975).

5 See my article 'Elements of the Classical Code of Beneficence Presupposed in Rousseau's Writing', *Studies on Voltaire and the Eighteenth Century*, 260 (1989), 279–303. This article overlaps in scope with this chapter and provides additional material not only on Seneca but also on other relevant intertexts. All quotations from Seneca are from the *Moral Essays*, translated by J. W. Basore (London, 1975).

6 Biblical teaching is assumed to be more familiar to the twentieth-century reader than that of, say, Seneca, and so I shall only allude to it in passing. For a discussion of the role of religious teaching in Rousseau's thinking, see P. M. Masson, *La Religion de Jean-Jacques Rousseau*, 3 vols. (Paris, 1916). Rousseau was exposed to numerous lengthy sermons during his boyhood in Geneva; he also read the Bible avidly through much of his life. Nevertheless, his moral thinking is largely based on a classical tradition.

7 Qu'est-ce que vertu? Bienfaisance envers le prochain. Puis-je appeler vertu autre chose que ce qui me fait du bien? Je suis indigent, tu es libéral; je suis en danger, tu me secours; on me trompe, tu me dis la vérité; on me néglige, tu me consoles; je suis ignorant, tu m'instruis: je t'appelerai sans difficulté vertueux. ('Vertu' in the *Dictionnaire philosophique*)

Voltaire's examples of beneficence are the classic ones and would be shared by the majority of writers on the subject including his erstwhile admirer turned detractor, Rousseau. The *Dictionnaire philosophique* was published in the same year as one of Voltaire's chief scurrilous and anonymous attacks on Rousseau.

8 To take the example of the society in which Plato and Aristotle

grew up: see, for instance, Sarah B. Pomeroy, *Goddesses, Whores, Wives, and Slaves: Women in Classical Antiquity* (New York, 1975), chapter 5, 'Private Life in Classical Athens':

> The separation of the sexes was spatially emphasized. While men spent most of their day in public areas such as the marketplace and the gymnasium, respectable woman remained at home. In contrast to the admired public buildings, mostly frequented by men, the residential quarters of Classical Athens were dark, squalid, and unsanitary. (p. 79) The separation of the sexes was expressed in private architecture by the provision of separate quarters for men and women. Women usually inhabited the more remote rooms, away from the street and from the public areas of the house. If the house had two stories, the wife along with female slaves lived upstairs. (p. 80)

In *The Human Condition*, Hannah Arendt argues that the ancient feeling was that privacy was privative, a state of being deprived of something (i.e. participation in the *polis*); Rousseau was, she claims, the first theoriser of intimacy, the first to accord value to privacy – not as withdrawal from the *polis*, but as withdrawal from the social.

9 Letter to Mme de Verdelin, *Correspondance complète*, XIII, p. 10, 4/9/1762. The retreat to Môtiers was not, of course, of Rousseau's choosing, but he had already decided to withdraw from 'the world'.

10 Thomas More's *Utopia* is another example known to Rousseau of a (hypothetical) state which would take over the provision of many services such as caring for the sick or even the provision of meals.

11 Sébastian-Roch Nicolas dit Chamfort, *Maximes et pensées*, CLX.

12 'But of all the bonds of fellowship, there is none more noble, none more powerful than when good men of congenial character are joined in intimate friendship' (Cicero, *de Officiis*, I, 17).

13 *Millenium Hall*, with an introduction by Jane Spencer, London, 1986, p. 41. I am grateful to Cath Sharrock for directing my attention to this work. Sarah Scott and her friend, Lady Barbara Montagu, themselves pooled their income and spent what they could afford on good works; Scott's sister reports in a letter that after early prayers Scott 'sits down to cut and prepare work for twelve poor girls, whose schooling they pay for; to those whom she finds more than ordinarily capable, she teaches writing and arithmetic herself. The work these children are usually employed in is making child-bed linen and clothes for poor people which Lady Bab Montagu and she bestow as they see occasion' (quoted in the introduction, p. viii). Importantly (in terms of Rousseau's scale of values) they do not only give money, but also time and

effort. The children are largely beneficiaries (as is Emile), but are acquiring skills which enable them to be benefactors.

14 Wind, *Pagan Mysteries in the Renaissance* (London, 1958), pp. 31–2.

15 Sarah Scott writes that

those who know all the pleasures of conferring an obligation will be sensible that by accepting it they give the highest delight the human mind can feel, when employed on human objects; and therefore while they receive a benefit, they will taste not only the comforts arising from it to themselves, but share the gratification of a benefactor, from reflecting on the joy they give to those who have conferred it; thus the receiver of a favour from a truly generous person, 'by owing owes not, and is at once indebted and discharged.' (*Millenium Hall*, p. 42)

16 One element of rational calculation is the benefactor's choice of beneficiary; according to Cicero he should first repay his benefactors, beginning with those to whom he owes most, for instance those who gave him well-considered gifts as opposed to those who gave on impulse.

17 Lewis Hyde, *The Gift* (New York, 1979).

18 This point has been made many times; for example Hélène Cixous, *La Jeune née* (Paris, 1975), pp. 114–19.

19 Rousseau maintains indeed that eros is not sustainable if merging has taken place. Furthermore, he insists that that specific eros which is erotic love between the sexes (amorous passion) requires greater dissimilarity, separation and firmer boundaries than beneficence does. That insistence ultimately challenges adherence to beneficence which relies on dynamic movement from one pole towards the other.

20 La Rochefoucauld, *Maximes et réflexions diverses*, edited by Jacques Truchet (Paris, second edition, 1972), no. 223.

21 See Sharon Kettering, 'Gift-giving and Patronage in Early Modern France', *French History*, 2, 1988, 131–51 for an account of the polite fiction of gift-giving in sixteenth- and seventeenth-century France.

22 Seneca does far more than provide general rules; he supplies a complex set of guidelines indicating that beneficience is far from spontaneous generosity. Changing circumstances must be taken into consideration – for example, if you have promised a benefit and then discovered that the intended recipient is unworthy or has a reputation for ingratitude (*de Beneficiis* IV, 34–9), what do you do? Seneca suggests that you keep your word if only as a reminder to yourself to be more discerning in future, unless this lesson would prove too costly and it would clearly be more prudent to retract. Seneca supports the possibility that you might go back on your word with a large number of examples and anecdotes covering all

kinds of eventualities. Another case for fine calculation is that of deciding when it is appropriate to remind a beneficiary of his obligation. Obviously if it is a matter of life and death then this may be done (*de Beneficiis*, v, 20), but it may also be a kindness, Seneca suggests, gently to remind a beneficiary of your needs if he is honourable but slow to repay – he will probably be pleased at the opportunity to show his gratitude (*de Beneficiis*, v, 22).

23 In 'Essai sur le don', in *Sociologie et anthropologie* (Paris, 1950), Marcel Mauss analyses the way in which many gift exchanges are motivated by the concern for honour; he writes of potlatch: 'L'on assiste avant tout à une lutte des nobles pour assurer entre eux une hiérarchie' (p. 153). This assumes that 'Donner c'est manifester sa supériorité, être plus, plus haut, *magister*; accepter sans rendre ou sans rendre plus, c'est se subordonner, devenir client et serviteur, devenir petit, choir plus bas (*minister*)' (pp. 269–70). Mauss links this phenomenon with ancient Roman law in which, he says, receiving a gift means being put under an obligation to the donor to the extent that the recipient is in a position of quasi-culpability, spiritual and moral inferiority. This legal situation must reflect a pre-existing conviction, such as that found in Aristotle's *Ethics*, of the superiority and power of the position of the donor.

24 Aristotle's theory persisted in spite of the fact that Hippocrates had already formulated a more accurate sexual biology – which may have influenced Plato's *Symposium* and *The Republic*, although the *Timaeus* is much closer to the views Aristotle expounds. See Anne Dickason, 'Anatomy and Destiny: The Role of Biology in Plato's View of Women' in *Women and Philosophy: Toward a Theory of Liberation*, edited by Carol Gould and Max Wartofsky (New York, 1976), pp. 45–53. Although medieval science finally refuted certain of Aristotle's particular claims, his general drift (masculine activity and feminine passivity) remains remarkably potent. It is interesting to note, for example, the way in which the first chapter of the first part of Simone de Beauvoir's magisterial feminist work *Le Deuxième Sexe* (1949) struggles to present the data of biology in a way which analyses hierarchical assumptions about activity and passivity rather than reproducing them. The weight of philosophical traditions, 'common-sense' perceptions, and language itself, is so heavy that Beauvoir may well be understood ultimately to reinforce notions of woman's enslavement to her thing-like body, as opposed to man's creative transcendence, in the acts of reproduction – as Toril Moi has pointed out.

25 *Allegories of Reading* (New Haven, 1979), p. 186. De Man points out that Rousseau's story has often been read as functioning according to a balanced economy of the harmonious exchange of properties

under the aegis of a totalising principle (the 'soul of the universe'), and yet Pygmalion's use of totalising rhetoric is by no means shown in an unambiguous light in the text.

26 See *De la grammatologie* (Paris, 1967). Derrida writes: 'Nous voyons donc se dessiner deux séries: 1. animalité, besoin, intérêt, geste, sensibilité, entendement, raison, etc. 2. humanité, passion, imagination, parole, liberté, perfectibilité, etc.' (p. 260).

27 'Economimésis' in *Mimésis des articulations*, Agacinski *et al.* (Paris, 1975), pp. 59–93.

28 An interesting link could be made to what Derrida writes of the feminine gift in 'Choreographies' in *The Ear of the Other*, ed. Christie McDonald, pp. 163–85; he stresses that it must not be an alibi for neglecting the patient and laborious struggles of feminism (p. 169).

29 Marivaux, *La Vie de Marianne* (Paris, 1933), p. 242.

30 Richardson, *Clarissa* (London, 1932).

31 In *The Sexual Politics of Jean-Jacques Rousseau* (Chicago, 1984), Joel Schwartz suggests that the connection between Rousseau's political philosophy and his theories of human sexuality is crucial.

32 See *The Politics*, translated by T. A. Sinclair (Harmondsworth, 1962).

33 *Les Vies des hommes illustres*, translated by Jacques Amyot (Paris, 1951).

3 THE PRACTICE OF BENEFICENCE AND MODEL BENEFACTORS IN THE MAJOR WORKS

1 Cf. for example, Pierre-Daniel Huet, *Traité de l'origine des romans* (Paris, 1670).

2 The true history which Rousseau sets out to tell is declared to be an inner history: 'j'ai dévoilé mon intérieur' (*Confessions*, p. 5), but it is told with precise reference to external events.

3 This chapter relates to the text of Rousseau's *Confessions* without, in general, raising the cognitive question of the degree of literal truth or falsity in Rousseau's version of any particular event. The *Confessions* are valuable in the context of this chapter in supplying the reader with Rousseau's beliefs concerning the events which formed him and his analysis of his motivations and emotions at certain crucial points. The notes in the Pléiade edition of the *Confessions* (edited by Bernard Gagnebin and Marcel Raymond) furnish historical details to corroborate or to modify Rousseau's account; clearly Rousseau's account is a personal one, and that, for example, of Mme d'Epinay, is quite different. As quite a large body of documentation has already been gathered and studied,

and it is extensively cited in the Pléiade notes, the present study has largely left such considerations aside in order to concentrate on the shaping of Rousseau's philosophy and fiction as that forming process is described by Rousseau himself. He appeals to an 'inner' rather than an external truth, and offers sincerity rather than accuracy, while not relinquishing accuracy by any means. The deliberate falsification of events (a theft of truth) to harm another would, of course, be maleficent; Rousseau discusses various kinds of lie in the *4ᵉ Promenade*, and the problems of verifiability or falsifiability haunt the *Dialogues*.

The insight that Rousseau employs social codes as tools for analysing relationships derives from the work of Felicity Baker on safekeeping (the *contrat de dépôt*).

4 The broken comb incident (*Confessions*, pp. 18–20) has been analysed by Jean Starobinski in *La Transparence et l'obstacle* (Paris, 1971), pp. 17–21. Starobinski comments: 'Ce souvenir a la valeur d'un archétype: c'est la rencontre de l'accusation injustifiée, Jean-Jacques paraît coupable sans l'être réellement. Il paraît mentir, alors qu'il est sincère. Ceux qui le châtient agissent injustement, mais parlent le langage de la justice.' The undeserved beating marks the loss of transparency for Jean-Jacques, and, from that moment onwards, transparency is not a given circumstance but something to be regained.

5 See Felicity Baker, 'Perverse Scenes of Writing', *Society for Critical Exchange*, 10 (1981), 57–71, for a reading of Book II which analyses, among other things, the question of Rousseau's assertions concerning salvation, and the undermining of these assertions by Jean-Jacques's progress from bad to worse in the narrative.

6 Some of the other examples are: the innkeeper who refuses Jean-Jacques's coat as guarantee of his unpaid bill (*Confessions*, pp. 146–7); Perrotet, another innkeeper (*Confessions*, p. 150); peasants who are afraid of the prohibitive taxation (*Confessions*, p. 163). In all these cases, Jean-Jacques's benefactors are of low social station.

7 For example, Rousseau writes: 'Je m'avisai pour ne pas vivre en sauvage d'apprendre à faire des lacets. Je portais mon coussin dans mes visites, ou j'allais comme les femmes travailler à ma porte et causer avec les passants' (p. 601). Jean-Jacques abandons breeches in favour of a long robe and happily spends much of his time with his 'voisines', in spite of his position that men and women should lead quite separate and different lives if both are to be happy and healthy.

8 Rousseau's friend Diderot often proffers advice or criticises Rousseau's decisions. He opposes Rousseau's stance of indepen-

dence, for example, when Rousseau decides not to attend an audience with the king which would have led to his being offered a pension. Rouseau comments on this occasion: 'Je perdais, il est vrai, la pension qui m'était offerte en quelque sorte; mais je m'exemptais aussi du joug qu'elle m'eût imposé. Adieu la vérité, la liberté, le courage. Comment oser désormais parler d'indépendance et de désintéressement?' (p. 380). Despite these reasoned objections to the pension, Diderot claims that Rousseau is failing in his duty to Thérèse and her mother. Diderot also opposes, on the same grounds, Rousseau's decision to live in the country. Rousseau declares himself 'excédé de son infatigable obstination à me contrarier éternellement sur mes goûts, mes penchants, ma manière de vivre, sur tout ce qui n'intéressait que moi seul; révolté de voir un homme plus jeune que moi vouloir à toute force me gouverner comme un enfant'. Rousseau rejects Diderot's attempt to act as moral adviser and would prefer him to carry out his role as a friend by visiting him more often, keeping appointments and so on.

9 In the *Confessions*, Rousseau cites a letter from Diderot which says: 'Le lettré a dû vous écrire qu'il y avait sur le rempart vingt pauvres qui mourraient de faim et de froid, et qui attendaient le liard que vous leur donniez.' Rousseau replies as follows:

Je crois avoir répondu au *lettré*, c'est à dire au fils d'un Fermier général que je ne plaignais pas les pauvres qu'il avait aperçus sur le rempart attendant mon liard qu'apparamment il les en avait amplement dédommagés; que je l'établissais mon substitut; que les pauvres de Paris n'auraient pas à se plaindre de cet échange; que je n'en trouverais pas aisément un aussi bon pour ceux de Montmorency qui en avaient beaucoup plus de besoin. (p. 459)

10 In the Pléiade edition of *La Nouvelle Héloïse*, Bernard Guyon points out (in a footnote to page 539) that Rousseau and Voltaire took up opposing positions on this as on so many matters. Voltaire wrote in 1738, concerning the beggars in Paris: 'C'est une vermine qui s'attache à la richesse' (*Observations sur MM. Jean Lass, Melon et Dutot*). Rousseau responds in an editorial footnote to *La Nouvelle Héloïse*: 'J'ai lu quelque part que les mendiants sont une vermine qui s'attache aux riches. Il est naturel que les enfants s'attachent aux pères; mais ces pères opulents et durs les méconnaissent, et laissent aux pauvres le soin de les nourrir' (p. 540).

11 Rousseau's stance of independence, even to the point of embracing poverty, is supported by his reading of Plutarch; see Jean-Emile Morel, 'Jean-Jacques Rousseau lit Plutarque', *Revue d'histoire moderne*, 1 (1926), 81–102.

12 See Judith Still, 'From Eliot's "Raw Bone" to Gyges' Ring: Two Studies in Intertextuality', *Paragraph*, 1 (1983), 44–59, for some remarks on modes of giving in the relations between author and reader.

13 Michel Foucault, Introduction to *Rousseau juge de Jean-Jacques Dialogues* (Paris, 1962), p. vii.

14 The term *bienfaisance* is invented (or revived) by the Abbé de Saint-Pierre; according to Voltaire:

> Certain législateur (l'abbé de St-Pierre)...
> Vient de créer un mot qui manque à Vaugelas,
> Ce mot est bienfaisance, il me plaît...

J. S. Spink gives a brief history of the word in his article 'From "Hippolyte est sensible" to "Le fatal présent du ciel"': The position of "bienfaisance"' in *The Classical Tradition in French Literature: Essays Presented to R. C. Knight*, edited by H. T. Barnwell *et al.* (London, 1977), pp. 198–9. He states that, although the term had been used before (as early as 1714), it was 'the Abbé de Saint-Pierre who launched it on its way, by giving a long description of this moral quality and its effects, and the public recognition of benefactions, in his *Projet pour mieux mettre en œuvre dans le gouvernement de l'Etat le désir de la distinction entre pareils*.' In that work, the Abbé writes:

> Ne point faire de mal, ne faire aucun tort à personne, rendre ce qu'on doit d'argent, de reconnaissance, de déférences, d'obéissance, voilà ce qu'on appelle *justice*, voilà le premier degré de la vertu; faire aux autres du bien qu'on ne leur doit point et surmonter pour cela des difficultés, n'attendre d'eux que de simples remerciements, c'est bonté, c'est générosité, c'est *bienfaisance*, et voilà le second degré vertu. (*Œuvres diverses* (Paris, 1730), p. 212)

It is against the background of such a definition, underlining the classical code of *beneficentia*, that Rousseau's account of the deliberate reversal of signification has its effect.

15 Words based on *bienfait* occur twenty-five times in the *Dialogues*, but only fifteen times in the *Confessions*, which are twice as long. Information on the occurrence of these terms comes from the Centre de Calcul at the University of Geneva.

16 The *Dialogues* contain some of the strongest statements concerning the moral power of Rousseau's works, for example:

> ayant lu plusieurs fois en entier les écrits que Jean-Jacques s'attribue, l'effet total qu'il en a résulté dans mon âme a toujours été de me rendre plus humain, plus juste, meilleur que je n'étais auparavant; jamais je ne me suis occupé de ces livres sans profit pour la vertu (p. 696)

ses livres me fortifièrent contre la dérision des esprits forts. Je vis que dans
ce siècle où la philosophie ne fait que détruire, cet auteur seul édifiait avec
solidité ... Le seul Jean-Jacques me parût chercher la vérité avec droiture
et simplicité de cœur. Lui seul me parût montrer aux hommes la route du
vrai bonheur en leur apprenant à distinguer la réalité de l'apparence
(*Dialogues*, p. 728)
[Jean-Jacques announces] Je vends le travail de mes mains, mais les
productions de mon âme ne sont à vendre; c'est leur désintéressement qui
peut seul leur donner de la force et de l'élévation. (p. 840)

17 Rousseau had long since claimed that his writing was an antidote
for a poisoned society; see Jean Starobinski, 'Le Remède dans le
mal', *Nouvelle revue de psychanalyse*, 18 (1978), 251–74. The closeness
of remedies and poisons makes the reversal of the one into the other
a particularly easy accusation. Writing itself is referred to as a
pharmakon in Plato's *Phaedrus*, and the question of whether it is a
poison or a remedy is debated; Jacques Derrida traces the
genealogy of that debate to Rousseau and beyond in *De la
grammatologie* (Paris, 1967). The reversal of any gift into poison is a
familiar one; see my 'From Eliot's "Raw Bone" to Gyges' Ring:
Two Studies in Intertextuality', *Paragraph*, 1 (1983), 44–59 for a
brief study of George Eliot's reception of Rousseau's gifts and her
wish to reciprocate with a vengeance.

18 See the *Confessions*, p. 9 for one example of the young Rousseau's
admiration for, and identification with, the heroes of Plutarch's
Lives.

Negative virtue means something quite different in Rousseau's
writing from the same term used by many other moral philosophers. There is a traditional division between negative virtues and
positive virtues; see André Lalande, *Vocabulaire technique et critique de
la philosophie* (Paris, 1960), pp. 113 and 138–9. This classes as
negative virtues all those duties which are essential, including
justice, and as positive virtues those acts which are supererogatory
like beneficence. This is similar to the division made by the Abbé
de Saint-Pierre between first degree and second degree virtue (see
note 14, above). By *negative virtue* Rousseau, however, means
inaction in a case where to act is to harm, that is to say, when *faire*
cannot be *bien faire*, but only *mal faire*. Negative virtue is virtue only
in a certain kind of situation, in which case it is the supreme (the
only) virtue. Thus it does not enter into a hierarchical relation
with any 'positive virtue' as it comes into play only when positive
virtue is out of the question.

19 There are, of course, many other *examples* of beneficence in these
works. The important case of Edouard will be discussed in Chapter
6.

20 *La Nouvelle Héloïse* is, of course, a love story; some readers have felt that Julie is first and foremost the heroine of the love story. Christopher Frayling, on the basis of study of manuscripts, has, however, claimed that the moral themes were not later super-imposed onto a romantic tale but were always an essential part of the novel. See Frayling, 'The composition of *La Nouvelle Héloïse*' in *Reappraisals of Rousseau* (Cambridge, 1980), pp. 181–214. Some earlier commentators have indeed always presented the work as a 'roman moral et philosophique'; see Daniel Mornet, Introduction to *La Nouvelle Héloïse* (Paris, 1925).

21 See Judith Still, 'Rousseau in *Daniel Deronda*', *Revue de littérature comparée* (1982), 62–77 for further discussion of the semantic incompatibility between *father* (blood bond) and *benefactor* (moral bond).

22 Jean Starobinski, *La Transparence et l'obstacle* (p. 138).

23 It is significant that Julie is the most devoutly religious character depicted by Rousseau. The title of the novel suggests a Christian source, Héloïse, for Julie; there is, of course, an important Christian tradition of female saints. However, Julie's role, and sphere of influence, is restricted to the hearth, to her family and household. Such a restriction has a source in Rousseau's image of the classical republic as much as in Christianity; it must not be forgotten that when Rousseau refers to Calvinist Geneva he cites Plutarch and gives Sparta as a model; see the *Lettre à d'Alembert*, pp. 181 and 183.

24 The code of feminine virtue is described in Chapter 4.

25 Rousseau is an anthropological optimist: he believes men are born free with the potential to be morally good; but he is an historical pessimist: he believes all societies have a tendency to degenerate, and once they have reached a certain point in their moral and political decline it is practically impossible for an individual who attempts to be virtuous to succeed in doing good. See Starobinski, Introduction to the *Discours sur l'inégalité*, p. LIX.

26 When Emile reaches puberty, the tutor must observe him all the more closely since it is at that point that his *positive education* begins:

C'est à cet âge aussi que commence, dans l'habile maître, la véritable fonction de l'observateur et du philosophe qui sait l'art de sonder les cœurs en travaillant à les former. Tandis que le jeune homme ne songe point encore à se contrefaire, et ne l'a point encore appris, à chaque object qu'on lui présente, on voit dans son air, dans ses yeux, dans son geste, l'impression qu'il en reçoit; on lit sur son visage tous les mouvements de son âme; à force de les épier on parvient à les prévoir, et enfin à les diriger. (*Emile*, p. 511)

27 Judith N. Shklar, *Men and Citizens* (Cambridge, 1969), writes: 'The reason Wolmar does not believe in God is that he *is* God to

all intents and purposes. Certainly he has all the attributes that Rousseau ascribed to God, self-sufficiency, justice, love of order. If he is not God, he certainly does God's work.' In the *6ᵉ Promenade* (analysed in Chapter 5), Rousseau imagines that he is like a god, invisible and all-powerful, as that would be the condition of his being a benefactor of perfect generosity.

Some readers of Rousseau have, however, found in the powerful roles played by Wolmar, Emile's tutor and the legislator something more sinister: the broad lines of modern totalitarianism. See, for example, Lester G. Crocker, *Jean-Jacques Rousseau: A New Interpretative Analysis of his Life and Works* (New York, 1968–73). In a review of that work (*The New York Review* (29 November 1973), 20–5, translated by Peter France), Starobinski shows the difficulties of sustaining that interpretation in the light of eighteenth-century intertexts and of careful analysis of the Rousseau text. He remarks, for example:

> If we look more closely we shall see that the hidden hand tactic is an expression of the aspiration to usurp the role of Providence which was fairly widespread among the *philosophes* of the eighteenth century. If Télémaque is still guided by a goddess in disguise and Zadig by an invisible angel, Emile is put into the hands of a superior man who foresees everything and makes everything happen according to his beneficent will. (p. 25)

The analogy with God is particularly useful since Rousseau's religion rests on the inner conviction of the individual rather than on any form of external authority. Likewise, the moral power of the benefactor is not ultimately an external force imposed on the beneficiary, but is something which stems from within.

28 It is interesting to compare Rousseau's distinction between the code of beneficence proper and the aristocratic code which attempted to appropriate it, with the account of (the aristocratic appropriation of) goodness given by Nietzsche in *On the Genealogy of Morals* (First Essay, 2). Nietzsche rejects the assumption that the concept 'good' originates in those to whom good is done, and who appreciate the benefit they receive from it. He writes: 'Rather it was "the good" themselves, that is to say, the noble, powerful, high-stationed and high-minded, who felt and established themselves and their actions as good, that is, of the first rank, in contradistinction to all the low, low-minded common and plebian' (translated by Walter Kaufmann and R. J. Hollingdale (New York, 1969), pp. 25–6). Nietzsche thus demonstrates the replacement of the utility of doing good with the lordly power of naming 'the good'.

29 *Emile et Sophie* will be analysed in Chapter 6.

30 In *De l'esprit des lois* Montesquieu argues that virtue in citizens was to be considered the outstanding characteristic of a democracy.

31 Rousseau's model of the legislator as outstanding benefactor owes something to examples of virtuous statesmen in Plutarch. Their virtue is said to lie in their readiness to sacrifice themselves, that is to say, to forget personal desires in the interest of the state; see 'Instructions pour ceux qui manient les affaires d'état' and 'Banquet des Sept Sages' in Plutarch's *Œuvres morales*, translated by Jacques Amyot. Rousseau's description of the legislator is, however, abstract rather than individual, and so has a greater affinity in character with the classical treatises on justice, benefi-cence and obligation discussed in Chapter 2 or with Plato's *Republic*.

4 THE PASSION OF PITY IN ROUSSEAU'S THEORY OF MAN

1 Rousseau claims in the *Confessions*: 'Je sentis avant de penser; c'est le sort commun de l'humanité' (p. 8). His emphasis on the passions and on the role of the senses has sometimes led commentators to assert that he abolishes reason. See Irving Babbitt, *Rousseau and Romanticism* (Boston, 1919) chapter 4, where he writes of Rous-seau's inversion of sense and sensibility; or Etienne Gilson, 'La Méthode de M. de Wolmar' in *Les Idées et les lettres* (Paris, 1932, second edition 1955), pp. 275–98, who refers to 'the resignation of reason' (p. 278). These assertions continue to convince some readers, for instance H. Gaston Hall, 'The Concept of Virtue in *La Nouvelle Héloïse*', *Yale French Studies*, 28 (1962), 20–33. This is in spite of the work on Rousseau which highlights the role which he allots to reason, see Robert Derathé, *Le Rationalisme de Jean-Jacques Rousseau* (Paris, 1948).

The functioning of social codes depends on the use of reason, yet the behaviour regulated by the code must be motivated by passion. Indeed, it is reason which analyses the importance of the passion, and emotion which confirms that reason is right.

2 The structure of supplementarity has been extensively treated by Jacques Derrida in *De la grammatologie* (Paris, 1967). Rousseau uses the noun *supplément* and its derivatives to describe a range of phenomena. Implicit (and sometimes explicit) in the use of the term is the suggestion that the thing which it designates is posterior, an additional after-thought, to some original whole, yet, at the same time, that the original whole is somehow lacking since it

requires a supplement. Derrida writes concerning the relation of law (which we can extend to social codes) to pity:

L'ordre de la pitié 'tient lieu de loi', il supplée la loi, entendons la loi instituée. Mais comme la loi d'institution est aussi le supplément de la loi naturelle lorsque celle-ci vient à manquer, on voit bien que seul le concept de supplément permet de penser ici le rapport entre la nature et la loi. (*De la grammatologie*, p. 247)

3 If this notion of appropriation by attachement is applied to beneficence (as the practice which is a manifestation of a positive emotion), then we have another formulation of the idea that the giver receives more than the receiver. The superiority of the position of the benefactor may be asserted following a number of different paths of argumentation.

4 *Amour de soi* makes us 'aimer ce que nous veut du bien' (*Emile*, IV, p. 583); it is thus the source of gratitude.

5 See Rousseau's note XV to the *Discours sur l'inégalité*; he describes the condition of natural man thus: 'Chaque homme en particulier se regardant lui-même comme le seul spectateur qui l'observe, comme le seul être dans l'univers qui prenne intérêt à lui, comme le seul juge de son propre mérite' (p. 219).

6 Jean Wahl applies the term *bipolarité* to Rousseau in his article, 'La Bipolarité de Rousseau' in the *Annales Jean-Jacques Rousseau*, 33 (1953–5), 49–55. Starobinski comments on Rousseau's alleged bipolarity: 'Elle ne consiste pas seulement en un passage du pour au contre, en une oscillation entre deux termes antithétiques: elle réside surtout dans le fait que Rousseau devant un même problème, recourt tour à tour à une rhétorique de l'antithèse, ou à une dialectique du dépassement' (*L'Œil vivant* (Paris, 1961), p. 165). The structure of *l'être-dans* is analysed by Jacques Derrida in *De la grammatologie* (p. 265). See also Paul de Man, *Allegories of Reading* (New Haven, 1979), especially the essay 'Self'. De Man writes:

The specular, reflective distance is postulated as already foremarked in the fictional state of nature where Rousseau is free to set up his scene as he pleases; as in all other instances, the differential relationships that will become the articulations and tensions of the historical world are already present 'en creux' and in the guise of equalities in the so-called state of nature. (p. 165)

7 Jacques Derrida, *De la grammatologie* (p. 262). My discussion of pity owes much to Derrida's analysis, see, for example, pp. 245–8 and pp. 258–72. Derrida's division of pity into animal and human stages is a response to Starobinski's suggestion, in the Pléiade footnotes to the *Discours sur l'inégalité*, that Rousseau's two accounts of pity correspond to two different stages in his thinking.

Starobinski suggests that the *Essai sur l'origine des langues* is a more mature formulation of Rousseau's theory of pity (*Œuvres complètes*, III, pp. 1330–1).

8 In the *Discours sur l'inégalité*, Rousseau describes the modern philosopher as indifferent to the suffering of his fellows; while pity brings men together, 'c'est la philosophie qui l'isole; c'est par elle qu'il dit en secret, à l'aspect d'un homme souffrant, péris si tu veux, je suis en sûreté' (p. 156).

9 The theory that the emotions most often provoked by (tragic) theatre are fear and pity dates back at least as far as Plato. In the *Republic* (Book x) Socrates suggests that dramatic poetry is morally, and hence politically, unsuitable because the more the author can move his audience the more he is admired, and yet giving way to grief is unmanly. He asserts: 'Few, I believe, are capable of reflecting that to enter into another's feelings must have an effect on our own: the emotions of pity our sympathy has strengthened will not be easy to restrain when we are suffering ourselves.' Rousseau's disapprobation of the effects of watching plays is based on the thesis that giving way to pity in the passive environment of the theatre dries up that emotion, rather than exciting it, in the long term. Rousseau is perhaps closer to Aristotle's influential theory that tragedy purges the spectator of fear and pity; see *On the Art of Poetry*, chapter 6, 'A Description of Tragedy'. However, for Aristotle, it seems, the theatre purged the spectator of *excessive* pity, restoring him to the healthy golden mean of pity. Aristotle's account of normal healthy pity, as seen in Chapter 1, is insufficient in Rousseau's framework – and so Aristotle's purged spectator is Rousseau's hardened one.

10 Jacques Derrida discusses amorous passion and its relationship with pity in *De la grammatologie* (Paris, 1967, pp. 2459–54). He writes, for example:

> Est-ce un hasard si la pitié protège l'homme (*homo*) de sa destruction par la fureur de l'amour, dans la mesure où elle protège l'homme (*vir*) de sa destruction par la fureur de la femme? Ce que veut dire l'inscription de Dieu, c'est que la pitié – qui lie l'enfant à la mère et la vie à la nature – doit nous garder de la passion amoureuse qui lie le devenir-homme de l'enfant (la 'seconde naissance') au devenir-femme de la mère. Ce devenir est la grande substitution. La pitié garde l'humanité de l'homme et la vie du vivant dans la mesure où elle sauve, nous allons le voir, la virilité de l'homme et la masculinité du mâle. (p. 249)

11 'Jamais l'animal ne saura ce que c'est que mourir, et la connaissance de la mort, et de ses terreurs, est une des premières acquisitions que l'homme ait faites, en s'éloignant de la condition animale' (*Discours sur l'inégalité*, p. 143). Derrida comments: 'Le

propre de l'homme s'annonce à partir de la double possibilité de la liberté et de l'anticipation expresse de la mort. La différence entre le désir humain et le besoin animal, entre le rapport à la femme et le rapport à la femelle, c'est la crainte de la mort' (*De la grammatologie*, p. 261).

12 Rousseau prided himself on his lack of jealousy, and created a hero (Saint-Preux) whose lack of jealousy is remarkable. In the *Lettres à Sara*, Rousseau writes: 'J'aimerais mon rival même si tu l'aimais; si tu ne l'aimais pas, je voudrais qu'il pût mériter ton amour' (p. 1291). With regard to Mme de Warens, he claims: 'La jalousie, la rivalité même cédait au sentiment dominant qu'elle inspirait' (*Confessions*, p. 178). See Robert Osmont, 'J.-J. Rousseau et la jalousie', *Annales J.-J. Rousseau*, 35 (1959–62), 73–91. Osmont points out the traces of jealousy in the *Confessions*, for example in the cases of Mlle de Vulson and Mlle Goton, and in the novel, the elements of frustrated desire, when Julie appears indifferent to Saint-Preux. However, he concludes that Rousseau sincerely tried to overcome what he regarded as negative emotions, hoping to find peace and harmony.

13 There is an extended analysis of Rousseau's treatment of women in *La Lettre à d'Alembert* in Sarah Kofman, *Le Respect des femmes* (Paris, 1982).

14 With regard to the supplementary structure see note 2 in this chapter, above. Derrida discusses *pudeur*, in particular, on pp. 254–7.

15 Since pudic women are experts in rationing sexual pleasure it is not surprising that one of Rousseau's main elaborations of this general economy of pleasure is in a description of Julie; she is one of those who are seen to 'sentir les charmes de la retraite...se plaire au sein de leur famille et s'y renfermer volontairement' (*La Nouvelle Héloïse*, p. 528). Saint-Preux tells Edouard that 'l'art de jouir est pour elle [Julie] celle des privations [...qui] servant d'assaisonnement au plaisir en préviennent le dégoût et l'abus' (p. 541). Julie only serves food and drink which is in season and locally available, but she adds to the charms of a particular dish by serving it only occasionally in spite of the abundance of the ingredients in her garden (p. 543).

16 Rousseau writes: 'La honte qui voile aux yeux les plaisirs de l'amour est qulequechose. Elle est la sauvegarde commune que la nature a donnée aux deux sexes dans un état de faiblesse et d'oubli d'eux-mêmes, qui les livre à la merci du premier venu' (*Lettre à d'Alembert*, p. 112).

17 See Derrida: 'L'on peut suivre partout, dans l'œuvre de Rousseau, une théorie de *l'innéité* comme *virtualité* ou de la naturalité comme

potentialité sommeillante. Théorie peu originale, certes, mais dont le rôle organisateur est ici indispensable. Elle commande de penser la nature non pas comme un donné, comme une présence actuelle, mais comme une *réserve'* (*De la grammatologie*, p. 263). Derrida uses the term *réserve* in a number of senses, for example, that which is stored up, present yet hidden, held back, potential. See also Sarah Kofman's analysis in *Le Respect des femmes* (Paris, 1982).

18 Henri Roddier suggests that these anecdotes may be considered as 'petites comedies morales' (*Les Rêveries*, edited by H. Roddier (Paris, 1960), p. LXXVI).

19 The casual beneficence which does not lead to lasting bonds between the benefactor and the beneficiary is regarded by Seneca and Cicero as scarcely beneficence at all. Rousseau relates the anecdotes of the *9ᵉ Promenade* with such lyricism and feeling that it is clear that, for him, this minimal beneficence is of far greater emotional importance than is acknowledged by the classical treatises.

20 See Michael Fried, *Absorption and Theatricality* (Berkeley, Calif., 1980). Fried insists on the importance of the negating of the beholder's presence: 'Only by establishing the fiction of his absence or non-existence could his actual placement before and enthrallment by the painting be secured' (p. 103). He also emphasises the priority in French painting after 1750 of the 'values and effects of the dramatic as such' (p. 75). Diderot not only admires theatricality in painting but also recommends 'tableaux' in a play. In the *Entretiens sur le fils naturel*, he defines a 'tableau' as 'Une disposition de ces personnages sur la scène, si naturelle et si vraie, que, rendue fidèlement par un peintre, elle me plairait sur la toile' (*Entretiens sur le fils naturel*, edited by P. Vernier (Paris, 1959), p. 88). Diderot gives pathetic scenes from real life as examples of theatrical tableaux, such as the woman whose husband is killed by her brother and who weeps at the foot of his corpse. Diderot also advises actors to behave as if the spectators did not exist, so that the spectators can forget that it is a play and imagine that it is real. The effacement of the beholder leads to a heightening of his imaginative involvement, an increase in his power as a spectator.

5 GYGES' RING: A READING OF ROUSSEAU'S *6ᵉ PROMENADE*

1 For the worldly counterpart of penetrating vision, see Peter Brooks, *The Novel of Worldliness* (Princeton, 1969): 'To "penetrate" someone is to find him out, to lay bare his true motives and

sentiments' (p. 16). In society *pénétrer* and *fixer* are used to control others; the experienced aristocrat does not permit himself to be penetrated or caught in others' definitions. He therefore employs a social mask or disguise. This is a tyrannical extreme of the conjunction of personal invisibility with perception of others.

2 The twentieth-century reader is reminded of Freud's use of personal anecdote in, for example, the *Psychopathology of Everyday Life*, in which a scientific approach is combined with autobiography. Rousseau's insight concerning the ultimate accessibility of motivation which is not immediately apparent is compared to Freud's theory of the unconscious by Edouard Claparède (see *Œuvres complètes*, I, p. 1803). Starobinski has written, 'il fallait Freud pour penser les sentiments de Rousseau' (*La Transparence et l'obstacle*, p. 142). Anecdotes, as opposed to hypothetical examples, were, of course, frequently used by classical moralists such as Seneca, but these were more often historical than personal. The effect of the personal anecdote is to heighten emotional intensity and to make the reader feel more closely involved with the writer.

3 Edgar Wind, *Pagan Mysteries in the Renaissance* (London, 1958), p. 32.

4 Rousseau's deviation from his route in the anecdote is a metaphorical return to nature. Rousseau refers to his literal and figural detour as 'un mouvement machinal', and he repeats the term 'machinalement' twice in the paragraphs describing his action. It might at first seem more usual to employ the image of a machine to characterise dutiful habit rather than rebellion. In this instance, rebellion is involuntary; it is not an exercise of will-power. This paradox may easily be resolved by reference to the *Discours sur l'inégalité*, where animality is defined as 'une machine ingénieuse'; in the state of nature 'la machine humaine' differs in kind from animals only in that man is a free agent with regard to natural law. In other words, animals have to follow their instincts, according to Rousseau, but human beings can choose to deviate from them. Thus a mechanical response implies an instinctual, natural reaction such as animals possess.

5 The passage in which Rousseau names the people whom he has helped, and who have betrayed him, gave him particular difficulty in composition. First of all he named the Comte des Charmettes and the Abbé Palais, then he added the Abbé de Binis and Moultou in the margin. Subsequently he crossed out the references in red crayon, but did not change the preceding or following sentences, and so the gap would be obvious: See *Les Rêveries*, edited by John S. Spink (Paris, 1948), p. xxxix. The question of whether

or not to name the guilty was one which Rousseau clearly found difficult to resolve; it is a particularly interesting question in this *Promenade* in which the successful circulation of his own name amongst his enemies puts an end to his beneficent exchange with the crippled boy.

6 See Marcel Raymond, *Jean-Jacques Rousseau: la quête de soi et la rêverie* (Paris, 1962), for example, p. 214.

7 Cf. Madeline B. Ellis, *Rousseau's Socratic Aemilian Myths* (Columbus, Ohio, 1977) for an (idiosyncratic) account of the influential roles played by Socrates and by Christ in *Emile* and *Du contrat social*.

8 For this detail see Leo Strauss, *The City and the Man* (Chicago, 1964). He claims that Glaucon is the motive for the *Republic*, referring to the *Memorabilia* of Xenophon (III, 6) in which we are told that Socrates cured Glaucon of his extreme political ambition. In the *Republic* Glaucon takes the side of injustice until he becomes one of the founders of the just city. Strauss suggests that 'Glaucon is the interlocutor of Socrates in the *Republic* whenever the highest themes are discussed' (p. 99).

9 See Marc Shell, *The Economy of Literature* (Baltimore, 1978). Shell claims that Gyges 'was the archetypal tyrant as he was the archetypal minter' (pp. 12–13). See also George Radet, *La Lydie et le monde grec au temps des Mermnades* (Paris, 1892) pp. 155ff. in which he discusses the invention of coinage and the belief that Gyges was the first coiner. He suggests that 'Gygès et ses successeurs ont possédé un merveilleux talisman: la science économique' (p. 224). P. N. Ure makes another link between Plato's tale and the historical association of Gyges with coinage: he connects the story of Gyges' descent into the earth after an earthquake with the fact that the precious metals of his kingdom were found underground in mines; see *The Origin of Tyranny* (Cambridge, 1922), pp. 146ff. Rings were, of course, at one time used as coins. Shell develops the link between rings and coins in greater detail.

10 *The Republic of Plato*, translated and annotated by F. M. Cornford, (Oxford, 1941), p. 44.

11 Socrates compares the soul to Glaucus just before he concludes: 'Let a man do what is just, whether he have the ring of Gyges or not' (Book X, 612b). Rousseau takes up this comparison in his preface to the *Discours sur l'inégalité*. Michel Butor suggests that Rousseau is himself the best incarnation of Glaucus. See *Répertoire III* (Paris, 1968), p. 73.

12 Roger Masters makes some interesting remarks about this in his book, *The Political Philosophy of Rousseau* (Princeton, 1968). He states that Rousseau 'puts his finger on an essential characteristic of the

Republic, namely its abstraction of *eros* or love from the political realm. Rousseau counters Plato's egalitarian treatment of women with the observation that love of one's own is essential to political life and patriotism' (pp. 22–3). He notes that Aristotle criticises the *Republic* on similar ground in *Politics*, II, 1261a–1264b.

Masters juxtaposes Rousseau's comments on Plato with his praise of Lycurgus for 'denaturing' the Spartans.

13 See Tony Tanner, *Adultery in the Novel* (Baltimore, 1979), chapter entitled 'Elysium', in particular pp. 146–8.

14 For a general account of Rousseau's identification with the Bible story, see Jean Starobinski 'Le moi accapare l'histoire sainte' in *L'Œil vivant* (Paris, 1961).

15 See Felicity Baker, 'La Route Contraire' in *Reappraisals of Rousseau*, ed. Harvey *et al.* (Manchester, 1980), pp. 132–62. Baker points out that *force* and *liberté* are co-hyponyms of *pouvoir*, and that they may be almost synonymous (as in the quotation from *Emile*) although they are often antonyms – in society where men attempt to use their strength to enslave others and are thus enslaved themselves. The synonymous relationship of the two terms is far from being a contradiction of the antonymous one. In the figure of God, man in nature, or Rousseau with Gyges' ring, there is a primitive fusion of these two concepts which are cleft asunder in human society: 'ce niveau de fusion est un en-deçà de toute contradiction, plutôt qu'un dépassement dialectique de celle-ci: malgre l'élévation morale de certaine de ses applications, cette fusion a quelque chose de primitif qui précède la division et l'opposition des concepts' (p. 139).

16 See *Œuvres complètes*, I, pp. 1806–7.

17 The reference to Glaucon is as follows:

Lisez-vous quelquefois la *République* de Platon? Voyez dans le second dialogue avec quelle énergie l'ami de Socrate, dont j'ai oublié le nom, lui peint le juste accablé des outrages de la fortune et des injustices des hommes, diffamé, persécuté, tourmenté, en proie à tout l'opprobre du crime et méritant tous les prix de la vertu, voyant déjà la mort qui s'approche, et sûr que la haine des méchants n'épargnera pas sa mémoire, quand ils ne pourront plus rien sur sa personne. Quel tableau décourageant, si rien pouvait décourager la vertu. (*Œuvres complètes*, IV, p. 1144)

18 Privacy, in this context, is a boundary which safeguards pudicity; it both requires and protects private property. There is a discussion of the Greek opposition of the public and the private in Hannah Arendt, *The Human Condition* (Chicago, 1958). She suggests that privacy, private property and the home are, in Greek thought,

necessarily associated with the bodily side of human existence and with women and slaves who are hidden away and excluded from the political speech and action (p. 72).

19 This is a footnote to an anecdote from Herodotus which Rousseau retells, which illustrates Lydian ingenuity in invention. This anecdote follows Herodotus' claim that the Lydians were the first people to use coinage and to introduce retail trade. There seems to be a recurrent association in Greek thinking of three semantic fields: Gyges, coinage and tyranny. See note 9 in this chapter, above.

20 This practice is, moreover, not altogether in conflict with that of modern readers of Herodotus. Seth Bernardete, *Herodotean Inquiries* (The Hague, 1969) follows Rousseau (whom he cites in an epigraph) in insisting that Herodotus should be interpreted like a literary text rather than treated as a slightly muddled chronicler of historical fact.

21 See Kirby Flower Smith, 'The tale of Gyges and the King of Lydia', *American Journal of Philology*, 23 (1902), 261–387. He claims that Gyges was the 'first great "barbarian" with whom the Hellenic world had come in close contact', and that Plato's account and that of Herodotus are two halves of an original folk tale.

22 It is not uncharacteristic that Rousseau should take up the position of voyeur (and then, ashamed, 'throw the ring away'). Starobinski relates one incident as follows:

A Lyon, Jean-Jacques guette une fille qui se baigne; au bout de quelques instants, il révèle sa présence en chantant un couplet. La jeune fille se trouble, rougit: plaisir intense pour l'indiscret, qui mesure ainsi, de loin, le pouvoir de sa présence: 'Que ne puis-je vous rendre tout ce qui se passa dans mon âme à l'aspect de votre confusion!' Beau sadisme visuel, où Rousseau, pour un instant, joue le rôle du tourmenteur. Mais il ne soutient pas longtemps ce rôle: la honte le gagne et tout s'inverse. Dès qu'il se sait regardé, le spectateur cruel devient un autre homme, un pauvre être humble et confus, qui découvre sa coupable image dans les yeux de sa victime. (*L'Œil vivant*, p. 113)

23 Translation of Herodotus cited by Gide in the *Préface de la première édition* of *Le Roi Candaule*. This is more enlightening than standard translations of Herodotus into English, because it draws on the same vocabulary as that employed by Rousseau (and indeed Gide), for example 'pudeur'; the Penguin version is 'off with her skirt, off with her shame' (translated by Aubrey de Belincourt (Harmondsworth, 1954)).

24 K. Flower Smith (see note 21 in this chapter, above) declares that

'Herodotus himself was more or less in the habit of rationalising a legend... In rationalising this story from the popular tale, the first step would be to expunge the ring and all the marvels connected with it... therefore the ring ought to fit best in the scars made by its removal' (p. 280). Smith convincingly postulates that in an original story Gyges used his ring to hide in Candaules' bedchamber on both occasions; on the first occasion he is seen by the queen because of her dragon-stone which gives her 'penetrating vision'. This last detail derived from mentions of Gyges' ring in Ptolemaios Chennos (via Photios) and Philostratos. However, it is not essential that the queen should have specifically magical powers; later versions of the story allow her to suspect Gyges' presence because of sounds he makes, because he steals one of her jewels or because he himself confesses to her.

25 The significance of the code of pudicity relies on the assumption that the sight of women is very likely to arouse uncontrollable desire in men.

26 On the whole from his position as unseen spectator of the theatre of the world Rousseau can, like Emile, pity his fellow man, seeing them as they are in all their folly and misery, 'voyant les hommes tels qu'ils sont et lisant aisément au fond de leurs cœurs, j'en aurais peu trouvé d'assez aimables pour mériter toutes mes affections, peu d'assez odieux pour mériter toute ma haine... leur méchanceté même m'eut disposé à les plaindre par la connaissance certaine du mal qu'ils se font à eux-memes en voulant en faire à autrui' (*Rêveries*, p. 1058).

27 See Norman Bryson, 'David's *Oath of the Horatii* and the Question of "Influence"', *French Studies*, 37 (1983), 404–25, for an eighteenth-century example of the concentration of power and sight in the masculine, and of the constitution of woman as 'that which is seen'.

28 See appendix.

29 See Seth Bernardete, *Herodotean Inquiries* (The Hague, 1969). Both Deioces and Gyges found dynasties and, in punishment for Gyges' murder of Candaules, Deioces' fifth descendant (Cyrus) destroys the fifth descendant of Gyges (Croesus). Deioces becomes king because of his reputation for impartiality and justice. Once king, he becomes invisible from his people because he lives in a specially constructed labyrinthine palace, fortified by a series of concentric or 'ring' walls. Thus, in a figural sense, he too is hidden from sight by ring power. He also has particularly penetrating vision because 'his spies were busy watching and listening in every corner of his dominions' (Herodotus, I, 103).

30 In the *Ebauches des Rêveries* (no. 22) there is a passage in which Rousseau describes himself in a position of absolute omnipotence: 'Maître et roi sur la terre, tous ceux qui m'entourent sont à ma merci, je peux tout sur eux et ils ne peuvent plus rien sur moi' (p. 1171). He does not imagine using his power for the good; on the contrary, he writes: 'Si j'avais des passions fougueuses je les pourrais satisfaire à mon aise et aussi publiquement qu'impunément.' This unused fragment is an example of visible revenge rather than invisible generosity. He is able to be visibly present *and* active, but at the cost of his moral superiority.

31 Projection of unpleasant thoughts is characteristic of the *Rêveries*: 'Ecartons donc de mon esprit tous les pénibles objets' (*Rêveries*, p. 999). See Starobinski, 'Rêverie et transmutation' in *La Transparence et l'obstacle*, pp. 415–29.

32 See Ralph Leigh, *Rousseau and the Problem of Tolerance in the Eighteenth Century* (Oxford, 1979). Leigh points out that *Du contrat social* is not about an ideal state, but about the institutions of a legitimate society (p. 3).

33 See Felicity Baker, 'Remarques sur la notion de dépôt, *Annales Rousseau*, 37 (1968), 57–93 for Rousseau's contractual thinking, and the 'réciprocité d'influence du sentiment et du droit' (p. 61) in his writing.

6 PUDICITY IN SOME OF ROUSSEAU'S MINOR WRITINGS: ITS RELATIONSHIP TO BENEFICENCE

1 *La Mort de Lucrèce* is an unfinished prose tragedy, which Rousseau was working on in 1754. He mentions it in the *Confessions*, p. 394. (The text is in *Œuvres complètes* II.) *Les Amours d'Edouard* is a condensed version of Edouard's adventures which was written for Mme de Luxembourg in 1760 (see *Confessions*, pp. 522–5). (The text is in *Œuvres complètes*, II.) *Le Lévite d'Ephraïm* was composed as Rousseau fled from Paris after the condemnation of *Emile*, 1762. (The text is in *Œuvres complètes*, II.) Rousseau was reading *Les Solitaires* aloud in 1762; his writing of it was interrupted by the crisis over the publication of *Emile*. He returned to it in 1768. See Pierre Burgelin, 'Introduction' in *Œuvres complètes*, IV.

2 *Les Amours d'Edouard* are a supplement to *La Nouvelle Héloïse*, intended to clarify certain mysterious letters in the novel; in reading the secondary text it is necessary to refer to letters in Part V and Part VI of the novel to supply the end of the story. For the sake of simplicity it will be assumed that *Les Amours d'Edouard* refers

to the story of Edouard's love affairs including information given in *La Nouvelle Héloïse*, except where it is relevant to be more precise.

3 There are two letters of *Les Solitaires*; the second one ends in mid-sentence. Certain passages in these two letters make it clear that Rousseau intended to reunite Emile and Sophie, and that they should have some time of happiness together before her death. Bernardin de St-Pierre gives a summary of what Rousseau confided to him about his plans for *Emile et Sophie* in *La Vie et les ouvrages de Jean-Jacques Rousseau* (edited by Maurice Souriau (Paris, 1907), pp. 170–3). According to Bernardin de St-Pierre, Emile goes to a desert island because he hears that it has a miraculous cave containing a statue of the Virgin, in which there is always food and drink for travellers. It turns out that this is due to the beneficence of an elderly Spaniard, who believes that he and his daughter were saved from a shipwreck by the Virgin. At the Spaniard's request Emile marries his daughter and lives happily with her in this earthly paradise. She makes it her duty to be like many women in one, by dressing differently and playing different musical instruments, making use of the echo on the island. When Sophie arrives Emile is forced to imitate the Patriarchs and enjoy two wives; there is no jealousy between them. After Sophie's death a letter explains how she was seduced by her false friend's husband. Another account of Rousseau's projected continuation is given by Pierre Prevost.

4 A variation on this theme is to be found in Fragment 4: 'Pauline, songez que je suis la femme de Collatin et qu'ainsi j'ai mieux fait de l'épouser.'

5 For a survey and analysis of different versions and reactions to the story of Lucretia, see Ian Donaldson, *The Rapes of Lucretia* (Oxford, 1982). Donaldson suggests that versions of the story which imagine Lucretia with a lingering fondness for Tarquin (such as Rousseau's or that of A. V. Arnault, *Lucrèce, ou Rome libre*, 1792) approached the sceptical or comic interpretations which infer that Lucretia enjoyed the rape (pp. 84–5).

6 Sextus says to Lucretia 'vous me faites aimer l'innocence et la pureté, j'adore en vous leur céleste image' (Fragment 1, *Œuvres complètes*, II, 1043). He is, of course, deceiving himself, if not Lucretia, about the order of his love for her purity; he realises that his actions will destroy what he desires (Act II, scene 1).

7 Wolmar says to Julie when he proposes leaving her alone with Saint-Preux for a few days: 'Je remets ma femme et mon honneur en dépôt à celle qui, fille et séduite, préférait un acte de bienfaisance à un rendez-vous unique et sûr' (*La Nouvelle Héloïse*, p. 498). The

fact that an act of beneficence took priority over Julie's passion shows that the relationship between Julie and Saint-Preux never became a criminal one. Wolmar assures Julie: 'Je jugeai que le même goût qui avait formé votre union la relâcherait sitôt qu'elle deviendrait criminelle' (p. 495).

8 Rousseau is, of course, following his source (the Book of Judges) in this respect. He has, however, made a decision to follow the Bible on this matter, whereas in the case of Axa he departs from the anonymity of the Old Testament.

9 In *Emile*, Emile and Sophie have similar fictional status; Emile is at first an example in a philosophical treatise, but by Book v where he encounters Sophie he is, as she is, a fictional character in what resembles a novel. *Les Solitaires* changes the balance of fictive power: Emile is now the narrator, the writer of the letters which would make up an epistolary novel; Sophie remains the written object, that which is written about, the object of the gaze not only of the reader (you or me) and the writer (Rousseau), but also of the reader addressed (Emile's tutor) and the writer (Emile) within the work.

10 See Livy Book I, 57, 7–11:

Every man fell to praising his own wife with enthusiasm and, as their rivalry grew hot, Collatinus said that there was no need to talk about it, for it was in their power to know, in a few hours time, how far the rest were excelled by his own Lucretia. 'Come! If the vigour of youth is in us let us mount our horses and see for ourselves the disposition of our wives. Let every man regard as the surest test what meets his eyes when the woman's husband returns home unexpected.' They were heated with wine. 'Agreed!' they all cried, and clapping spurs to their horses were off for Rome. Arriving there at early dusk, they thence proceeded to Collatia, where Lucretia was discovered very differently employed from the daughters-in-law of the King. These they had seen at a luxurious banquet, whiling away the time with their young friends; but Lucretia, though it was late at night, was busily engaged upon her wool, while her maidens toiled about her in the lamplight as she sat in the hall of her house. The prize of this contest in womanly virtues fell to Lucretia. As Collatinus and the Tarquinii approached, they were graciously received, and the victorious husband courteously invited the young princes to his table. It was there that Sextus Tarquinius was seized with a wicked desire to debauch Lucretia by force; not only her beauty, but her proved chastity as well, provoked him. However, for the present they ended the boyish prank of the night and returned to camp.

La Mort de Lucrèce opens with Lucretia saying to her companion 'allez, Pauline, préparer la pourpre et le lin pour nous remettre à l'ouvrage '. Jacques Scherer suggests that this is inspired by Livy's account of Lucretia working at her wool (*Œuvres complètes*, II p. 1870).

11 Machiavelli and Montesquieu, for example, are more interested in the revolution and in questions relating to the exercise of public office; they suggest that Lucretia is no more than a pretext for Brutus. See Donaldson, *The Rapes of Lucretia*, chapter 6, for the fashioning of a political myth.

For some Christian writers (in a tradition dating from Saint Augustine's remarks in *The City of God*) Lucretia's suicide is a sin in itself and also implies a sentiment of guilt. See E. R. Dodds, *The Greeks and the Irrational* (Berkeley, 1951) for the historical shift from a shame culture to a guilt culture. Rousseau's attitude is quite different; he not only admires Lucretia but also Cato, the most celebrated male suicide of antiquity. In *De l'honneur et de la vertu* (*Fragments politiques*, p. 506), Rousseau criticises Saint Augustine for his 'pleasanteries' concerning Brutus' killing of his children (an action which is significantly related to Lucretia's suicide). In fact, Saint Augustine quotes the *Aeneid* (see *Œuvres complètes*, III, p. 1525). Rousseau's remark could equally well apply to the attitude towards Lucretia:

> Les pères de l'église n'ont pas su voir le mal qu'ils faisaient à leur cause en flétrissant ainsi tout ce que le courage et l'honneur avaient produit de plus grand; à force de vouloir élever la sublimité de christianisme ils ont appris aux chrétiens à devenir des hommes lâches et sans... (*Fragments politiques*, p. 506)

12 Charles Duclos's *Histoire de Madame de Luz* (1740) is an interesting reworking of some of these issues. Mme de Luz – whose name, like Lucretia's, seems to connote light – is a woman of outstanding virtue. She is an exceptional woman, especially set against characters in Duclos's wordly novel, *Les Confessions du Comte de ***,* which portrays the majority of women in a highly cynical manner. Mme de Luz, married to a man she does not love is assailed by a number of suitors some of whom will stop at nothing in order to satisfy their desires. Her confessor drugs her and then rapes her while she is deeply asleep. Despite the opium she finally awakens and discovers him. Her first thought is to kill herself (by stabbing herself with a knife), and her second, when the knife is seized from her, to make public his misdeed. The priest prevents her by his threat to tell his own besmirching version of her story. Mme de Luz finally dies of misery, having told the tale on her deathbed.

13 See F. van Laere, 'Jean-Jacques Rousseau de phantasme à l'écriture les révélations du *Lévite d'Ephraïm*' in *Archives des lettres*

modernes, 81 (1967), for this association with *Olinde et Sophronie*. Van Laere refers to the Levite as 'l'homme qui livre à la luxure d'autrui la femme qu'il aime' (p. 33); this generalised description would also apply to Candaules, even though the circumstances are very different.

14 Sophie reacts quite differently from Lucretia to her predicament; Rousseau's admiration for the heroism of Lucretia does not mean that he considers suicide to be an appropriate response in general to a woman's loss of honour. Sophie's suicide would be meaningless, an escape from an unpleasant situation without regard for the responsibilities she may have to bear.

15 It is important that Sophie is envisaged as 'estimable' as well as 'malheureuse'; this means that it is just to pity her. Emile does not wish to gloat over her downfall: 'Contempler Sophie avilie et méprisable... Ce tableau était le seul que je ne pouvais supporter' (p. 895). The spectacle of the pitiable Sophie calms Emile as a theatrical spectacle cannot. Rousseau decides that Emile, without any element of conscious decision, should be taken to the theatre shortly after his discovery of Sophie's infidelity (p. 893). The theatre epitomises the artificiality of the world into which he has brought his wife, and which has led her astray. The fact that he hears her name mentioned (at which point he can no longer control himself and cries aloud) demonstrates the extent to which she has departed from the code of pudicity and its confinement of the woman, even the name of the woman, to her home. The theatre is the locus of sterile pity according to the *Lettre à d'Alembert*; Emile must find release in action, not in amusement.

16 For silent erotic communication, see P. W. Lasowski, *Libertines* (Paris, 1980), for example:

C'est que le langage du corps est l'idéolecte féminin que, de tous temps la Nature a fixé: 'Consultez leurs yeux, leur teint, leur air craintif, leur molle résistance: voilà le langage que la nature leur donne pour vous répondre... D'autant plus expressif est le corps de la femme qu'elle ne saurait passer à l'écriture. (pp. 143–4)

Lasowski maintains, however, that Rousseau's own writing can be particularly feminine, and that 'seul un homme sous le nom de Julie aura pu dire en effet le désir féminin' (p. 144). For further discussion of rhetoric and the feminine as it touches upon *La Mort de Lucrèce*, see Judith Still, 'Lucretia's Silent Rhetoric', *The Oxford Literary Review*, 6 (1984), pp. 70–86.

17 According to Livy and Plutarch (*Vie de Publicola*, v), Brutus feigns stupidity in order to escape death under Tarquin's rule and this is how he acquires his name:

He therefore deliberately assumed the appearance of stupidity, and permitted himself and his property to become the spoil of the King; he even accepted the surname Brutus, that behind the screen afforded by this title the great soul which was to free the Roman People might bide its time unseen. He it was who was then taken by the Tarquinii to Delphi, more as a butt than as a comrade; and he is said to have carried a golden staff inclosed within one of cornel wood, hollowed out to receive it, as a gift to Apollo, and a roundabout indication of his own character. (Livy, I, 56, 8–10)

Brutus literally means 'dullard'. Donaldson writes that Brutus is often represented as 'a man who *hides himself*: as a man expert in political self-camouflage' (*The Rapes of Lucretia*, p. 119). As the story is reshaped by various writers this side of Brutus may be presented as a tyrannical one; as was pointed out with regard to Gyges, the combination of invisibility and penetrating vision (in Rousseau's play Brutus is the only character to perceive Lucretia's love for Sextus) is associated with tyranny. Brutus' action in ordering the death of his own sons is sometimes represented unfavourably, but Rousseau is unequivocal in celebrating it as virtue.

18 In Book I of his *Confessions* (p. 9), Rousseau recalls:

Plutarque surtout devint ma lecture favorite. Le plaisir que je prenais à le relire sans cesse me guérit un peu des romans, et je préférai bientôt Agésilas, Brutus, Aristide à Orondate, Artamène et Juba. De ces intéressantes lectures, des entretiens qu'elles occasionnaient entre mon père et moi, se forma cet esprit libre et républicain, ce caractère indomptable et fier, impatient de joug et de servitude qui m'a tourmenté tout le temps de ma vie dans les situations les moins propres à lui donner l'essor. Sans cesse occupé de Rome et d'Athènes; vivant, pour ainsi dire, avec leurs grands hommes, né moi-même citoyen d'une république, et fils d'un père dont l'amour de la patrie etait la plus forte passion, je m'enflammais à son exemple; je me croyais Grec ou Romain; je devenais le personnage dont je lisais la vie: le récit des traits de constance et d'intrépidité qui m'avaient frappé me rendait les yeux étincellants et la voix forte.

One of the characters with whom the young Rousseau identifies is Brutus (see also *Confessions*, p. 24). Jacques Scherer doubts that this Brutus is Lucius Junius (the avenger of Lucretia) on the grounds that Plutarch devotes an entire *Life* to Marcus Junius Brutus (who killed Julius Caesar) whereas Lucius Junius Brutus principally features in the *Vie de Publicola*. Scherer suggests that Rousseau 'a pu mêler tous ces souvenirs, confondant plus ou moins les deux Brutus dans un même idéal d'héroïsme romain et républicain' (*Œuvres complètes*, II, p. 1870). Such a conflation of the two men does indeed occur in the creation of a political myth. Plutarch states, in the *Vie de Marcus Brutus*, that Marcus was descended from Lucretia's contemporary; this possible blood link fuelled desire to transpose associations from the one to the other. However, it is sometimes quite plain which Brutus is in question. In the letters on suicide in *La Nouvelle Héloïse* the Brutus whom Saint-Preux cites must be Marcus (who did commit suicide) since Lucius died in battle. This difference in their ends suggests that it is Lucius whom it is natural to want to resemble 'mourant pour son pays' (*La Nouvelle Héloïse*, p. 224).

19 The relationship between Edouard and Saint-Preux follows the course which Julie predicts for it in Part II of *La Nouvelle Héloïse*; it conforms to that which is laid down by the classical code of beneficence. Julie writes to Edouard (pp. 209–10):

> Oui, soyez son consolateur, son protecteur, son ami, son père, c'est à la fois pour vous et pour lui que je vous en conjure; il justifiera votre confiance, il honorera vos bienfaits, il pratiquera vos leçons, il imitera vos vertus, il apprendra de vous la sagesse. Ah, Milord! s'il devient entre vos mains tout ce qu'il peut être, que vous serez fier un jour de votre ouvrage!

20 The term 'hospitality' etymologically contains within it the terms 'host', 'guest', 'stranger' and 'enemy'.

21 See J.-P. Vernant, *Mythe et pensée chez les Grecs* (Paris, 1966). Mobile Hermes presides over the predominantly masculine world of exchanges and contracts, 'le contact avec l'autre que soi', whereas the stationary Hestia (goddess of the interior, the hearth) represents 'le repli du groupe humain sur lui-même'.

22 As suggested in Chapter 2, Rousseau's account of beneficence tends towards equality and reciprocity; beneficiaries should aim to be benefactors in their turn (as Saint-Preux does). Women, on the other hand, should not aim to be like men. Rousseau himself, in common with other writers, explicitly began as a reader; see the early books of the *Confessions*, for example, 'je ne sais comment j'appris à lire; je ne me souviens que de mes premières lectures et de leur effet sur moi: c'est le temps d'où je date sans interruption la conscience de moi-même' (p. 8). Rousseau's very awareness of his self is mediated from the outset by reading, as it will later be by writing his self in autobiography. However, in general, most readers should not aim to be writers; there are too many poor writers, according to Rousseau.

23 The reader who refuses to read, or who reads refusing to understand, occurs in other works; Rousseau caters for him in the *Confessions* with the well-known phrase: 'Quiconque, même

sans avoir lu mes écrits, examinera par ses propres yeux mon naturel... et pourra me croire un malhonnête homme, est lui-même un homme à étouffer' (p. 656).

24 This is not to say that there are not many female benefactors in Rousseau's writing, particularly, of course, in the autobiographical works (see Chapter 3). But on a linguistic level, the code of beneficence has associations of masculinity, of virile action, of stoical reasoning. Pity, the inspirational force, has a 'gentle voice', and enjoys feminine connotations: this is the role of the mother with the baby (in Mandeville's example) or the image of the unhappy Sophie. When pity is put into practice as virtuous action it loses its feminine connotations and takes on those of, for example, Plutarch's *Vies des hommes illustres*.

25 The Théâtre de la Foire tradition is one which turns Tarquin into Arlequin; see Scherer, *Œuvres complètes*, II, p. 1869.

26 Rousseau meditates on his plan for *La Mort de Lucrèce* during solitary walks around the lake at Geneva, where he hoped to settle in preference for Paris (a hope that was not to be fulfilled). At the same time he ponders on his projected *Institutions politiques*, a history of the Valais, and a translation of Tacitus; the textual juxtaposition of these items is not idle. Lucretia is a strand in a web of thought which binds Geneva, walks by the lake, political institutions, the Valais, history and Tacitus. The associations evoked are both moral and political rectitude, a configuration which is opposed to that of the French theatre and French amusement at simple virtue, the virtue of the Roman republic (and the idealised Genevan republic), and the virtue of women.

27 Saint-Preux intends to devote his life to repaying Edouard; he writes to him 'Faites, Milord; ordonnez de moi; vous ne serez désavoué sur rien' (*La Nouvelle Héloïse*, p. 377). Edouard can thus say with confidence to him that when he returns from his sea voyage 'nous nous rejoindrons pour ne nous séparer jamais' (*La Nouvelle Héloïse*, p. 395).

28 Edouard writes to Julie on the same subject: 'La première fois que je vis votre amant, je fus frappé d'un sentiment nouveau, qui n'a fait qu'augmenter de jour en jour, à mesure que la raison l'a justifié' (*La Nouvelle Héloïse*, p. 198). This emotion precedes the reasoning; the reasoning confirms the emotion. The reciprocity of the heart and the mind is central to Rousseau's adoption of the code of beneficence, indeed of his thinking in general.

29 Edouard's passionate nature is a strength which carries its own weakness. He argues fiercely in favour of Saint-Preux to Julie's father to no avail; later he realises that he has only made the Baron

d'Etanges more firm in his resolve, and considers that he acted with 'zèle inconsidéré' (*La Nouvelle Héloïse*, p. 181).

30 While Sophie's father acts with the best interests of his daughter at heart, there is another 'Sophie' (whose name, Rousseau tells us, is not Sophie) with another father who becomes 'un père irrité oubliant ses premiers engagements et traitant comme une folle la plus vertueuse des filles' (*Emile*, p. 763). This 'Sophie', who is, Rousseau claims, real, but whose reality will not be credited by the reader (*Emile*, p. 759), could have had the story of her death told by Rousseau, but, he writes, 'Non, j'écarte ces objets funestes' (*Emile*, p. 763). 'Sophie' dies for love of a fictional character, Télémaque; her story suggests the danger of allowing a girl to read edifying books, let alone corrupting ones. 'Sophie' is the spectre of the sacrificed daughter in *Emile*.

31 For another discussion of the question of fathers and benefactors see Judith Still, 'Rousseau in *Daniel Deronda*', *Revue de littérature comparée*, January–March 1982, pp. 62–77.

32 See Jean Starobinski, 'Rousseau's Happy Days', *New Literary History*, 11, 1 (1979), pp. 147–66. Starobinski links terrifying nocturnal separation with the imaginary which separates us from reality. He suggests that Rousseau's night readings with his father represent the shadowy side of life and are also the source of the imaginary beings which enrich the waking hours (see *Confessions*, 1). Rousseau describes reading the tale of the Levite of Ephraim at the end of the Book of Judges during the night which ends in a particular separation, the flight from Paris (*Confessions*, p. 579). Starobinski suggests that the material in the biblical story is peculiarly akin to Rousseau's circumstances; he could superimpose 'the biblical night time incursion of the villains into the house of the old man upon the sudden arrival of those who interrupted his half sleep to bring a letter warning of danger' (p. 162). Canto II narrates the unfolding of an entire night which ends with the dismemberment of the dead woman's body. Starobinski thus relates the episode particularly to Rousseau's experience of writing as well as to writing in general.

33 Quand le Lévite d'Ephraïm voulut venger la mort de sa femme, il n'écrivit point aux tribus d'Israel; il divisa le corps en douze pieces, et les leur envoya. A cet horrible aspect, ils courent aux armes en criant tout d'une voix: *Non jamais rien de tel n'est arrivé dans Israël, depuis le jour que nos pères sortirent d'Egypte jusqu'à ce jour*. Et la tribu de Benjamin fut exterminée. De nos jours, l'affaire, tournée en plaidoyers, en discussions, peut-être en plaisanteries, eût trainé en longueur, et le plus terrible des crimes fût enfin demeuré impuni. (Chapter 1)

34 This analysis of the allegory of writing owes much to an analysis by Paul de Man in *Allegories of Reading* (New Haven, 1979), chapter 12, 'Excuses'.

35 Chapter 20.

36 Ainsi pour réparer la désolation de tant de meurtres ce peuple en commit de plus grands, semblable en sa furie à ces globes de fer lancés par nos machines embrasées, lesquels, tombés à terre après leur premier effet, se relevant avec une impétuosité nouvelle, et dans leurs bonds inattendus renversent et détruisent des rangs entiers. (*Le Lévite d'Ephraïm*, p. 1221)

37 See Pierre Burgelin, 'Introduction' in *Œuvres complètes* IV, pp. cliii–clxviii. Burgelin also points out the similarities between *Les Solitaires* and Rousseau's autobiographical writing.

38 'Le cœur ne reçoit de lois que de lui-même: en voulant l'enchaîner on le dégage, on l'enchaîne en le laissant libre' (*Emile*, p. 521).

39 After Julie's death a beautiful veil (a gift from Saint-Preux) is placed over her face. Starobinski concludes: 'Le voile *est* la séparation et la mort' (*La Transparence et l'obstacle*, p. 146). He goes on to suggest that her death may also be a transcendence of the veil in that it permits her to accede to unmediated communication with God. Such a transcendence does not, however, resolve the question of justice in social relations, nor does it render that question any less important. While Rousseau takes and offers a final comfort from faith in an afterlife, priority is afforded to the problems of earthly existence.

APPENDIX: GENEROSITY AND PUDICITY IN *GYGES UND SEIN RING* AND *LE ROI CANDAULE*

1 There have been other literary versions of the story; indeed, it was probably first made into a play in classical antiquity (see D. L. Page, *A Chapter in the History of Greek Tragedy* (Cambridge, 1951)). Other modern versions include a poem by E. R. B. Lytton in *Chronicles and Characters* (1868) and Théophile Gautier's *Le Roi Candaule* (1893). The former portrays Candaules as a foolish 'heart-sick' king, the latter as an aesthete.

2 André Gide, *Le Roi Candaule* (Paris, 1942), p. 158. All references to *Le Roi Candaule* are to this edition.

3 André Gide, *Journal 1889–1939* (Paris, 1939), pp. 188–9.

4 Théophile Gautier, *Le Roi Candaule* (Paris, 1893).

5 C. F. Hebbel, *Werke*, II, edited by Gerhard Fricke, Werner Keller and Karl Pornbacher (Munich, 1964). All quotations from Hebbel are from this edition. Translations from Hebbel are my own, and are intended to err towards the literal rather than the poetic.

6 In Herodotus' *Histories* the queen is not given a name; Hebbel names her Rhodope, Gide Nyssia, and other writers have chosen other appellations. It seems appropriate that she is to this extent nameless, and that names can almost arbitrarily be given to her, since she is regarded as a possession and occupies an analogous (although much loftier) position to that of a slave, who may be renamed by his or her master at will.

7 Letter to Karl Werner, 16 May 1856, reproduced in C. F. Hebbel, *Werke*, II, p. 698.

Bibliography

WORKS BY JEAN-JACQUES ROUSSEAU

EDITIONS USED THROUGHOUT THE BOOK

Œuvres complètes, edited by Bernard Gagnebin and Marcel Raymond, 4 vols., Paris, 1959–69
Correspondance complète, edited by Ralph A. Leigh, 40 vols., Oxford, 1965–82
Essai sur l'origine des langues, edited by Charles Porset, Paris, 1970
Lettre à d'Alembert sur les spectacles, edited by M. Fuchs, Geneva, 1948

OTHER EDITIONS CONSULTED

The computer analysis of the vocabulary of Rousseau's published writings made available by the Faculté des Lettres of the University of Geneva.
Le Discours sur l'inégalité, edited by J.-L. Lecercle, Paris, 1971
La Nouvelle Héloïse, edited by Daniel Mornet, 4 vols., Paris, 1925
Les Rêveries du promeneur solitaire, edited by Raymond Bernex, Paris, 1970
edited by Robert Niklaus, Manchester, 1942
edited by Marcel Raymond, Lille, 1940
edited by Henri Roddier, Paris, 1960
edited by J. S. Spink, Paris, 1948
edited by Jacques Voisine, Paris, 1964

CLASSICAL WORKS CONSULTED

Aristotle, *Ethics*, translated by J. A. K. Thompson, Harmondsworth, revised edition 1976
L'Ethique à Nicomaque, translated and edited by René Antoine Gauthier and Jean Yves Jolif, 2 vols., Louvain, 1958
The Politics, translated by T. A. Sinclair, Harmondsworth, 1962
La Politique, translated by J. Tricot, 2 vols., Paris, 1962

Aristotle, Horace and Longinus, *Classical Literary Criticism*, translated by T. S. Dorsch, Harmondsworth, 1965
Augustine, Saint, *The City of God*, translated by John Healey, 2 vols., Edinburgh, 1909
   The Confessions, translated by R. S. Pine-Coffin, Harmondsworth, 1961
La Bible, translated by P. R. Olivetan, Geneva, 1546
   translated by David Martin, 2 vols., Amsterdam, 1707
   translated by M. le Maistre de Saci, 15 vols., Paris, 1707
Cicero, *Les Devoirs*, translated by Maurice Testard, Paris, 1965
   On Moral Obligation, translated by J. Higginbotham, London, 1976
   Les Offices, translated by M. Du Bois, Paris, 1729
   de Officiis, translated by Walter Miller, London, 1913
Herodotus, *The Histories*, translated by Aubrey de Selincourt, Harmondsworth, revised edition 1972
Homer, *L'Odyssée*, translated by Médéric Dufour and Jeanne Raison, Paris, 1935
   The Odyssey, translated by E. V. Rieu, Harmondsworth, 1945
Horace, *Ars Poetica*, translated by T. S. Dorsch, Harmondsworth, 1965
Livy, *Ab Urbe Condita*, translated by B. O. Foster, London, 1926
Plato, *The Dialogues*, translated by Benjamin Jowett, ed. R. M. Hare and D. A. Russell, London, 1970
   The Laws, translated by Trevor J. Saunders, Harmondsworth, 1970
   The Republic, translated by Francis Macdonald Cornford, Oxford, 1941
   The Republic, translated by Allan Bloom, New York, 1968
   La République, translated by L. le Roy, Paris, 1600
Plutarch, *The Age of Alexander*, translated by Ian Scott-Kilvert, Harmondsworth, 1973
   The Fall of the Roman Republic, translated by Rex Warner, Harmondsworth, 1958
   Makers of Rome, translated by Ian Scott-Kilvert, Harmondsworth, 1965
   Les Œuvres morales et meslées, translated by Jacques Amyot, edited by M. A. Screech, 2 vols., Paris, 1971
Plutarch, *The Rise and Fall of Athens*, translated by Ian Scott-Kilvert, Harmondsworth, 1960
   Les Vies des hommes illustres, translated by Jacques Amyot, edited by Gérard Walter, 2 vols., Paris, 1951
Seneca, *de Beneficiis*, translated by John W. Basore, London, 1935
   Des bienfaits, translated by François Préchac, 2 vols., Paris, 1926
   Des bienfaits, translated by F. de Malherbe, Paris, 1650

Les Epistres, translated by Pintrel, 2 vols., Paris, 1681
Xenophon, *The Memorable Thoughts of Socrates*, translated by Edward Bysshe, London, 1903

AUTHORS CONSULTED FROM THE
RENAISSANCE TO THE EARLY TWENTIETH
CENTURY

Chamfort (Nicolas Sébastien Roch), *Maximes et pensées*, edited by Ad. van Bever, Paris, 1922
Corneille, Pierre, *Œuvres complètes*, edited by Pierre Lièvre, 2 vols., Argenteuil, 1934
Diderot, Denis, *Œuvres complètes*, edited by J. Assezat and M. Tourneux, 20 vols., Paris, 1875–7
Duclos, Charles, *Les Confessions du Comte de ****, edited by Laurent Vertsini, Paris, 1969
  Histoire de Madame de Luz, edited by Jacques Bengues, Saint-Brieuc, 1972
Emerson, Ralph Waldo, *Works*, London, 1883
Freud, Sigmund, *The Standard Edition of the Complete Psychological Works*, 24 vols., London, 1953–74
Fustel de Coulanges, N. D., *La Cité antique*, Paris, 1864
Gautier, Théophile, *Le Roi Candaule*, Paris, 1893
Gessner, Salomon, *Œuvres*, translated by M. Huber *et al.*, 3 vols., Paris, 1786–93
Gide, André, *Journal 1889–1939*, Paris, 1939
  Le Roi Candaule, Paris, 1942
Hebbel, Friedrich, *Werke*, II, edited by Gerhard Fricke *et al.*, Munich, 1964
Hobbes, Thomas, *Leviathan*, edited by C. B. Macpherson, Harmondsworth, 1968
Huet, Pierre-Daniel, *Traité de l'origine des romans*, Paris, 1670, Facsimile edition, Stuttgart, 1966
La Bruyère, Jean de, *Œuvres complètes*, edited by J. Benda, Paris, 1951
Laclos, Cholderlos de, *Les Liaisons dangereuses*, Lausanne, 1960
La Rochefoucauld, François, duc de, *Maximes et réflexions diverses*, edited by Jacques Truchet, Paris, second edition, 1972
Lee, Nathaniel, *Lucius Junius Brutus*, London, 1967
Locke, John, *Two Treatises of Government*, edited by Peter Laslett, Cambridge, 1960
Lytton, E. R. B., *Chronicles and Characters*, I, London, 1868
Machiavelli, Niccolo, *The Prince*, translated by George Bull, Harmondsworth, revised edition, 1975

Mandeville, Bernard de, *La Fable des abeilles*, translated by J. Bertrand, 4 vols., London, 1740

Marivaux, Carlet de Chamberlain de, *Le Paysan parvenu*, edited by Abel Farges, Paris, 1939

La Vie de Marianne, edited by M. Duviquet, Paris, 1933

Montaigne, Michel Eyquem de, *Essais*, edited by Albert Thibaudet, Paris, 1950

Montesquieu, Charles de Secondat, Baron de la Brède et de, *De l'esprit des lois*, edited by Gonzague Truc, 2 vols., Paris, 1944

More, Thomas, *Utopia*, London, 1974

Nietzsche, Friedrich, *Beyond Good and Evil*, translated by R. J. Hollingdale, Harmondsworth, 1973

The Gay Science, translated by Walter Kaufmann, New York, 1974

On the Genealogy of Morals, translated by Walter Kaufmann and R. J. Hollingdale, New York, 1969

Racine, Jean, *Œuvres complètes*, edited by Raymond Picard, 2 vols., Paris, 1951

Radet, Georges, *La Lydie et le monde grec au temps des Mermnades*, Paris, 1892

Richardson, Samuel, *Clarissa*, edited by Ernest Rhys, 4 vols., London, 1932

Pamela, edited by Ernest Rhys, 2 vols., London, 1906

Rollin, Charles, *De la manière d'enseigner et d'étudier les belles lettres* or *Traité des études*, Paris, 1726–8

Sablé, Mme de, *Maximes*, edited by D. Jouaust, Paris, 1870

Sade, Donatien Alphonse François de, *Œuvres complètes*, edited by Jean-Jacques Pauvert, Paris, 1959

Saint-Pierre, Bernardin de, *Œuvres complètes*, edited by L. Aimé-Martin, 12 vols., Paris, 1818

La Vie et les ouvrages de Jean-Jacques Rousseau, edited by M. Souriau, Paris, 1907

Scott, Sarah, *Millenium Hall*, London, 1986

Shakespeare, William, *The Rape of Lucrece* in *The Complete Works*, edited by Peter Alexander, London, 1951

Smith, Adam, *The Wealth of Nations*, first edition 1776, revised edition by Andrew Skinner, Harmondsworth, 1970

Voltaire, François-Marie Arouet, *Œuvres complètes*, edited by Theodore Bestermann *et al.*, Geneva, 1968–77

Wollstonecraft, Mary, *A Vindication of the Rights of Woman*, New York, 1975

TWENTIETH-CENTURY WORKS CONSULTED

Agacinski, Sylviane, *et al.*, *Mimésis des articulations*, Paris, 1975

Altmann, Janet G., 'The "Triple Register"': Introduction to Temporal Complexity in the Letter-Novel', *Esprit Créateur*, 17 (1977), 302–10

Ambri Berselli, Paola, 'Influences italiennes sur *La Nouvelle Héloïse*', *Annales Jean-Jacques Rousseau*, 32 (1950–2), 155–65

Annales de la Société Jean-Jacques Rousseau, Geneva, 1905—present

Ansart-Dourlen, Michèle, *Dénaturation et violence dans la pensée de J.-J. Rousseau*, Paris, 1975

Arendt, Hannah, *The Human Condition*, Chicago, 1958

Atkinson, Geoffrey, *The Sentimental Revolution*, Seattle, 1965

Aulagnier-Spairani, Piera et al., *Le Désir et la perversion*, Paris, 1967

Austin, J. L., *How to do Things with Words*, Oxford, 1962

Babbitt, Irving, *Rousseau and Romanticism*, Boston, 1919

Bachelard, Gaston, *L'Eau et les rêves*, Paris, 1942

La Formation de l'esprit scientifique, Paris, 1938

Baczko, Bronislaw, *Rousseau: Solitude et communauté*, translated by Claire Brendhel-Lamhout, Paris, 1974

Badinter, Elizabeth, *L'Amour en plus*, Paris, 1980

Emilie, Emilie ou l'ambition féminine au XVIIIᵉ siècle, Paris, 1983

Baker, Felicity, 'L'Esprit de l'hospitalité chez Emile', *Romantisme*, 4 (1972), 90–9

'Perverse Scenes of Writing', *Society for Critical Exchange*, 10 (1981), 57–71

'Remarques sur la notion de dépôt', *Annales Jean-Jaques Rousseau*, 37 (1968), 57–93

'La Scène du lac dans *La Nouvelle Héloïse*', *Le Préromantisme hypothèque ou hypothèse, Actes et Colloques*, 18 (1972), 129–52

Barber, W. H., *The Age of the Enlightenment*, Edinburgh, 1967

Barnett, H. G., 'The Nature of the Potlach', *American Anthropologist*, 5 (1938), 349–58

Barthes, Roland, *L'Empire des signes*, Geneva, 1970

S/Z, Paris, 1970

Bataille, Georges, *Œuvres complètes*, Paris, 1970

Baudrillard, Jean, *Pour une critique de l'économie politique du signe*, Paris, 1972

Beauvoir, Simone de, *Le Deuxième Sexe*, Paris, 1949

Becker, Gary, *The Economic Approach to Human Behaviour*, Chicago, 1976

Bennington, Geoffrey, *Sententiousness and the Eighteenth-Century Novel*, Cambridge, 1985

Benot, Yves, *Diderot de l'athéisme à l'anticolonialisme*, Paris, 1970

Benveniste, Emile, *Problèmes de linguistique générale*, Paris, 1966

Bernardete, Seth, *Herodotean Inquiries*, The Hague, 1969

Blanchot, Maurice, *Le Livre à venir*, Paris, 1959

L'Entretien infini, Paris, 1969

Bloch, Jean H., 'Knowledge as a Source of Virtue: Changes and Contrasts in Ideas concerning the Education of Boys and Girls in Eighteenth-Century France', *British Journal for Eighteenth-Century Studies*, 8 (1985), 83–92

'Women and the Reform of the Nation' in *Woman and Society in Eighteenth-Century France*, London, 1979

Bloom, Harold, *The Anxiety of Influence*, Oxford, 1973

A Map of Misreading, Oxford, 1975

Poetry and Repression, New Haven, 1976

Wallace Stevens, The Poems of our Climate, Cornell, 1977

Bloom, Harold *et al.*, *Deconstruction and Criticism*, New York, 1979

Bourdieu, Pierre, *Algérie 60*, Paris, 1977

Brandt, Richard B., 'The Concept of a Moral Right and its Function', *Journal of Philosophy*, 80 (1983), 29–45

Bretonneau, Gisèle, *Stoïcisme et valeurs chez Jean-Jacques Rousseau*, Paris, 1977

Brooks, Peter, *The Novel of Worldliness*, Princeton, 1969

Brown, Norman O., *Hermes the Thief, the Evolution of a Myth*, Madison, Wis., 1947

Brownmiller, Susan, *Against our Will, Men, Women and Rape*, New York, 1975

Bruss, Elizabeth W., 'L'Autobiographie considérée comme acte littéraire', *Poétique*, 17 (1974), 14–26

Bryson, Norman, 'David's Oath of the Horatii and the Question of "Influence"', *French Studies*, 37 (1983), 404–25

Word and Image, Cambridge, 1981

Burgelin, Pierre, *La Philosophie de l'existence de Jean-Jacques Rousseau*, Paris, 1952

Butor, Michel, *Répertoire III*, Paris, 1968

Cahiers pour l'analyse, 8 (1969), 'L'Impensé de Jean-Jacques Rousseau'

Cassel, Gustav, *The Theory of Social Economy*, II, translated by Joseph McCabe, 2 vols., London, 1923

Cassirer, Ernst, *The Question of Jean-Jacques Rousseau*, translated by Peter Gay, Columbia, 1954

Cazeneuve, Jean, *Sociologie de Marcel Mauss*, Paris, 1968

Chambers, Ross, 'Change and Exchange? Story Structure and Paradigmatic Narrative', *Australian Journal of French Studies*, 12 (1975), 326–42

'Commentary in Literary Texts', *Critical Inquiry* (1978) 323–7

Chase, Cynthia, 'Paragon, Parergon: Baudelaire Translates Rousseau', *Diacritics*, 11 (1981), 42–51

Chesseguet-Smirgel, J. *et al.*, *Recherches psychanalytiques nouvelles sur la sexualité féminine*, Paris, 1964

Cixous, Hélène and Clément, Cathérine, *La Jeune née*, Paris, 1975

Clément, Pierre-Paul, *Jean-Jacques Rousseau de l'éros coupable à l'éros glorieux*, Neuchâtel, 1976

Codere, Helen, *Fighting with Property*, Monographs of the American Ethnological Society, 18, New York, 1950

Conroy, William Thomas, Jr., 'Diderot's *Essai sur Sénèque*', *Studies on Voltaire and the Eighteenth Century*, 131 (1975)

Cousins, Mark, 'The Logic of Deconstruction', *Oxford Literary Review*, 3 (1978), 70–7

Cranston, Maurice, and Peters, R. S., ed., *Hobbes and Rousseau: A Collection of Critical Essays*, New York, 1972

Crocker, Lester G., *Jean-Jacques Rousseau: A New Interpretative Analysis of his Life and Works*, New York, 1968–73

Culler, Jonathan, *On Deconstruction*, London, 1982
    The Pursuit of Signs, London 1981

Dagen, Jean, *L'Histoire de l'esprit humain*, Paris, 1977

Dawson, John P., *Gifts and Promises*, New Haven, 1980

Deleuze, Gilles, *Présentation de Sacher Masoch*, Paris, 1967

Derathé, Robert, *Le Rationalisme de Jean-Jacques Rousseau*, Paris, 1948

Derrida, Jacques, *La Carte postale*, Paris, 1980
    'Choreographies' in *The Ear of the Other*, edited by Christie V. McDonald, Lincoln, Nebraska and London, 1985
    L'Ecriture et la différence, Paris, 1967
    Eperons, Paris, 1978
    De la grammatologie, Paris, 1967
    Marges de la philosophie, Paris, 1972

Dickason, Anne, 'Anatomy and Destiny: The Role of Biology in Plato's View of Women', in *Women and Philosophy: Toward a Theory of Liberation*, edited by Carol Gould and Max Wartofsky, New York, 1976

Dodds, E. R., *The Greeks and the Irrational*, Berkeley, 1951

Donaldson, Ian, *The Rapes of Lucretia*, Oxford, 1982

Eagleton, Terry, *The Rape of Clarissa*, Oxford, 1982

Earl, Donald, *The Moral and Political Tradition of Rome*, London, 1967

Ehrenberg, Victor, *From Solon to Socrates*, London, 1967

Eigeldinger, Marc, *Jean-Jacques Rousseau et la réalité de l'imaginaire*, Neuchâtel, 1962

Eliade, Mircea, *The Sacred and the Profane*, translated by Willard R. Trask, New York, 1961

Ellis, Madeleine B., *Rousseau's Socratic Aemilian Myths*, Columbus, Ohio, 1977

Ellrich, Robert, *Rousseau and his Reader: The Rhetorical Situation in the Major Works*, Chapel Hill, 1969

Fabre, Jean, 'Rousseau et le Prince de Conti', *Annales Jean-Jacques Rousseau*, 36 (1963–5), 7–48

Fages, Jean-Baptiste, *Comprendre Jacques Lacan*, Toulouse, 1968

Felman, Shoshana, 'Turning the Screw of Interpretation', *Yale French Studies*, 55 (1977), 94–207

Figes, Eva, *Patriarchal Attitudes*, London, 1970

Finley, Moses, *Ancient Slavery and Modern Ideology*, Harmondsworth, 1980

Aspects of Antiquity, London, 1968

Economy and Society of Ancient Greece, edited by R. P. Saller and B. D. Shaw, London, 1981

Finley, Moses, ed., *Studies in Roman Property*, Cambridge, 1976

Fish, Stanley, *Is there a Text in this Class?* Cambridge, Mass., 1980

Foucault, Michel, Introduction to *Rousseau juge de Jean-Jacques: Dialogues*, Paris, 1962

La Volonté de savoir, Paris, 1976

France, Anatole, *M. Bergeret à Paris*, Paris, 1966

France, Peter, 'Jacques or his Master? Diderot and the Peasants', *British Journal for Eighteenth-Century Studies*, 7 (1984), 1–13

Francon, M., 'Chronologie rousseauiste. Quand Rousseau composa-t-il la 9ᵉ *Promenade*?' *Annales Jean-Jacques Rousseau*, 32 (1950–2), 189–91

Fried, Michael, *Absorption and Theatricality*, Berkeley, Calif., 1980

Galliani, Renato, *Rousseau, le luxe et l'idéologie nobiliaire*, Oxford, 1989

Gans, Eric, 'The Victim as Subject: The Esthetico-Ethical System of Rousseau's *Rêveries*', *Studies in Romanticism*, 21 (1982), 3–31

Garver, Newton, 'Derrida on Rousseau on Writing', *Journal of Philosophy*, 74 (1977), 663–73

Gasché, Rodolphe, 'Deconstruction as Criticism', *Glyph*, 6 (1979) 177–215

'L'Echange héliocentrique', *L'Arc*, 48 (1972), 70–84

'"Setzung und "Übersetzung": Notes on Paul de Man', *Diacritics*, 11 (1981), 36–57

Gauthier, R. A., *Magnanimité*, Paris, 1951

Geffriaud Rosso, Jeannette, 'Montesquieu, Rousseau et la fémininité, de la crainte à l'angélisme', *Studi francesi*, 25 (1981), 482–9

Genette, Gérard, *Figures III*, Paris, 1972

Introduction à l'architexte, Paris, 1979

Genovese, Eugene D., *The Political Economy of Slavery*, New York, 1965

The World the Slaveholders Made, Harmondsworth, 1970

Gilot, Michel *et al.*, *Le Vocabulaire du sentiment dans l'œuvre de Jean-Jacques Rousseau*, Paris, 1980

Gilson, Etienne, 'La Méthode de M. de Wolmar' in *Les Idées et les lettres*, Paris, 1932

Girard, René, *La Violence et le sacré*, Paris, 1972

Giraudoux, Jean, *Pour Lucrèce*, Paris, 1953

250   *Bibliography*

Goffman, Erving, *The Presentation of Self in Everyday Life*, Harmondsworth, 1971
Goldschmidt, Victor, *Anthropologie et politique: les principes du système de Rousseau*, Paris, 1974
Gosse, Edmund, 'Rousseau en Angleterre au XIXe siècle', *Annales Jean-Jacques Rousseau*, 8 (1912), 131–60
Goulemot, Jean-Marie, '*Les Confessions*: une autobiographie d'écrivain', *Littérature*, 33 (1979), 58–74
Green, André, *Un Œil en trop*, Paris, 1969
Grimsley, Ronald, *The Philosophy of Rousseau*, Oxford, 1973
Gruner, Shirley M., *Economic Materialism and Social Moralism: A study in the History of Ideas in France from the Latter Part of the Eighteenth Century to the Middle of the Nineteenth Century*, The Hague, 1973
Guillaume, P. and Meyerson, I., 'Les Fonctions psychologiques et les œuvres' in *Etudes de psychologie et de philosophie*, Paris, 1948
Hagstrum, Jean H., *Sex and Sensibility*, Chicago, 1980
Hall, Gaston H., 'The Concept of Virtue in *La Nouvelle Héloïse*', *Yale French Studies*, 28 (1962), 20–33
Harvey, Simon et al., *Reappraisals of Rousseau: Studies in Honour of R. A. Leigh*, Manchester, 1980
Hendel, G. W., *Jean-Jacques Rousseau, Moralist*, Oxford, 1934
Hillis Miller, J., 'Ariachne's Broken Woof', *Georgia Review*, 131 (1977) 44–63
Hirsch, Marianne, 'A Mother's Discourse: Incorporation and Repetition in *La Princesse de Clèves*', *Yale French Studies*, 62 (1981), 67–87
Hoffman, Paul, *La Femme dans la pensée des lumières*, Paris, 1977
Howard, Martha Walling, *The Influence of Plutarch in the Major European Literatures of the Eighteenth Century*, Chapel Hill, 1970
Hyde, Lewis, *The Gift*, New York, 1979
Imbert, Francis, 'Eléments pour une théorie du changement chez Jean-Jacques Rousseau', *Revue de Métaphysique et de Morale*, 87, 1 (1982), 82–103
Irigaray, Luce, *Ce sexe qui n'en est pas un*, Paris, 1977
Iser, Wolfgang, 'Indeterminacy and the Reader's Response' in *Aspects of Narrative*, ed. J. Hillis Miller, Columbia, 1971
Jakobson, Roman, and Halle, Morris, *Fundamentals of Language*, The Hague, 1956
Kamuf, Peggy, *Signature Pieces*, Ithaca, 1988
Kavanagh, Thomas, *Writing the Truth*, Berkeley and Los Angeles, 1987
Kelly, George Armstrong, *Idealism, Politics and History: Sources of Hegelian Thought*, Cambridge, 1969
Kettering, Sharon, 'Gift-giving and Patronage in Early Modern France', *French History*, 2 (1988), 131–51

Klein, Melanie, 'Envy and Gratitude' (1957) in *Collected Works*, III, London, 1975
Klein, Richard, 'Kant's Sunshine', *Diacritics*, 11 (1981), 26–41
Klossowski, Pierre, *Les Lois de l'hospitalité*, Paris, 1965
Kofman, Sarah, *Le Respect des femmes*, Paris, 1982
Kristeva, Julia, *Semiotike*, Paris, 1969
Kusch, Manfred, 'Landscape and Literary Form: Structural Parallels in *La Nouvelle Héloïse*', *L'Esprit créateur*, 17 (1977)
'The River and the Garden: Basic Spatial Models in *Candide* and *La Nouvelle Héloïse*' in *Eighteenth-Century Studies*, 12 (1978), 1–15
Lacan, Jacques, *Les Quatre Concepts fondamentaux de la psychanalyse*, ed. Jacques-Alain Miller, Paris, 1973
Lafrance, Guy, 'Remarques sur le Rousseau de Victor Goldschmidt', *Dialogue*, 16 (1977), 281–97
Laforgue, René, 'Etude sur Jean-Jacques Rousseau', *Revue française de psychanalyse*, 1 (1927), 370–402
Lagache, Daniel, *La Jalousie amoureuse*, Paris, 1947
Lalande, André, *Vocabulaire technique et critique de la philosophie*, Paris, eighth edition, 1960
Lasowski, Patrick Wald, *Libertines*, Paris, 1980
'Un Souffle unique', *Glyph*, 6 (1979), 68–89
Launay, Michel, *Rousseau, écrivain politique*, Cannes, 1972
Le Vocabulaire politique de Jean-Jacques Rousseau, Geneva 1977
Leclerc, Annie, *Origines*, Paris, 1988
Leigh, Ralph Alexander, *Rousseau and the Problem of Tolerance in the Eighteenth Century*, Oxford, 1979
Leigh, Ralph Alexander, ed., *Rousseau after Two Hundred Years*, Cambridge, 1982
Leiris, Michel, *L'Age d'homme*, Paris, 1946
Lejeune, Philippe, *Le Pacte autobiographique*, Paris, 1975
'Le Peigne cassé', *Poétique*, 7 (1976), 1–29
'La Punition des enfants', *Littérature*, 10 (1973), 31–56
Lévi-Strauss, Claude, 'Jean-Jacques Rousseau, fondateur des sciences de l'homme' in *Jean Jacques Rousseau*, Neuchâtel, 1962, pp. 239–48
Anthropologie Structurale, Paris, 1958
Introduction à l'œuvre de Mauss in Marcel Mauss, *Sociologie et anthropologie*, Paris, 1966
Lodge, David, *The Modes of Modern Writing: Metaphor, Metonymy, and the Typology of Modern Literature*, Cornell, 1977
Lyotard, Jean-François, *Economie libidinale*, Paris, 1974
'One of the Things at Stake in Women's Struggles', translated by Deborah J. Clarke, *Sub-Stance*, 20 (1978), 9–17
MacCannell, Juliet Flower, 'Nature and Self-Love: A Reinterpre-

tation of Rousseau's "Passion primitive"', *PMLA*, 92 (1977), 890–902

McDonald, Christie V., 'Jacques Derrida's Reading of Rousseau', *The Eighteenth Century*, 20 (1979), 82–95

McDougall, Joyce, 'Primal Scene and Sexual Perversion', *International Journal of Psychoanalysis*, 53 (1972), 371–91

'Le Spectateur anonyme', *L'Inconscient*, 6 (1968), 39–58

Mackenzie, Lionel A., 'Rousseau's Debate with Machiavelli', *Journal of the History of Ideas*, 43 (1982), 209–28

Macpherson, C. B., *The Political Theory of Possessive Individualism*, Oxford, 1962

Maddox, James H. Jr., '*Ressentiment* in *Clarissa*' in *Texas Studies in Literature and Language*, 24 (1982), 271–92

Man, Paul de, *Allegories of Reading*, New Haven, 1979

Blindness and Insight, Oxford, 1971

'Structure intentionnelle de l'image romantique', *Revue internationale de philosophie*, 14 (1960), 68–84

Marsden Gillis, Christina, 'Private Room and Public Space; the Paradox of Form in *Clarissa*', *Studies on Voltaire and the Eighteenth Century*, 176 (1979), 153–68

Massey, M. and Moreland, Paul, *Slavery in Ancient Rome*, Basingstoke, 1978

Masson, P. M., *La Religion de Jean-Jacques Rousseau*, 3 vols., Paris, 1916

Masters, Roger D., *The Political Philosophy of Rousseau*, Princeton, 1968

Mauss, Marcel 'Essai sur le don', in *Sociologie et anthropologie*, Paris, 1950, 145–279

'L'Expression obligatoire des sentiments', *Journal de psychologie*, 18 (1921), 425–34

'Une catégorie de l'esprit humain: la notion de personne, celle de "moi"', *Journal of the Royal Anthropological Institute*, 68 (1938), 263–81

Mauzi, Robert, *L'Idée du bonheur dans la littérature et la pensée française au 18ᵉ siècle*, Paris, 1960

Mercken-Spass, Godelieve, 'Some Aspects of the Self and the Other in Rousseau and Sade', *Sub-Stance*, 20 (1978), 71–7

Michel, Jacques H., *Gratuité en droit romain*, Brussels, 1962

Moi, Toril, 'Existentialism and Feminism: The Rhetoric of Biology in the Second Sex', *Oxford Literary Review*, 8 (1986), 88–95

Morel, Jean-Emile, 'Jean-Jacques Rousseau lit Plutarque', *Revue d'histoire moderne*, 1 (1926), 81–102

Morrow, Glenn R., *Plato's Cretan City*, Princeton, 1960

Plato's Law of Slavery, New York, 1976

Moscovici, Serge, *La Psychanalyse: son image et son public*, Paris, 1961

Nacht, S., *Le Masochisme*, Paris, 1948

Okin, Susan M., *Women in Western Political Thought*, Princeton, 1979

Olivecrona, Karl, *Law as Fact*, London, 1971

Oltramare, Andre, 'Plutarque dans Rousseau', in *Mélanges offerts à Bernard Bouvier*, Geneva (1920), pp. 185–96

Onians, Richard Broxton, *The Origins of European Thought*, Cambridge, 1951

Osmont, Robert, 'Contribution à l'étude psychologique des *Rêveries*', *Annales Jean-Jacques Rousseau*, 23 (1934), 7–135

'Jean-Jacques Rousseau et la jalousie', *Annales Jean-Jacques Rousseau*, 35 (1959–62), 73–91

'Un événement aussi triste qu'imprévu...', *Revue d'histoire littéraire de la France*, 65 (1965), 615–28

Page, D. L., *A New Chapter in the History of Greek Tragedy*, Cambridge, 1951

Perelman, Chaim, and Olbrechts-Tyteca, L., *Traité de l'argumentation*, Brussels, 1970

Pierce, Christine, 'Equality: *Republic V*', *Monist*, 57 (1973), 1–11

Pire, G, 'De l'influence de Sénèque sur les théories pédagogiques de Jean-Jacques Rousseau', *Annales Jean-Jacques Rousseau*, 33 (1953–5), 57–92

'Du bon Plutarque au citoyen de Genève', *Revue de Littérature Comparée*, 32 (1958), 510–47

Stoïcisme et pédagogie, Liège, 1958

Planiol, Marcel and Ripert, Georges, eds., *Traité pratique de droit civil français*, Paris, 1952

Pollard, Patrick, 'Gide and Antiquity' (unpublished Ph.D. dissertation, University of London, 1965)

Pomeroy, Sarah B., *Goddesses, Whores, Wives and Slaves: Women in Classical Antiquity*, New York, 1975

Poulet, Georges, *Les Métamorphoses du cercle*, Paris, 1961

Pringsheim, F., 'Animus in Roman Law', *Law Quarterly Review*, 49 (1933), 43–60

Proust, Jacques, 'Le Premier des pauvres', *Europe*, 391–2 (1961), 13–21

Ragland-Sullivan, Ellie, 'Jacques Lacan: Feminism and the Problem of Gender Identity', *Sub-Stance*, 36 (1982), 6–20

Rawls, John, *A Theory of Justice*, Oxford, 1971

Raymond, Marcel, *Jean-Jacques Rousseau: la quête de soi et la rêverie*, Paris, 1962

Ricatte, Robert, *Réflexions sur 'Les Rêveries'*, Paris, 1960

Richebourg, Marguerite, *Essai sur les lectures de Rousseau*, Geneva, 1934

Ricœur, Paul, *Finitude et culpabilité*, Paris, 1960

Riffaterre, Michel, 'L'Intertexte inconnu', *Littérature*, 41 (1981), 4–7

Robinson, Philip, 'Awakening to Music: Two Autobiographical Passages of Rousseau', *Nottingham French Studies*, 18 (1979), 22–36

'Jean-Jacques Rousseau and the Autobiographical Dimension', *Journal of European Studies*, 8 (1978), 77–92

'Rousseau's Second *Discours*: Preciosity, Politics and Translation', *French Studies Bulletin*, 10 (1984), 1–3

'Virginie's Fatal Modesty: Bernardin de Saint-Pierre and Rousseau', *British Journal for Eighteenth-Century Studies*, 5 (1982), 35–48

Rorty, Richard, 'Derrida on Language, Being and Abnormal Philosophy', *Journal of Philosophy*, 74 (1977), 673–81

Rosenberg, Aubrey, 'Rousseau's View of Work and Leisure in the Community', *Australian Journal of French Studies*, 18 (1981), 3–12

Rossard, J., *Une clef du romantisme: la pudeur*, Paris, 1974

Rousseau et Voltaire en 1978: Actes du colloque international de Nice, Geneva, 1981

Ruegg, Maria, 'Metaphor and Metonymy: The Logic of Structuralist Rhetoric', *Glyph*, 6 (1979), 141–57

Runcimann, W. G. and Sen, A. K., 'Games, Justice and the General Will', *Mind* (1965), 554–62

Russell, Bertrand, *The History of Western Philosophy*, London, second edition, 1961

Rustin, Jacques, *Le Vice à la mode*, Paris, 1979

Sage, Lorna, 'Ravishment Related', Review of Ian Donaldson, *The Rapes of Lucretia*, *The Times Literary Supplement* (24 December 1982), 1410

Scanlan, Timothy M., 'The Dynamics of Separation and Communication in Rousseau's *Julie*', *Esprit Créateur*, 17 (1977), 336–48

Scherer, René, *Emile perverti*, Paris, 1974

Schuhl, Pierre Maxime, *La Fabulation platonicienne*, Liège, 1968

Schwartz, Joel, *The Sexual Politics of Rousseau*, Chicago, 1984

Shapiro, Stephen A., 'The Dark Continent of Literature: Autobiography', *Comparative Literature Studies*, 5 (1968), 421–54

Shell, Marc, *The Economy of Literature*, Baltimore, 1978

Shklar, Judith N., *Men and Citizens: A Study of Rousseau's Social Theory*, Cambridge, 1969

Simons, Madeleine Anjubault, *Amitié et passion: Rousseau et Sauttersheim*, Geneva, 1972

'Rousseau's Natural Diet' *Romanic Review*, 45 (1954), 18–29

Smith, Kirby Flower, 'The Tale of Gyges and the King of Lydia', *American Journal of Philology*, 23 (1902), 261–387

Smith, Louise Z., 'Sensibility and Epistolary Form in *Héloïse* and *Werther*', *Esprit Créateur*, 17 (1977), 361–76

Smock, Ann, 'Literary Economies and Critical Gifts', *Diacritics*, 10 (1980), 37–48

Spengemann, William C., *The Forms of Autobiography*, New Haven, 1980

Spink, J. S., 'From "Hippolyte est sensible" to "Le fatal présent du ciel": The Position of "bienfaisance"', *The Classical Tradition in French Literature: Essays presented to R. C. Knight*, ed. H. T. Barnwell *et al.*, London, 1977, pp. 191–202

'Lévesque de Pouilly et David Hume: "bienveillance" et "justice", "sentiments agréables" et "calm passions"', *Revue de Littérature Comparée* (1982), 157–75

Srabian de Fabry, Anne, 'L'Architecture secrète de *La Nouvelle Héloïse*', *Australian Journal of French Studies*, 19 (1982), 3–10

Starobinski, Jean, *L'Invention de la liberté*, Geneva, 1964

J.-J. Rousseau: La Transparence et l'obstacle, revised edition, Paris, 1971

L'Œil vivant, Paris, 1961

La Relation critique, Paris, 1970

'Le Remède dans le mal', *Nouvelle revue de psychanalyse*, 18 (1978), 251–74

'Rousseau and Modern Tyranny', Review of Lester G. Crocker, *Jean-Jacques Rousseau: A New Interpretative Analysis of His Life and Works*, translated by Peter France, *The New York Review* (29 November 1973), 20–5

'Rousseau et Baudelaire', *Nouvelle revue française*, 338 (1980), 37–50

'Rousseau's Happy Days', *New Literary History*, 11 (1979), 147–66

Still, Judith, 'The Disfigured Savage: Rousseau and de Man', *Nottingham French Studies*, 24 (1985), 1–14

'Elements of the Classical Code of Beneficence presupposed in Rousseau's writing', *Studies on Voltaire and the Eighteenth Century*, 260 (1989), 279–303

'From Eliot's "Raw Bone" to Gyges' Ring: Two Studies in Intertextuality', *Paragraph*, 1 (1983), 44–59

'Lucretia's Silent Rhetoric', *Oxford Literary Review*, 6 (1984), 70–86

'Rousseau in *Daniel Deronda*', *Revue de littérature comparée* (1982), 62–77

'Rousseau's *Lévite d'Ephraïm*; the imposition of meaning (on women)', *French Studies*, 43 (1989), 12–30

Strauss, Leo, *The City and the Man*, Chicago, 1964

Natural Right and History, Chicago, 1953

Tanner, Tony, *Adultery in the Novel*, Baltimore, 1979

Thomson, Donald F., *Economic Structure and the Ceremonial Exchange Cycle in Arnhem Land*, Melbourne, 1949

Trousson, Raymond, *Jean-Jacques Rousseau Le deuil éclatant du bonheur*, Paris, 1989

Ulmer, Gregory L., 'Jacques Derrida and Paul de Man on/in Rousseau's Faults', *The Eighteenth Century*, 20 (1979), 164–81

Ure, P. N., *The Origin of Tyranny*, Cambridge, 1922

Van Laere, François, 'Jean-Jacques Rousseau du phantasme à l'écriture, les révélations du *Lévite d'Ephraïm*', *Archives des lettres modernes*, 81 (1967)

Vernant, Jean-Pierre, *Mythe et pensée chez les Grecs*, Paris, 1966
Mythe et société en Grèce ancienne, Paris, 1966
Mythe et tragédie en Grèce ancienne, Paris, 1972

Wade, Gail G., 'A Lacunian Study: de Man and Rousseau', *Eighteenth-Century Studies*, 12 (1979), 504–13

Wahl, Jean, 'La Bipolarité de Rousseau', *Annales Jean-Jacques Rousseau*, 33 (1953–5), 49–55

Watson-Williams, Helen, *André Gide and the Greek Myth*, Oxford, 1967

Weil, Eric, 'Jean-Jacques Rousseau et sa politique', *Critique*, 56 (1952), 3–28

Wexler, Victor, '"Made for Man's Delight" Rousseau as Anti-Feminist', *American History Review*, 81 (1976), 226–91

Wind, Edgar, *Pagan Mysteries in the Renaissance*, London, 1958

Wright, Derek, *The Psychology of Moral Behaviour*, Harmondsworth, 1971

Young, Robert, ed., *Untying the Text*, Boston, 1981

Index

257

Cambridge Studies in French

GENERAL EDITOR
Malcolm Bowie (*University of London*)
EDITORIAL BOARD
R. Howard Bloch (*University of California, Berkeley*), Ross Chambers (*University of Michigan*), Antoine Compagnon (*Columbia University*), Peter France (*University of Edinburgh*), Toril Moi (*Duke University*), Naomi Schor (*Duke University*)
Also in the series (* denotes titles now out of print)

(39) (188)

1 Dhicⁿ crucial — sees fantasy underpinning &
117 profound issues — really good
∨ g reading of _LG_ 143

170 moral codes _shd_ work togr but don't always